THE MURDE[R]

MARY MAGDALENE

Synchronicity and the Scarlet Saint

DAN GREEN

Healings Of Atlantis Ltd
Devon
England
UK

www.healingsofatlantis.com

Published in Great Britain, 2013
by 11th Dimension Publishing

ISBN: 978-1-907126-14-7

A catalogue record for this book is available from the British Library.

ACKNOWLEDGEMENT:

The author would like to thank the following for their kind permission for reproduction of some images used in this book; 'The Death of Mary Magdalene', Courtesy of The Hispanic Society of America, New York, The Masonic Dog on the platter, Re-printed with permission of *The Lincolnshire Echo*, James Robinson, Royston Cave, Elona Rogers, Simon Brighton and Andrew Gough.

MARY·HATH·CHOSEN·THAT·GOO D·PART·WHICH
SHALL·NOT·BE·TAKEN·AWAY·FROM·HER✠

Erected to the Glory of God in loving memory of
Mary Forrest of Ardow. Died 23rd October, 1904,
by her affectionate sister, Isabella D. Forrest,

FOREWORD

While lecturing on 'The Psychology and Sociology of Unexplained Phenomena' for Cambridge University's Extra-Mural board back in the seventies, we were forever on the look-out for new, intriguing, unexplained mysteries to explore on site, and then share with our students. This sent us off to Rennes-le-Chateau in 1975 during what were the pioneering years of the Rennes mystery – and it is undoubtedly one of the greatest unsolved mysteries of all time. Various hoax theories have been put forward as attempts to explain away the Rennes mystery during the thirty intervening years – BUT NONE OF THEM HAVE DESTROYED THE MYSTERY COMPLETELY.

Mysterious contributors to the Rennes enigma, such as Monsieur Plantard, may have clouded the water a little, but a hard core of inexplicable facts remains. SUPPOSE that Plantard really had close to some cataclysmic secrets known to the Cathars, the Templars and the Priory of Sion. Was he subsequently told that unless he came up with a contradictory 'confession' that his so-called 'disclosures' were all a hoax, he would go the same way as the hapless Father Gelis (whose axe-battered body was found in his Presbytery at Coustaussa?) If a traumatically powerful secret society real DOES exist, what better way to conceal its existence than to proclaim that it is merely a hoax? How many of the most vocal Rennes detractors might secretly be members of a society whose existence they are denying?

The important elements in Dan Green's work are his honesty, his integrity and his intelligence. These shine through in everything he has written, and are the cornerstones of all his research. He also has the gift of seeing connections - of finding meaningful synchronicities – which is the way that great and enduring riddles are finally answered.

His subject is an enormous one, with cosmic implications. Rennes and Lincoln Cathedral provide valuable clues – but they are only clues. Much, much more waits to be discovered.

This is an intriguing and thought-provoking book. You will enjoy it. As Rennes researchers for over thirty years, we are impressed by his findings.

Lionel and Patricia Fanthorpe,
Cardiff

INTRODUCTION

The *Murder of Mary Magdalene - Synchronicity and the Scarlet Saint* is a deliberate attempt at trying to approach that age-old chestnut of 'the mystery of life' that has gnawed at our collective ankle area since the dawning of our civilization. Living in the vastness of an ever-expanding universe that the brightest of our minds can only struggle to hope to speculatively understand a mere percentage, we have to concede that if we cannot understand the mechanics of that cosmos that contains this speck of dust we call earth, then any understanding of our miniscule component part must also be speculative. And yet, today in this troubled arena, all focus on enlightening developments on centre stage, there is an air of a consciousness of the movement of something – 'something' is happening around and about us, a change. Tangible evidence is that of our environmental crisis, global warming, and Greenhouse effects, all indicators of a certain change. Seeking reassuring escape exits and a way out from the anticipation of having to face these consequences, bred from the fear of uncertainty in our generation, has many desperately seeking a consoling religion, the older version of which is in its own state of confusion, having been challenged by technology and historical detectives such as myself. Alternatively, they are rushing into that vastness of the frontier of space seeking communion with their hopeful interpretation of that most popular archetype of the UFO and its saviour pilots. Our belief in spaceships and aliens may well be the product of us attempting to deal with an 'alien' situation fast approaching us, such as our mounting monumental global problems.

Archetypes have been introduced into our way of learning since 1947 courtesy of the daring and self-enforced self-discoveries of the psychologist Jung, to cover all aspects of religion and mythologies. As author of this work, I have allowed archetypes and its closest companion, the phenomenon of the synchronicity, to be my tools in my own attempt to tackle understanding of the mysteries that so frustrate us and encapsulated within religiosity and myth, a struggle to seek a spirituality providing security. Feeling that we do not understand enough about ourselves – we live and die only accessing a fifth of our brain capacity – coupled with puzzling aspects of natural phenomenon that the planet can manifest, which if we did understand it would explain away most of the mystery including the UFO. I follow, unapologetically, that well worn path of that historical and psychic detective and ask a staggeringly simple question 'Do we own our own brains?' One thing we do know for certain about life on earth is that we live it and die to it with the hope that somewhere, somehow there is a re-birth or continuance of life after we wear out our protoplasm. This book suggests that the uneasiness we are now conceding to be conscious of – that 'movement' – is a strange awareness of an imminent birth, a global one of consciousness changing from a current frightened, full of thoughts seeking meaning, pregnant state of mind.

The most popular, current, archetype concerning mystery and pregnancy arises from the healthy curiosity concerning the biblical figure of Mary Magdalene, and whether she actually was the mother of a child by the figure Jesus, to propagate a bloodline. Key to a global birth of consciousness, we explore this serious issue contributory to the disruption of an already faltering religious system and whether clues to this hidden drama have been placed for centuries by secret societies, one secret society or establishments like the Freemasons. It will have a surprising conclusion. This book posits that there is an alternative, and flawless mechanism that is helping us along to a greater awakening concerning a global pregnancy and birth, and that it is the medium of Jung's Collective Unconscious, working through the sensitivity and randomness of the human agency, even if the recipients are themselves unaware of the communication.

In my case, I am aware and of the confirmatory synchronicities that will pop up here, there and everywhere. If the Gaia hypothesis, and theory propounded by Lovelock in the seventies, announcing our planet as a thinking 'super organism' is correct – as good a theory as any, and following on from where Blavatsky's Theosophy left off a century earlier – it can easily solve our mysteries by virtue of uncovering the 'clues' it has left for itself throughout history, rather like the anamnesis of a patient recalling their medical history, or an occultist attempting to tap the Akashic record. The end product may well be to raise our consciousness in attunement with earth's own evolution which means as guest on this Host we have to adapt and change how we think. The adventure contained within this book led the author, through an often undesired assault of synchronicities and archetypes, to the city of Lincoln, England, and to assume the individual responsibility of unlocking the hidden aspect of its magnificent Gothic Cathedral and, through the common denominator of the figure of the scarlet Saint, Mary Magdalene, recognising a connection to the popular mystery of the small village of Rennes-le-Chateau in France.

Herein, a great mystery is solved involving the archetypes of 'treasure' and the 'Grail', but more importantly its emphasis on this recurring theme of pregnancy and birth dwarfs any 'localised' consequences that would only have its significance earth based. As our quantum mechanics and physicists are now attesting, everything in the universe is connected to everything else, and so from the precise placing of cathedrals on pole positions on the ground at the behest of the Collective Unconscious, there will be complimentary stars winking down at us from above. Some connections are far more obvious than others, but all are equally important and there to be detected, as there is no such thing as a meaningless coincidence. Theory and hypothesis are nothing to be ashamed about, but sometimes, with the handicap of only that low percentage of brain capacity, we have to stop and confess, 'This is beyond my comprehension.' As far as my own comprehension will go, and I was a student of Kalachakra and Vajrayana Tibetan Buddhism and psychology, my own intuitive feelings – I expect it is trickling through from that global Collective Unconscious – shares the discovery this author has been pushed through a personal hoop to unveil, showing the story of the scarlet Saint Mary to be a microcosmic version of a macrocosmic universe full of the continual birthing of galaxies and stars. A planet about to give birth would want any scar tissue in its history to heal, and this is why the case of the Magdalene must be highlighted. To hear the voice of Mother Earth translating, this book will also demonstrate a lost mother Tongue, a matrix behind all attempted coding employed by those who have ever felt a need to encode, be it in signs or symbols – the only Code of any importance worth cracking being that of the language-containing DNA of the parent Mother, assisting us to understand the 'scar' content within the scarlet.

MARY·HATH·CHOSEN·THAT·GOOD·PART·WHICH
SHALL·NOT·BE·TAKEN·AWAY·FROM·HER

Erected to the Glory of God in loving memory of
Mary Forrest of Ardew, Died 23rd October, 1904,
by her affectionate sister Isabella D. Forrest,

CHAPTER ONE
SYNCHRONICITY AND THE COLLECTIVE UNCONSCIOUS

To both fully understand and appreciate how our Lincoln Cathedral Code operates and works, we will have to tarry a short while to learn a little about the concept of both the Collective Unconscious, the mechanism of synchronicity, and a wondrous hypothesis, the Gaia theory. Many books have attempted to solve mysteries involving treasure hunts and the Knights Templar based on the trust that a secret society, or societies, have guarded and left clues throughout the passing of time, helpful or certain in such a search. Some of this may well be true, but an optional way of thinking is this; secrets may easily have been distorted or lost throughout time lapsing centuries, and we are all aware of the effects of 'Chinese whispers'. If this be the case, then truly lost or buried items, or artefacts, will remain precisely that – lost. I stand alone in my suggestion that there may be another and solitary agency that can impinge 'clues' upon individuals to lead them to a prize, and that this may well become operational even without the knowledge or interest of its founder! Hopefully, to keep this explanation in basic layman's terms – as we will need to take a crash course in psychology and neurology – we will start a little learning of the work of a Swiss psychiatrist, influential thinker and founder of analytical psychology, and inspiration behind depth psychology.

The Collective Unconscious, described as a reservoir of the experiences of our species (alternatively known as the Collective Subconscious), is a term belonging to the realms of analytical psychology, coined by Carl Gustav Jung (1875-1961).

Whereas Sigmund Freud, (1856-1939) the Austrian psychiatrist and founder of the psychoanalytical school of psychology and inspiration behind the theory of the Unconscious Mind, his Mentor, did not distinguish between individual psychology and collective, Jung made a distinction between this collective unconscious and the personal, particular to each individual human. Whilst Freud made one and all aware of the goings on activated and abound within their own hidden and individual selves, Jung disseminated the notion that almost everyone the world over drew from a common denominator, a matrix pool of ideas, images and meanings, and that these ideas that have the same basic meaning are scattered across all continents, and throughout history dating back to the earliest dawning of civilization. These basic forms he called 'archetypes' which are found in the form of visual symbols and graphics, a part of our psychological makeup and built in us, so that we are generally unaware of them and may never even experience them – but they are inherently there, awaiting a trigger. Aren't we born with a basic understanding within us of what is conceptually 'right' and what is 'wrong'? (Even if we choose to go against it!) Who put that there? Baby chicks have an awareness of shapes and shadows of predatory birds – who put that there? Jung's explanation of a Collective Unconscious explains how this can be.

Synchronicity, the experience of two or more events casually unrelated to occur together in meaningful or revelatory manner, and unlikely to occur together by chance provide access to archetypes that are located in the Collective Unconscious rather than originating in our world of senses, existing independently of our world, known directly to the Mind. Jung announced that archetypes arise spontaneously in Mind especially at times of a crisis. You may have heard about the phenomenon of 'poltergeist' manifesting when teenage girls are experiencing puberty, a type of crisis for the child...strange brain activity responsible for objects being thrown about amidst kinetic activities and turbulence, whilst chemical changes are occurring in the brain. Crisis becomes a gateway for the Collective Unconscious to let pour out revealing archetypes informing deep hidden truths stowed away from our the ordinary consciousness we use to go to work, catch buses and buy milk from shops. I think we will all agree that presently, and for some time now, not only is our planet going through a crisis of sorts with its problems of global warming and related hazards, but individuals too, not only from a knock-on effect, but from a very real spiritual crisis – this is the generation that needs to know where it has came from, why it is here and where will it be going.....is life entirely random, is there a meaning, is there a continuance of life beyond physical expiry? We have reached crisis point, and need some answers fast. The Collective Unconscious is replying to this plea, and archetypes and synchronicities are pouring through thick and fast to assist us in our spiritual Quest, and at this point it may be sensible to take a look at another unexpected mechanism that has been gaining acceptance since 1979..the Gaia Hypothesis.

During the decades spanning the '60-'70s, NASA was looking out for signs indicative of any forms of life on Mars. James Lovelock (born 1919) who was assigned the task, assumed that conditions to look for would echo those we know of on earth, and so began looking out for evidence of essential chemicals, but before long queried his experiments when doubt entered his mind – would any Martian way of life reveal to tests designed on the life style of the earth? Realising that as there was no actual life detecting experiments based on a broader definition of life as a physical process, maybe he should go about designing one. Inspired by a suggestion from a colleague, both began to work on a hypothesis of life detection by atmospheric analysis, which convinced them that the improbable atmosphere of our planet was being manipulated on a daily basis, the manipulator being Life itself. Taking the discovery one further, and one controversial step further, Lovelock declared that if the earth was acting like a living organism, it must be because it is one. The Gaia Theory was born, with its inventor rapidly becoming a 20th Century equivalent of Darwin. As early as the mid-1700s, a Scots physician, philosopher and farmer, James Hutton, had described earth as a 'living world', Russian scientist Vladimir Vernadsky, born in 1863, referred to the biosphere (a term coined in 1875 by an Austrian geologist and philosopher) as a living organism. The Gaia Hypothesis soon took on a spiritual concept – the earth female is alive, and her spiritual energies manifest as life, through form flowing through us all, and all that is upon and within her planetary playground connecting us and making us one (as ecology attests) with topography, oceania, and every living thing, and touching every aspect of human behaviour, whether we care to believe that or not. Excited adherents embracing the Gaia Hypothesis take it even one further step again - the earth, as it is alive, must think!

The admired English mathematician, Alan Turing states that when an entity acts in such a complex and coherent way it looks like it is conscious and thinking, then the only conclusion must be that it is! Gaia may not have a physical brain we can locate and point to, but it may well be that her brain is our brain, using each and every one of the world's population of seven billion, and not only that, but all of the residents of the aggregate kingdoms too, animal, vegetable, plant, mineral, as all are part of the earth super-organism, making our minds part of Gaia, who is self-conscious through all of us. On this basis, can you try to imagine the wisdom contained in the genetic memory of our four billion year old host? Occultists have their equivalent library in what they call the Akashic record, where every thought and event ever having occurred on the planet has been recorded and may be located or tapped, rather like borrowing a book from a library filing system. In 2013, Gaia is facing changing times, and it is her responsibility to deal and adapt the problems we have caused her, with our polluting of her seas and atmosphere. She will deal with the change, she has seen numerous cyclic ones before, but can we? What are these changes emulating? In consistency with Lovelock's hypothesis, using the metaphor of the biosphere as a single organism, a pregnant woman, humanity becomes the biosphere's reproductive system which is experiencing a problem by way of unsustainable growth – its increasing human population. Body chemistry changes in a pregnant woman, which parallels how current changes in air and water chemistry have been brought about by our pollution. In the same way that people recoil at the tarot card 'Death' when it produces itself in a reading when all it implies is a fresh start, doom and gloom merchants are already declaring our planet to be dying, and yet I don't think this is so, for it is pregnant, and about to give a new consciousness birth.

My training in Tibetan Kalachakra and Vajrayana at the Samye-Ling monastery in Dumfries, Scotland, taught me that there is one and only genuine Buddhist rebirth, that of the planet, and of the spiritual transference of a 'Starchild' born of Mind – it is underway now. Denizens of this plane are living at a time and phase giving way to great change. Most of us are unwittingly alive at a time that has entered into the 'death' cycle of our earth, giving way to a new birth. This death is in the mode of our usual decaying physical body passing away, but is afforded a slightly more illuminating exegesis in the Tibetan opus 'Book of the Dead', the stages referred to here are paralleling with the death experience of our mother globe. This is not an alarmist statement that earth will 'die' – surely never – for it will always have the means to adapt to whatever its inhabitants will bring upon it or be guided to; the meaning expressed is that a 'death' will occur when a separation from the giver of birth is distinguishable from the born – in that moment of parting we not only have the birth but also the 'death'. Death, as the Tibetans know it, is the separation of mind from body. There is a rapid evolving new consciousness arising from this planet presently, a new mind and birth to be that will separate from the planet earth body as we pass through certain and definite stages of the dying process. As it is with the human frame so it is with the planetary body – there is a gradual loss of consciousness involving each element of earth, water, fire and air in turn. The dying procedure has long been described in Tibetan tantric texts, going to lengths to explain how first the earth element sinks, dissolving into the water element, water sinking into fire, fire into air and air into consciousness. Currently, we are at the stage of earth sinking into water, as experienced by the increased global rise in sea level as polar caps melt from greenhouse effects of absorption of solar radiation from the earth, its conversion and re-emission in the infra-red, the absorption of the infra-red radiation by atmospheric ozone, water vapour, and carbon dioxide, and the consequent rise in temperature of the atmosphere, as this global Gaia pregnancy moves into the birthing stages.

Today, the understanding of the term 'Holy Grail' has moved focus and is understood to be the bloodline or child of a pregnant Mary Magdalene. It is of no wonder that this is our philosophical and spiritual way of thinking right now, as we are clearly keeping in alignment with the planetary condition, and as we search for the physical treasure that is Magdalene related we are also acting out our craving for spiritual truth and direction. This yearning is rather like the phenomenon displayed by pregnant mothers, referred to as 'pica', a craving for unnatural food such as mud, dirt, plaster, coal or cloth, pickles, ice cream and a whole host of wonderfully inappropriate others. Authorities state that there is no specific nutritional need that would be asserted this way, the cravings put down to either hysteria, or a bid for sympathy, such cravings thought to be the signs of iron deficiency. The search for this Holy Grail and its sundry connotations has never been more prevalent, and in the mystery of Rennes-le-Chateau has been packaged in a most simple and convenient form for all to investigate. Events that are synchronous unfold to show an underlying pattern, an encompassing conceptual paradigm, that is larger than all of the systems displaying the synchronicity. The most favoured of Jung's quotes on the mechanism of synchronicity, we find from Lewis Carroll's classic *Through the Looking Glass*, when the White Queen remarks to Alice, 'it's a poor sort of memory that only works backwards.'

We now know a little more about Jung and his contribution to our Cathedral Code Mystery, so now let us spend a short while investigating exactly how he did arrive at his conclusions, as it was from his own direct and inner experiences much the same as the one I have described myself as having during the eighties. In the main, they have now stopped! At least I can say I am in good company! His personal dreams and visions became the formulation of his scientific work. (We will later include the poet Lord Tennyson as a key player in our Code, in a similar vein) Jung was 37 when he broke ties with Freud in 1912, and as a psychologist he tried developing his own orientation to his patients' treatment. I believe Jung was the first empirical and compassionate psychiatrist in this respect, trying out his own experiences before he came to formulate them into a catalogue to help him understand similarities that would be related to him by his patients, by experiencing his own flood of archetypes, synchronicities and revelations from the Collective Unconscious reservoir. If ever there had been a man destined to deal with this task for humanity, it was Jung, and he did so by recording it all in over 1,000 private handwritten pages and illustrations. In 1916 Jung experienced what he described as 'The seven sermons to the Dead'. Visitations from spirits claiming they were from Jerusalem, fully of strange language and imagery, and whom Jung announced as the voices of the 'Unanswered, the Unresolved and Unreedemed', souls, like our troubled generation today, who were looking for answers they were unable to discover in their lifetime, the content of the conversations becoming the prelude to what he would be about to announce to the world about the unconscious and its workings, focusing on a marriage between the conscious and unconscious elements of our psyche, for religious teaching had failed us in preserving key knowledge that is exemplified and given expression in spirit through nature and instinct, and deliberately thrown us out of balance by neglecting the feminine principle in our culture, we now appreciate the abandonment of the Magdalene and her role as a perfect example. Before I leave the subject of Jung and his Mentor Freud behind, let me show you the ironic sympathy concerning these two, once best of, friends, and another example of how we cannot escape how synchronicity links us. Sigmund Freud was known affectionately as 'Siggy'. If you take the initial letter of each of Carl Gustav Jung's name , and allow for the fact that his surname is actually pronounced 'Yung', you will have C-G-Y, to be pronounced as... 'Siggy' !

To have employed that almost playful deduction was to have used an understanding of an unsuspected Mother Tongue, a form of Esperanto that can link up languages and sciences into a cybernetic fashion, not a code but more correctly the Mother of all code cracking! It is the so-called and obscure 'Rabbit Language' of the Knights Templar, presumably called so because it is underground like a rabbit, and takes more than a small amount of burrowing to locate! (It has, to be fair, also been described as 'The Green Language') This lost Mother Tongue resides deep in the Collective Unconscious, and if tapped is a means whereupon all languages of the many thousands of residents of the world's countries are placed into a cosmopolitan melting pot. A common matrix producing flawless Esperanto capable of providing accurate and endless information deduced from any one word, a word that will without fail metamorphose, constantly changing, never running dry, on and on to link the vastness of all known alphabets and their words, as first the ancient Buddhism taught that everything is linked to everything, and now modern physics is saying the same. If everything is linked to everything, then so too, must all language be. The 'paper chase' of the living word is as infinite as the mathematical figure Pi. This is not a game, nor ingenious wordplay as is the pastime of keen wordsmiths, who would lose their way quite hopelessly. Words formed by re-ordering total, or partial, letters of another word; play on words, sometimes on a different sense of the same word, sometimes in a similar sense or a sound of different words; the sounds of speech, their production, reception, combination, description and classification from a written word – all the property of the Language of the Dream World of an inaccessible lingual 'computer', an ethereal locality that performs high speed calculations assembling, storing and correlating information derived from coded data in accord with a predetermined program.

Professors of comparative philology do not know anything at all about this lost Mother Tongue or 'rabbit language'. They are only able, at best, to reconstruct the parent language of English/Latin/Greek/ /Sanskrit/Hittite/Slavic which they call Indo-European, but this is simply the parent of a specific family of languages, and not a Mother Tongue at all. In fact, they do not even know whether there is such a Mother Tongue, or if language arose separately in different places. They concede that there are scholars who believe in a 'Proto-World' language, but the vast majority of 'reputable' scholars do not accept this. Nor would they accept the language spoken by Gaia. Freemasons may have employed fragments of the language in attempting to code words, and even the High Priests in Egypt would use visual puns on their heiroglyphs, but total access through the Gateway of the Unconscious has been the privy of a rare few....language that comes from all natural sound and phenomena. This is why, and herein lay a great secret, everything can talk to us. We can read the unwritten, hear conversations in the wind – everything has its own speak...the onomatopoeia of a whispering brook, the howling gale of a banshee-like wind that gives rise to ghost stories, the pitter-patter of the earliest drops of precipitous rainfall, the buzz of the busy honey gathering bee, the 'bless you!' and 'atchoo!' of the forceful sneeze, the booming snore of the person deep in sleep.

This Mother Tongue has in one word revealed to me many explanations that would normally take sentences or even a paragraph. I will demonstrate here my most favourite and illumined two. As a teenager, I was fascinated by the High Lama Masters of Tibet who, until the invasion of their Homeland in 1959, would congregate at the Pothala Summer Palace, residency of HH the Dalai Lama. Well, we find these high lamas and the Pothala in the word 'hypothalamus', the tiny cluster of cells in the brain and an essential link between brain and pituitary gland, which is sometimes called the 'Master gland'... 'Hy...(high)....at the beginning of the word, and 'lamus' (lamas) at the end, with 'pothala' in the middle! The intention of these so-called primitive lamas' meditations were to raise consciousness to unite with deep space and the cosmic unity. Today, in our much advanced push button technological world of computers and the micro-chip, we find that we have a similar device to the struggling brains of our lama friends high up their mountain tops, used to amplify long range radar and radio astronomy signals. It is called the Maser – and you can find it hidden in our word 'Lamaseries'. My other example explains why as long as we have had the human race, it has been unable to cease warring with one another; it is almost as if the urge to fight is inbuilt. War has been not such a necessity, as more of an inevitability, for we are a sexual planet. From 'gamete', a sexual reproductive cell, we have 'gametophyte' – in alternation of generation, a plant of the sexual generation, producing gametes. 'Gametophyte' = 'game to fight' = war.

And so now having taken a necessary look at the wonder and tools of the Collective Unconscious, synchronicity and Gaia, Gaia who assembles synchronicities through the unconscious, to provide what it wills, using the neurology of a brain whose capacity we only use a percentage. Now we can move on and follow one of those contemporary provisions...exactly how a timely Code initially instigated and thought out in France, and incorporating the mental and physical dexterity of many people from architects to religious bodies, is brought to discovery to culminate in the Gothic Cathedral of Lincoln.

MARY·HATH·CHOSEN·THAT·GOOD·PART·WHICH
SHALL·NOT·BE·TAKEN·AWAY·FROM·HER

Erected to the glory of God, in loving memory of
Mary Forrest, of Ardow, Died 23rd October, 1904,
by her affectionate sister Isabella D. Forrest,

CHAPTER TWO
PSYCHIC CASES AND PREGNANT PLACES

Some say start as you mean to go on. I was born in 1956; a breach birth and thus entered into this world feet first in topsy-turvy fashion, spending many of my following years rushing in with them to firmly 'put a foot in it', 'it' being any number of circumstances whereby hastiness would have been a preferred non option – except maybe in the area of being precocious. My first encounter with the synchronicities of this life, I recognised as early as the tender, naïve age of being seven when I sat in the silhouetted stalls to watch the very beautiful Ursula Andress rise from the foam like Aphrodite in the voted most favourite James Bond movie of all time, *Dr No*, in 1963. Ursula was the personification of female and/or young woman in her bikini-clad role of Honey Ryder. Like many millions, I may have been mesmerised. I met up with Ursula on screen only a few short years later in the screen adaption of *She*, Ayesha, 'Who must be obeyed' ... an even more beautiful personification of female. The movie was an adaption from the first Ayesha book by the possibly mystical Rider Haggard, with 83 million copies sold in 1965, one of the bestselling books of all time. Yes, Rider Haggard. Along with Ursula-Ayesha, here was 'Ryder/Rider' again. My flirtation with synchronicity, if not with Ursula, was born, but - on reflection - I feel she had triggered something in my psyche...the search for the Ultimate Woman. Not bad for a ten-year-old!

The following years were pretty mundane, living in the small fishing village of South Shields in a tiny corner of the north east of England – I must have gone a little bit shy on Ayesha. My mother referred to herself as a spiritualist medium, and for company would easily persuade me to accompany her on her many regular jaunts to the nearby spiritualist church in the town. With a dawning of an early scientific mind, I was happy enough to go, after all even at 14 you can't consider contact with the dead as passé. She would often recount the tale of how, just before my birth, she had had a vision of an angelic figure she interpreted as no less than Jesus, presenting her with a string of pearls, but alas, one was missing on the broken link. As I was born in June, which has the pearl as its stone, maybe that was the simple solution to that.

After numerous visits over a short period, in which my fascination began to wane, I was told the familiar sort of messages many, many people hear and in many cases hope to hear. They are gifted, special, should be a healer and have a spiritual task to fulfill. I suppose I imbibed as much of this promise as would any other kid in his mid-teens. Still, to be fair, there was still a 'something' in there somewhere, indeed a quest but not a one mollified by almost anybody who could call themselves a spiritualist, and relate to you mainly stuff you already knew, or who you could fall asleep listening to. I did have more than a fair share of what is loosely referred to as 'psychic phenomenon' occur in my presence or nearby. Too numerous to mention here, and maybe a percentage of them clearly having rational explanations that I would resist accepting at the time, after all nothing more natural for a teenager to rebel, and so in this case, against orthodox sciences.

Mind, there was one good vision in which I was awake in bed when suddenly I found I couldn't move. My head was gently turned to the left by a presence and when I tried to shout out of fear, nothing would come out. I was now in direct alignment with my closed bedroom curtains...but as I was, I suppose, forced to watch, they slowly opened and a table appeared before them with a vase containing dead or withered flowers.

As I watched, the flowers suddenly came into bloom as if reincarnating (maybe they WERE rein-carnations!) then the vision faded and my limbs could function again.

We're told this phenomenon is called 'night terrors' caused by increased brain activity, confusional arousal and partial awakening from non REM, or non-dream, sleep. Maybe it is, but it certainly is a strange experience. I was living in a house – number 13 as it happens – that had previous Jewish occupants, and when we arrived there they had some of their religious icons about. On my mother's side I have a Jewish connection, her surname was Laban, a tribe mentioned in the bible. My father was Danish who had arrived in this country from Canada. With icy-cold Scandinavian blood in my system courtesy of Dad and hot blood in my ancestral blood from the Middle East courtesy of Mother, I could, indeed, blow cold or hot with equal ease. I had also experienced the state of going into epileptic seizure at 10 when one of my tonsils had poisoned me to such a point that I was slowly choking to death as my windpipe was shrinking, and the lack of oxygen would hurl me into unconsciousness. It's a condition called peritonitis. This was hurriedly remedied by the emergency removal of the nasty tonsil, but at least I can say I have experienced the state of aura – the imminence of the fit approaching. It is weird and most likely mystical ... once epilepsy was known as a sacred disease as during the state of convulsion communication was being made with the Gods. Maybe it threw me up a neurological circuit to join the one that may have followed the delivery of breach birth, another condition that can affect the brain owing to oxygen. Maybe neither.

Still, the Inner search was still on, not completely dormant and beginning to twitch a little. It twitched in the direction of Buddhism. Brought up in a Christian country and actually being quite good at school, I decided that I knew enough of this Christianity thing and was intrigued when I first heard of the Buddha chap. A bit confusing mind – if he ate so little and regulated, why did he look so fat in his statues? By the time I was 20 I also decided it was time to make a move. I had been absolutely astounded to learn that the Tibetans had categorised 49 levels of consciousness, when we in the West only knew two – sober and drunk. I had to know more or learn and earn, about these other states. I didn't do drugs unlike so many other mystics who can only access inner planes by doing so, and had no intention or interest to. I was relatively confident I had already been born with psychedelic vision. If ever I heard a wild or far out claim I would think, 'I must investigate that'. So you can imagine the many unbelievable anecdotes I had read after having read every worthwhile esoteric book from the age of 10-20 (I think the first may have been Adamski's iconic, and kind of silly when you get older, *Flying Saucers have Landed*, brought into class by our English teacher Mr Roberts who spent the entire lesson reading it to us!). Consequently, I was struggling to get my head around the more scientific investigations of physicist Jacques Vallee on the subject in his *Anatomy of a Phenomenon*. At the tender age of ten, that one was a difficult one to read with its contents of physics, but I wasn't giving up, and I'll explain why. As that ten-year-old, my interest in dinosaurs had been challenged overnight, when the front page of our local newspaper read one night in 1967, 'Flying Saucers over Tyne Dock'. Yes, here was my very first introduction to the pesky phenomenon that simply will not leave popular culture, or dinosaurs, alone.

Tyne Dock was a part of my town that I had never visited, it may as well have been in Australia, and I'd have never worked out the right bus to get me there. But one night some UFOs hung over a block of flats there long enough for residents to look out and up from their windows to witness these three stationary bright lights early in the morning, before the trio decided to whizz off at alarming pace. One family in particular were so concerned that they contacted the friendly, persuasive, Ministry of Defence, who assured them that what they had seen was a weather balloon that had blown over from Aughton, Liverpool. Oh dear, a difference of opinion there then. The poor chap who was afforded this reply went on to be stuck with the nickname 'Ronnie Rocket' for his troubles. Our alien weather balloon saga didn't end above Ronnie's flat, though. For that entire week, the town of South Shields was host to a 'UFO flap', the 5am gathering of early morning workers awaiting the first ferry of the day, all witnessing numerous 'flying crosses' in the sky being one of the better sightings. The local newspaper 'the Gazette' continued to carry a number of interesting sightings and reports from the townsfolk, as it certainly did look as if something was going on in their airspace that week. Naturally, I was out there each night too hoping to spot my quota. I didn't, just a false alarm with low flying seagulls, but it was jolly exciting and full of inspiring hope, despite being bloody freezing. Could you blame me for deciding there and then that this 'UFO' thing was something worthy of investigating? Obviously at the time I would be thinking here were the deliberately tantalizing space folk although I couldn't work out why they wouldn't just land and have done with it. However, they were going to re-enter into my life at a later stage, if not re-enter our atmosphere for all to see, by which time I wouldn't be thinking 'aliens', but something more psychological - as we will see.

In 1975, having been impressed by another 'good at the time but silly when older' book - George Hunt Williamson's saucer effort *Other Tongues, Other Flesh* - I had copied a logo from out of his pages, the emblem of the 'Knights of the Solar Cross'. After meditating on it for weeks and trying hard to relate to it in any way, one night I had a response. At the time, I was sleeping on the floor in a bedroom upstairs - I think I was trying to be disciplined - which meant I had a great panoramic view through my bay window. One late night/early morning whilst awake, I noticed a golden explosion in the sky above St Michael's Church, which was in direct line with my house in the not too far distance. Excitedly running to the window, I watched how this golden orb wobbled itself off to the left and out of vision. I was convinced that this was a response from my Solar Cross brethren. Sceptics will say it was probably a flare, but it wasn't. Unsure what it was, but I'm quietly confident now that it was an appropriately presented archetypical response to my meditations, I - of course - filed it under 'UFO'. Anyway, as I was by now starting to become a little restless and frustrated at not being able to suss out these mysteries of the Universe, I decided during my teens - the best time for rebellion against science - that there was nothing for it other than to became a magician and/or alchemist! A natural born loner, I wouldn't join any of the group, or order, or cult, or even work with any other individual. My path was a lonely one, and started with an investigation into the psychological realm of Jung - and Crowley's - archetypes.

As a child of nature, and a male, I wondered if I could experiment becoming 'one with the male force in nature'. The only way to find out would be to try. Having read about the liaison with Ogilvy Crombie, a 73-year-old chap in Edinburgh who was surprised one day by the unexpected appearance of the God Pan and his faerie folk, and further adventures with the Findhorn community in Scotland (they found a horn alright, two in fact!), I - too - was inspired to see if I could befriend the Goat God, saturating myself in thoughts, poetry, drawings and literature concerning his presence. In my second stage of experimenting with archetypes, the first being that of the 'UFO', I again eventually met with success and the archetypal Pan. The first time remains still quite fresh in my ailing memory, it was August 10th 1981. To some, purely Dreamland and therefore inconsequential, to others an Inner plane with meaning, I was led in the sequence by a figure whose voice I could only hear without seeing the person. 'So you want to see faeries,' it said, and an arm and hand pointed me in the direction...I was in some sort of garden with rocks and shrubs along a path. As I followed the natural direction, I began to feel an overwhelming force, which I will try to explain by saying it would feel like trying to push yourself forward through a sea of treacle! I had never felt such a force or feeling ever before, although I would encounter it, this amazing 'Panic', many years later whilst in the physical in June 2005 upon the tor at Glastonbury. Approaching an alcove I was finding myself forced to the ground by the invisible force, and then a stone pedestal appeared and upon it an open book. The figure of the God Pan appeared along with it. I remember nothing else, neither did I at the time but I do 'know' that some conversation did take place.

Thus began an intense archetypical interlude that lasted seven years until my interest in the God began to wane, and with it the interaction, but not after a number of Inner Plane encounters - some that are too ludicrous to mention! During these years I discovered that photographs I had taken in innocence of natural landscape had picked up subtle images, the camera apparently being able to pick up some activities that are too sensitive for the human eye. Strange creature-like figures that for all the world met with the archetype of faeries would often appear and be seen to move about from photo to photo! When I showed these pictures to people, some would see the figures without a problem, some would need time and others would see nothing. It's no fun showing photos to people highlighting elfin type figures when the viewer can't see anything! They obviously think you're barmy, but then I learned of a neurological condition called Scotoma, whereby some people CAN see certain content in a photograph whilst others simply can't. Much of it has to do with 'programming' in the brain, i.e., you only see what you expect to see and also from what brain lobe of the two the viewer may satisfactorily normally reside in. When I was 18, I decided that I would start writing with my left hand instead of my trusty right, and found that I could do it with equal ease. What I probably didn't know at that time was by changing to my left I would enforce functioning in my opposite and right brain lobe, wherein resides the faculty of intuitiveness and an open door to mysticism, and that I was actually making a neurological shift. Where the idea, or more correctly, impulse came to do that I'm unsure! I contacted ASSAP – the Association for the Scientific Study of Anomalous Phenomenon, who put me in touch with a retired photographer from the Royal College, a Vernon Harrison who lived in Surrey, who could see what I was indicating. He scrutinised the negatives to announce that they were entirely genuine with no touch-ups or composites. Vernon said that in order to take my claim of snapping elves further he'd have to come to personally visit the conducive wood in which they were appearing, and take photographs himself. If he picked up the faerie folk, and they were to be seen moving whilst retaining their identity from snap to snap he would have to declare that I was photographing dimensional denizens. Vernon taught me how to rotate pictures 360 degrees, and that if the figures still retained their identity then they would have to be ruled out as illusion. He sent his fairly balanced report to his superiors asking for the funding to travel to conduct his experiment and, surprisingly to him, he heard nothing more! Content with my own findings, I let the matter go. But what were my findings? I had conducted psychological experiments to attempt to 'tap' a powerful archetype - the God Pan, who is associated with the faerie realm. It worked, and next I was having representatives of his kingdom appear on photography. Had the archetype had a knock on effect, producing another powerful and global archetype, that of the faerie folk? That they could appear on photographic film, as did the God Pan, suggests that Mind can impress itself in any form it wishes on chemical film.

Years later in 1989, I was visited by Joe Cooper from Leeds, author of *The Case of the Cottingley Fairies*, with whom I had acquainted myself owing to our common interest, having been brought together in 1982 by Colin Wilson. Joe had a dilemma. For years and years he had, I suppose, pestered Elsie and Frances, the two sisters who shook the world in 1917 by producing photographs of faeries taken alongside a beck in Cottingley, Yorkshire. Joe was adamant that one day he would get them to confess that the pictures were fake, and how they had done it. Both girls stood firm and so Joe was within weeks of having his book and life's work published in support of their claims when the girls fell out, and Elsie announced that they were fake. Joe didn't know what to do – should he keep the disclosure to himself and have the book published or cash in on the scoop to tell the world but lose his book deal? How could I advise him? In the end, the book did survive and a compromise was reached – three of the four photos were fake, but the fourth was genuine. No way was I going to get embroiled in all that stuff, so I moved on from fairyland and photography, my last ever faerie encounter being during a visit at Trow Rocks one day, on the South Shields coastline. From behind a rock a short distance from where I was standing, I heard the weirdest sound, or music, I had ever heard, drifting over. I couldn't describe it then and from what I recall of it I couldn't now. Why did I recognise it as faerie music then? Thinking that somebody must be sitting behind this huge rock, and therefore out of my vision and possibly fiddling with some radio off station, I hopped over the few rocks between to confirm this. The music stopped as I approached, and sure enough there was nobody there. I now understand there are such things as audio hallucinations, and I'll settle for that, having soaked my pysche for a long time then with all things faerie. To my mind, I had satisfactorily attained a direct link with a global archetype. Where to next?

I'd had a fair smattering of astral projections, although not the sort where you could consciously step out of your heavy protoplasmic shell. My encounters started with a lucid consciousness, moments after separation during sleep; hey, it's fun bouncing off your bedroom wall because your still alert, rational mind tells you that you can't walk through that wall! I'd just wander about outside amazed that physical people out there couldn't see me, nothing much more exciting than that! One weird encounter that must have been astral was when my consciousness became lucid as I found myself strapped on some sort of trolley that you'd expect to find in a hospital, travelling along tight, windy corridors that appeared to be flanked by stone walls. I wasn't happy with this and so decided to wake myself up, as you usually can in these sorts of scenarios, but this time I couldn't. It was like an enforced ride through your visiting fair's ghost train. Next up, I'm in this sort of mosque-type building and can even hear the sort of Arabic calls they make to round up their own for prayer. An appropriately attired, Persian-type fellow approached, and - so nervously, but happy to be at last free from restraint - I asked him the obvious one. 'Where am I?' I remember his reply clearly, although it still doesn't make much sense. 'Well... you could be in an element...or you could be in Nempis or Lillyland.' A conversation followed that I can't remember, but could when I woke up in a pool of sweat soon after. The Mastery type looking fellow in the turban had told me,

'You are going to be well known, and then....' Just like the shot gangster in the movie who is going to name a name, but then takes his last breath, I was left in limbo over the 'and then..' bit. Oh well, just as well I simply record these experiences for you. I sure can't fathom them, let alone dare to even want to. I had, at this stage, developed a taste for investigating anything that, on the face of it, sounded too good to be true. When I read the 1981 book *The Lost World of Agharti* by Alec McLellan I knew at once what was next on my agenda. Alec claimed that whilst on a walking trip along the Wharfe Valley in Yorkshire during the '70s he had spotted a light shining high up at a point almost mid-way between the small villages of Starbotton and Kettlewell. Taking himself up the slope through the foliage, he approached the area of the light and found a cave entrance. Alec says he went along the tunnel until he heard a rumbling noise and saw an eerie green light. He left in a hurry never to return, but included the tale in his book nominating this entrance as being one of the many across the globe that can lead to the subterranean realm of Agharti – pretty much one and the same as the Tibetan Shamballah! In Yorkshire!

It seemed unlikely to me that a person having made such a fortuitous find, and the implications he announced, would never return, so I wrote to him through his publisher to see if he would release any further assistance in pinpointing where the tunnel lay. Having waited long enough to deduce that I was unlikely ever to hear, I visited the valley on an icy February day in 1982 when the landscape was devoid of natural covering. With two intrepid people to help me out, we split into three solitary groups mid-way between the two villages as recounted in the book, and ascended the slope; that same slope in the valley to which he had alluded. After considerable time, and just as we were about to give up what we thought was fast becoming a hopeless task, one of my men shouted over. I won't repeat what he shouted, but there he was facing a cave entrance sealed by frozen ice. To cut a long story short, I kicked the ice in, and ventured along the tunnel which has water running outwards up to half way up the knee. I did reach an end to the tunnel after ten or so nervy and lonely minutes, as my companions waited outside. No ongoing tunnel, no weird green light, no rumbling. I have no doubt this was the same place Alec was describing, but to me it appeared to be nothing other than an old worked mine, the kinds of which are plentiful in the area. Again through his publishers, I sent him photos of both inside, and of the cave entrance for him to recognise, but again I never received any correspondence. What I had received from this venture though, was well worth it - confidence. Don't believe a thing until you can check it for yourself. In the following years, I would do just that.

This form of investigation also extended to people. From 1982-85, I had made contact with the late Mr Alex Sanders, self-proclaimed 'King of the Witches', and a big media celebrity during the sixties. Much of Alex's claims were outrageous to say the least, and as I viewed him as the logical successor to arch rogue and occultist Aleister Crowley, I thought I should check out the chap for myself to see what made him tick. Alex, it seems, was branching out from his previously restricted witchcraft-only activities. He was 69 at the time I met up with him (although to everyone else he was a mere 59) and drawing his pension, and reckoned six covens that were out to get him for having upset them were chasing him! I was always wary of Alex as he was a notorious bi-sexual, which in some ways I found peculiar as he claimed to be the head of a natural religion and practice, and I made it abundantly clear to the promiscuous fellow that I was a red-blooded male with only eyes for the female. He reckoned he was now being bothered by UFOs and wasn't too happy about it, even telling me that a car he had been travelling in had a disc-shaped object tail it as close as the car bumper. My interests in Alex were purely to ascertain, as I had done with my stay at Samye-Ling, how valid people's experiences with the hidden side of life could be, and how valid, for example, witchcraft could be. As usual, my findings were that most, if not all, of it was subjective and a matter of belief and/ or hearsay and anecdotal stories. Mind you, you just couldn't keep those nosey UFOs out of the picture, and impinging themselves upon people's lives, whatever they were. He had also mentioned reluctant communications that were involving those around him in Rennes-le-Chateau.

Next up, I thought it was high time (pun intended!) that I visit the Tor at Glastonbury, although to be fair, it might just have been that the Tor was 'drawing' me to it. There's nothing like timing in this Game. Staying with a friend who was living nearby I couldn't wait, as my original intention was to go up there on Hallowe'en night – nothing like a bit of drama! And so my first actual ascension up this world famous mound was at about 4pm in October. The Tor at Glastonbury is a natural 520' conical hill set in the Somerset landscape. Its legends and accolades are many, ranging from a faerie hill, the entrance to the Underworld of King Gwyn Ap Nudd, a global energy point where ley lines cross, and tales of people suddenly being levitated whilst up there, as sworn by a group of Buddhist monks in 1969. So many are these stories that it is really difficult to write anything refreshingly new. A book in 2005 by author Nicholas Mann who lives in the area, *The Secret Energies of Glastonbury Tor*, goes some way in trying to explain electro-magnetic vortices at work with a scientific approach. Can this hill justify the wondrous tales of coloured lights seen emanating from it, earth lights that can spiral, the least optical phenomena associated with any self-respecting faerie hill? I personally know of two friends who, individually on separate occasions, have experienced what they describe as a 'beam' coming down from the night sky to pass from their head right through and down their body. And once I had an email from a previous Mayor of Glastonbury who saw a reddish orange light appear one night above the Tor and sink into the summit, but not come out of it as its coloured light displays mostly do, and himself referring to it as a 'spaceship'. And so it goes on! If it is an energy point then one fact that people of Glastonbury can't be denied is that every year the rock music festival that first started in 1970 now draws approximately 180,000 visitors into the area, all camping out over its three days in June - that's a lot of energy to soak up!

Does it draw these people's energy to itself for some reason, as if it needs, or can utilise it? Did it draw me? There was no wind about, but as I began a slow ascension from the bottom of Chalice Well a small breeze began to whip up, and whip up, and whip up until by the time I reached the Michael Tower at the summit a full scale gale was blowing and I feared I would be blown off the top! An interesting introduction! I did, as planned, return on Hallowe'en but not at the night-time as I'm pretty certain I wouldn't have been the only one with that thought in mind, and so I visited at 11.30pm on the 30th staying until 1.30am, the actual morning of the Hallowe'en date. I did well, as I didn't come across a soul up there throughout, and did even better when - after only a few moments having reached the summit - a silent flash of silver shot horizontally only feet above my head. A few minutes later what I can best describe as a rapid, short-lived bombardment of tiny grey 'ping pong' type balls whizzed past me on either side of the slopes. I've since read that other people have experienced this impromptu game of table tennis. The Tor, with its carved stone representation of the Phoenix on its Michael Tower, fascinated me. Whether it did anything else to me on a subtle level I can't be sure, but, as we shall soon see, circumstances may have been priming me for an even more astounding encounter relating to this bird.

Many years later, on the bright day of February 26th, 2007 at 4.33pm Mike Chenery, a resident of Glastonbury whom I was destined to meet, was walking up Well House Lane when his attention was drawn to the fact that all the singing birds had stopped their song. This stillness and suspension was reminiscent of what occurs at the time of a solar eclipse, when birds temporarily become disorientated. He was then at the gate that provides a vantage point view of one of the un-arched sides of the Tower. Casually looking up, he saw a dazzling white 'something' that, in his words 'glided' a short distance from within the Tower. At first it showed itself as thin, but then moved its perspective facing Mike's direction and - in doing - so widened, rather like at first being like a door seen sideways on and then full frontal. As he always carries a camera during his numerous excursions, he only just found the time to take a picture, and then the apparition that had only lasted seconds, simply 'popped off'! There had been nobody upon the Tor at the time. The result on his digital camera confirmed what he had seen with his own eyes. I have met Mike and have no doubt about the sincerity of his account, and the authenticity of his photograph. Was it what is referred to by UFO enthusiasts as a Portal? I now have definite thoughts on what exactly certain points on the globe are, those that are celebrated by criss-crossing of ley lines and such, and I'll return to this subject later, for Lincolnshire has a most impressive network!

My drive for travelling to investigate other places of personal interest was fuelled by a spiritual petrol. Next stop was the wonderful subterranean Temple of Hal Saflieni on the wondrous island of Malta, island of the Knights of St John of Jerusalem. I had read strange accounts of goings on at Hal Saflieni, a three level, underground temple discovered by accident when a tractor hit a stone in a field in 1902. There were reports of individuals, and an entire school party of children, having gone missing after entering a burial chamber entrance at the bottom level. Such was the concern of the Maltese Government with rumours of never-ending tunnels, and reports of strange sightings of 'Giants' along there, that they put an end to it by selling off the chamber in 1972. Some researchers believe that the entire Maltese island can be traversed from end to end via a subterranean network. Having waited ten years to get there, I eventually visited this Wonder of the World and had a déjà vu experience when enunciating the word 'Ma' into the strange oracle there that repeats what you say in echo. For a person who had had his fair share of this strange phenomenon some call a mild form of epilepsy, this happened to be the very last time I was to experience it. The Oracle is the only part within the Temple where this effect occurs. I saw for myself the sealed chamber, and was confident, albeit disappointed, when I had to concede there were no other apparent uninvestigated entrances. Crossing Hal Saflieni off my list at last, I also visited the megalithic sites, Tarxien and Tas silg (finding time to nip under the ground at St Paul's catacombs) on the island and on its smaller sister island of Gozo. At one of these sites, Gigantija, I was unaware at the time that it was associated with pregnancy.

Whilst I had been staying with friends at Chapel St Mary's during my Glastonbury jaunt, they had also taken me to visit the Cerne Giant etched out in chalk in Dorset. It had been so misty that morning you couldn't even see right in front of you, and so when we parked up and ascended small hills in the area we didn't even know we were standing on him until the mist slightly cleared, and I realised I was standing on his erect penis! The Cerne Giant is also associated with pregnancy and is visited by many infertile couples who later have success in becoming pregnant. And so, at least two unwitting visits to specific zones associated with childbirth. Was I in preparation for some sort of destined birthing – or re-birth – event? If so, two other areas I had been drawn to – presumably when some time scale beyond my senses was right – was the Castlerigg Carles stone circle at Keswick, Cumbria, one of the most beautiful stone circles in Britain dating from around 3,000BC, and where I was destined to meet my wife for the first time. And also the mystical 3.4 mile long and 1.7 wide Scottish island of Iona within the Inner Hebrides, an isle with past faerie associations, both in 1985. No particular, or obvious, pregnancy associations there. Or so I thought at the time until the Lost Mother Tongue taught me how to delve deeper. The anagram of 'Carles' is 'Lescar', a commune in the Aquitaine area of South West France, site of the Roman city known as Benearnum, the capital and origin of the name of the ancient province of Bearn. 'Bearn' is the Old English word meaning 'to bear' and gives birth (pun intended!) for the Scottish word 'bairn' – a child. There is an even more impressive confirmation. Traditionally, it is considered impossible to accurately count the number of stones within the Carles circle. Why? Erosion around the stones from heavy traffic of visitors is responsible for several smaller stones having 'appeared' next to some of the larger ones. Owing to this, some count the total as being 38, others 42, the official number, say the National Trust, is 40. The gestational age in human birth occurs normally at about 40 weeks though a normal range is from 37-42. The Castlerigg stone circle is spot on for birth! As for the Inner Hebridean Iona, we find the name concealed within the word 'amnion', the inner of the two fetal membranes enclosing the amniotic sac that surrounds and protects the embryo.

CHAPTER THREE
A DATE WITH THE RENNES VALLEY

S ince 1982, when a million or more of us read the controversial TV advertised *Holy Blood, Holy Grail* by Baigent, Leigh and Lincoln, I was longing to visit what had fast become the top of the mystery list, way above the pyramids and life after death, and even our friends in their UFOs ... Rennes-le-Chateau. What on earth, or possibly under it, was going on over there in this small mountaintop village at the foothill of the Pyrenees? Something, it appeared, to do with what we refer to as the Holy Grail, Jesus and Mary, and a treasure hunt. The mystery was hard to miss. There seems to be something deep in the human psyche that simply loves a treasure hunt. Maybe the perceived challenge, in some way, plucks it out from something hidden deep within our psychology, the culmination of finding some sort of catharsis, or required emotional release. From simple acrostics found in any weekly, coffee-break puzzle magazine to complex cryptology employing computers, there is a startling cross-section of people who enjoy both the eventual satisfaction, and interim frustration, of the pleasure-pain of working out the cracking of codes. Man's fascination with this search in its myriad forms, from the ridiculous to the sublime never seems to wane. After the Meaning of Life, the one enduring Quest – and perhaps entwined with it – seems to be the fabled search for the Holy Grail, to some a spiritual or psychological object, and to others perhaps a real, tangible object or treasure of immense religious significance. Since the 12th Century this Grail Quest has taken many forms in many places, the most famous and popular - no doubt - that of the semi-legendary British King, Arthur and his chivalrous Knights of the Round Table.

Arthur himself is reputedly buried at approximately sixteen different sites scattered throughout the British Isles! In fact, the search for Arthur's grave alone has been the goal of many treasure hunters. Along with these archaeological intrepid, there is another category that continues to fascinate. That of the conspiracy theorist, be it the Kennedy assassination, the American moon landing, UFOs , and the death of Princess Diana and Dodi Fayed, (not to mention the alleged faked deaths of Elvis, Bruce Lee and Jim Morrison) all of which are being argued over today. However, there is now a new contender above all contenders, which does appear to combine both treasure hunt and conspiracy theory rolled into one. The Line of David – a genealogical paper chase that twists and spirals like DNA throughout history claiming to have its origins in an undisclosed family emanating from the biblical Jesus himself, has now become the premier 'fact or fiction' investigation...the finding of any such 'treasure' is the ultimate hunt, the disclosure of its secret the ultimate conspiracy. Whereas modern conspiracies have little or nothing to do with ciphers, word games and puns, this finely attuned mystery most certainly does, often to the point of vexation and discouragement, inviting us into, without any real option, an arena almost exclusively dominated by the controversial society known as Freemasonry. To some, the very mention of the word conjures up scenes of men in this exclusive male order doing silly things like rolling up their trouser leg and swopping funny handshakes, but to others it is a very serious, if not aloof, social standing of favoured individuals. Either way, the Freemasons are viewed in such a controversial light it enables them to compete with any conspiracy theory!

In the beginning was the Word...and from the word 'treasure', Old French 'tresor', Latin 'thesauros', we find that a thesaurus is 'a storehouse of knowledge...a dictionary'. Maybe treasure = dictionary, for certainly without the word play we will face, there will be no chance of a fortuitous or guided find.

Three years after the blockbuster that was the brainchild of Baigent, Leigh and Lincoln, there arrived a new book on the steady stream of books attempting to solve the mystery at Rennes. It was the geometrical handiwork of a surveyor from Tunbridge Wells in Kent, England by the name of David Ronald Wood. David's book *Genisis-The First Book of Revelations* caused more than a stir, packed with stark graphic sexual imagery as revealed in his geometrical appraisal; and finds within the Rennes Valley. His work was innovative and caught most expectations off guard. In a way, David nominated a location within the book, calling it his 'seed', and seemed happy enough to more or less present where it lay within the pages of his self-published epic. (At a later date he confided to me that he had moved it a bit!) After considerable amounts of interchange with David by mail, it made sense to pay the author a visit if he was happy with that. He was, understandably, guarded about such things and later told me he believed there had been an Israeli attempt to have him kidnapped and taken out of the country for assassination, as his book could be interpreted as revealing where might be the location of the biblical Ark of the Covenant...his possible identification with the treasure. At the time, he was living at 'Owl's Nest Wood', something of a fortress befitting an individual who may have to be aware of people out there who would wish him harm. Rennes-le-Chateau in those days, was a dangerous place to involve yourself with, as previous investigators had found...as a snooping outsider you clearly weren't made welcome...at all.

Some of David's own personal revelations, made in confidence, were alarming to say the least. He said that he had a man in the French Government who made sure that his work would be placed in President Mitterrand's tray. Most unexpected of all was a series of verse that he showed us, which read like gobbledegook as words and rhymes ran into one another in pun-like fashion, to give a convoluting and tantalising prose concerning Rennes-le-Chateau, its environs, and the search for a 'treasure'. As if needing to have to show it to somebody for reassurance in some way, David explained that he had been made to sit up in bed at night against his will to receive and jot down the bizarre recitals, and that they were being put into his head! I still remember today, the opening line, at least. It went, 'One knows one now we will allow from the nest of the owl to note the Al...' I had no resistance in believing the man, as he was far too dedicated in his relentless researching, a serious and rational man in early middle-age who appeared to possess strength, will and knowledge. The obvious question to ask was placed in his head by whom, and how? I remember clearly how he was afraid of sharing this for fear of being branded a lunatic, and who could blame him? We all thought that this mystery was nothing other than involving physicality, not craziness from who knows where. I later found that a number of Rennes researchers had all rubbed shoulders with this aspect of the Unknown and would always find it difficult should they ever dare to share it to a sympathetic ear, in case their earlier credibility was dismissed on the spot. From my own experiences in life it read like water off a duck's back, for who gives the authority for us to assume life to be as we think it? I couldn't really help David with the verses, and to this day wouldn't know if he had ever shown them to anyone else, though I'm quite certain he never did make head nor tail of any, if not all, of it. David at the time was a close friend of the French authoress Elizabeth Van Buren who had written both books, *The Sign of the Dove* and *Refuge of the Apocalypse* concerning Rennes. She was living at Les Labadous in the valley, and at the time we visited in April '86 she was having trip wires installed across her property, and David and her would meet at his home to trade ideas and liable discoveries.

Elizabeth did my wife and me a great disservice when we met her at her farm in the valley the following year. She inaccurately, and I don't know why, told David that we had said we thought he wasn't to be trusted and that we didn't like him, when in fact it was herself who had said to us, that if only he were working for good, he would be a powerful force! This relayed mischief certainly, as one would expect, soured our relationship with David Wood. Whilst at his home, and after a few drinks, he had taken me into his drawing room and instructed me to do a simple piece of geometry on his huge Ordinance Survey maps of the valley; it was nothing more than join a few places up in a straight line that led to Pech Cardou. 'There's no need for geometry', he said, 'It's Cardou'... an entirely different conclusion to the one stated in his book. Years later in 1995, in their book *The Tomb of God* authors Andrews and Schellenberger announced the same. Their book sat at the top of the bestseller list, and may have stayed longer had they not been well and truly stitched up by appearing on the BBC documentary programme 'Horizon'.

Anyway, such was the continuing controversy with David's 'Genisis' that I gather his unpopularity in France made him so unwelcome at Rennes that he was just about banned from the region. I last spoke with him in 1989 when he was still experiencing problems. He said that one night eleven cars pulled up unannounced outside his property and gained entrance with warrants to leave, helping themselves to as much correspondence and paperwork of his as they wanted. He further told me they were trying to frame him for trumped-up tax evasion, for which he wasn't at all guilty, and which could have led to a term in prison. Apparently, a similar thing had just occurred in America with a researcher who had gone to jail, after he had claimed there was evidence that there had been physical life on Mars. David had also had his share of UFO intervention. On one occasion, whilst conducting research into his geometry in the valley, he was unsure about which direction to go. At the precise moment he indicated with his hand whether he should carry on in that particular direction, one solitary clap of thunder directly overhead him persuaded him he should! To some, this sort of stuff might sound incredulous but as you will learn, there is little or nothing that cannot be ruled out concerning this exceptionally strange place we call Rennes-le-Chateau.

We liked David Wood. He came at precisely the right time to open up new frontiers in attempting to solve the enigma. His final word on the matter was revealed in his second and last book in 1994 – *Geneset - Target Earth*, co-written with Ian Campbell, in which he announced that the clues and geometry all led to telling us that there was a comet on the way that would hit the planet, and that this would happen in 2085. David, sadly, passed away on November 19th 2012 aged 83, the first and last of his kind. We send him our respect through Time and Space.

It was now getting time for us to visit Rennes for ourselves to see what lay in store, and we had a time and date to meet, again arrived at by unorthodox means. Avril, the lady who was soon to become my wife, had already been there in 1984, having been instructed – here we go again! –in a series of informative, strangely lucid, dreams. She had been told that she was going to find, 'A treasure..a golden helmet encrusted with diamonds and rubies with a bird flying out of the top'. She was then, as today - and in tandem with myself - an individual totally unconcerned and disinterested in commercial gain, let alone treasure. The two most unlikely treasure-hunters make we! Whilst visiting the Poussin tomb, which once stood off the roadside at Serres until it was blown up by its owner in 1989, she had taken a photo from that nearby road. When the photograph was developed it showed a huge circular form rising up from below the tomb. Cynics would dismiss it simply as a hair on the lens - as did the world famous physicist Paul Davies when I showed him it in person that year at a lecture in Newcastle-upon- Tyne. But upon closer, and more serious scrutiny, it clearly resembled a biological cell! More on this later.

It was an amazing photo, and I sent a photocopy version to David Wood, and later we included in a specific dossier sent to both Head Lodges of 33rd Degree Freemasons in both England and Scotland in 1989. As I had discovered many years earlier, the camera can pick up things invisible to the eye, imprinting itself on chemical film. My wife also has a photo taken in Sauniere's graveyard, and behind her - clearly visible to most, if not all who saw the photo - you could see a knight on a horse smiling at the camera! How preposterous, but absolutely true. As easily as we had been gifted these unique photos, we had them taken from us when a theft involving a temporary caravan-home that we had in 2000, meant all the contents were stolen by opportunists whilst we were at work and our whereabouts known. Maybe a case of easy come, easy goes.

In 1969, Avril along with her mother, saw a UFO outside their home in Washingborough, Lincolnshire. At first they thought it was no more than car headlights coming over the hill, but then a huge grey conical object completely blocked their view of the sky. As reported the following day in the local press, the local RAF base at Waddington had tracked a UFO on radar that night and followed it some distance down the coast. Avril has had many unexplained experiences throughout her life, and this may be due to the fact that she has a different brain-wiring to the norm, the complex and puzzling neurological condition known as Asperger's Syndrome, which allows her access to areas of the brain that are usually 'out of bounds' to others. She is known to Professor Darold Treffert at his Research Centre for autistic savants at Wisconsin, USA, and her life story is also known to Professor Simon Baron-Cohen, the UK's leading expert in autism at his Research Centre at Cambridge University. A limited edition book I wrote for academics in 2,000, *Buddha and the Autist*, put forward my observation that there is a tangible connection between various Schools of the Eastern Buddhist's search for enlightenment and the unfolding and ongoing evolution of the autistic consciousness, as evinced in the common aspiration of turning within, detachment and elaborate ritual. Simon described my book as 'very interesting and thought provoking'.

Regarding my own Rennes-le-Chateau visit, I too, had been given specific information whilst in the dream state. It clearly impressed upon me a date – April 24th - and with that the word 'Lacombe'. This was about seven or eight months before the following April, so I assumed it meant then: April 24th 1986. Old Halley's Comet whizzed by the earth on 9th February of '86, and as the months whizzed past almost as fast, it was soon approaching April. Avril and her son Rene, only fourteen at the time, and I, left for the Chateau in a mobile home and a van, enjoying every phase of the fantastic scenery that accompanies you as you near the South of France. To undertake to relate the entirety of our adventure at Rennes would probably warrant a book in its own right, and so I hope you'll accept that I will keep the experiences of our three week unannounced stay to the minimum.

Rennes-le-Chateau may be like a theme park now, but it certainly wasn't then. It was dark and unwelcoming, and that was just the locals. Still, it was nice of an impromptu rainbow, with no apparent rain, to welcome us at 8.20 in the evening when we arrived, that second week in April, parking up at the foot of Pech Cardou. The vulture sitting at the top of the mountain would let people know for far around any move that you would make. Our move the following morning was to head off for the Chateau, and there, stopping for a break, we met up with a Frenchman who had left Bordeaux, in his own full knowledge that he had been 'drawn' to give up his current existence, and move to Rennes. He had actually, in time, built his own

Navaho Indian style stone hut and hung his choice of name on it. He had chosen 'Lacombe'. This young shaman was Daniel, and there wasn't a thing he didn't know about the valley. He told us he had been waiting for a specific arrival...a couple. I guess we fitted the bill. Daniel allowed us to stay on his little bit of land, an offer we were gracious to accept. Daniel would be something of a guide to us whilst we stayed in this strangely atmospheric valley. Whilst we shared our travels, all four of us visiting places of specific interest to us, and given that then - as even now - you couldn't be wandering about Rennes without the slight hope that you were going to hit lucky and discover somewhere meant to be hidden, the permutations would sometimes vary, and it would just be me and Avril out and about.

It was the day of the 24th, and what a day we had in store. We had visited the small church of Bugarach, where Avril - when she went into the church alone - had a weird experience whereby she burst into an operatic-type vocal, and was freaked out by her own ability to have suddenly and unexpectedly let rip! On an earlier day, Avril, Daniel and I found ourselves drawn to the area known as 'Green Rocks', finding our way up a winding path where Daniel wiped some soil away on the ground to reveal a small Templar Cross etched on a stone slab. Then, after crossing a small stream, we came upon a natural rock in the shape of a kneeling angel. High up in a mountainous area, you could look across Green Rocks to see Rennes-le-Chateau on the left and Cardou on the right. To the left of our stone angel there was a natural circle in the rock at the very edge of the cliff face. Avril felt she had to sit inside, and from this point you could see right across the valley. She felt, and still does feel, that this was some sort of place and appointment to be met. Well, met it we did.

The previous day had been, until then, just as eventful and weird. I know that I may put my credibility on the line a few times during these pages, but I don't particularly care, for as long as I am telling what I know to be true, why should I care? And I say this because - and David Wood would know this is true as he told me a similar experience - one solitary thunderclap above a terrain prompted us to visit and find a sealed, rock-crop cave. It had two points of entry filled with rubble and debris and I can tell you it is highlighted at the top of one of Leonardo Da Vinci's two versions (Mary without halo) of his 'Virgin of the Rocks', so somehow he must have been aware! A babbling brook runs nearby, and there is a stone marker dolmen. There is an alcove on it that begs out for flowers to be placed there. When Avril arrived, running here first she burst into tears, sobbing and repeating over and over what sounded like 'Artoora'. I have yet to locate any such word in any language although that's not to say it is not out there. When we returned with Daniel, he too knew of the location and told us he had seen a man and woman digging there once. David Wood calmly knew of it and so, she claimed, did Van Buren, saying it was her 'special place', where she would visit and sprinkle holy water. Whether anybody else knew of it then or now, I'm unsure. My own thoughts and feelings are that Mary Magdalene once was entombed here, hence all the legends and her associations with the area. People today still searching for her at Rennes will be either disappointed, hoaxed or misled.

Later, on that fateful day of April 24th, even that encounter would be eclipsed. Whilst on that subject, we didn't know until many years afterwards, that there had been a rare total lunar eclipse that same day, rare owing to the fact that the moon was in conjunct with Pluto, a scarce astronomical event. In today's interpretation, Pluto represents explosive events and nuclear technology. A short few minutes after 8pm in the evening, it was young Rene who first noticed the three bright lights in the sky high above the mountain range in the distance. Bright and rounded, but like stars. Suddenly there, they couldn't help but hold your eye. And then, as we all checked with each other, we could clearly see they were on the move. As suddenly as they had appeared they were gone, but now heading our way came a huge orangey cloud, flashing bolts of lightning from within itself, but in absolute silence, and in a clear blue sky. There was no thunder either and so our thoughts were not with some storm. We were all in Daniel's hut area, which he enclosed with a huge circle of small stones, and then Avril instinctively knew that she had to cover her hair, which she did with a shawl. It was the weirdest thing as it slowly moved silently through the valley and over our heads; it really gave the impression that Time had stood still. The silence was a sound in its own right.

All around us we saw no other signs of life, as the cloud made its way over to the Chateau around the back of the tower there and made off. Only Daniel broke the silence within, in his broken English, 'I think it was a spaceship'. Well, whether it was or not, there are seventy verses describing 'cloud ships' in the *Bible*, my favourite being Ezekiel Chapter I, verse 4:

> 'And I looked, and, behold a whirlwind came out of the north, a great cloud, and a fire infolding itself, and a brightness was about it, and out of the midst thereof as the colour of amber, out of the midst of the fire.'

The following passages go on to describe beings coming out of this midst, but I will settle for that initial description, which is very reminiscent of our own encounter in the valley. That night Avril had this message in a dream, 'When the bird leaves its nest, look to the West'. However that was meant to be interpreted, we left for England the following day, only stopping off to see what Van Buren had thought of the encounter. She wasn't at home having left a day earlier and would be away for weeks, her maid told us. Elizabeth, I feel, hadn't a date with destiny and had missed the phoenix leaving its nest.

This phoenix, in mythology, is a bird with a beautiful voice and with feathers of gold and red, (the golden helmet and rubies Avril received in her message?) and as a bird of Arabia it was so called because it possessed a scarlet colour. In ancient Grecian times, the phoenix managed an association with the bennu bird of Egyptian mythology, and interestingly enough the planet Venus was called 'The star of the ship of the Bennu-Ausar (Osiris)'. Kenneth Grant, in his book *The Magical Revival*, assures us that the phoenix was also an ancient constellation in which Sothis, or

Sirius, was the chief star, this constellation probably corresponding to the complex of stars now known as Cygnus (the Swan of St Hugh) and Aquila. The constellation of Phoenix in the Southern hemisphere has been known by the Arabs as 'The boat'. A ship? Daniel's 'space' ship?

So what had it all been about? Critics - who weren't there – will try and say we had witnessed a strange electrical storm or a supercell thunderstorm and nothing else. I can't accept that I received a time date in my sleep months earlier just to come and witness a freak storm. Can you? Having since read British author Jenny Randles' excellent book *Time Storms*, I'm more inclined to accept that maybe that is what we witnessed. Jenny describes a time storm as involving a peculiar glowing energy cloud that can incur all manners of phenomenon from synchronicities, the opening of alternate dimensions, disorientating the viewers, gravity anomalies and other weird goings on, as part of a scientific reality that we do not understand yet. What I do understand is that a little over a day later, villagers at Chernobyl reported seeing a stationary orange cloud in the sky hours before the disaster at the nuclear power plant that occurred there. Coincidence, or was it related? The explosive and technological aspect of the Pluto configuration? Was the heat of nuclear energy requiring an extraction for some reason beyond our understanding? In 1992 Richard Stanley, an award winning South African-born filmmaker, posted on his online journal dated 31st October 2007, 'Lachrymae, Chapter III, Devil's chessboard' about a visit he had made in 1992 to the ruined castle at the village of Montsegur in the South of France, where the Grail is supposed - by many - to have temporarily been kept in the custody of Cathars. What is of interest, is the 'storm' that came out of nowhere to batter Richard and his crew!
He recalls:

> 'A golden spume of cloud boiled up out of the west moving so fast it was as if we were watching real-time animation or some form of time lapse photography. In fact it put me in mind of another Spielberg movie entirely and this being the 90's and UFOs being all the rage, we half expected the Mothership of Close Encounters to show up at any moment.'

He goes on to describe how the violent storm came right at them with forked lightning flickering within the thunderhead. Richard's encounter, then, did have thunder, but I must tell you this as far as synchronicities go, and he did bump into Daniel when he was over at Rennes on the same expedition. You will recall Daniel's Navaho hut in the Rennes Valley was named 'Lacombe'. Claude Lacombe was the name of the French scientist in the 'Close Encounters' movie who made the alien contact, and the fictional character was styled on real French physicist Jacques Vallee. In the movie, the Mothership made contact at a landmark that actually exists in Wyoming, USA, called 'The Devil's Tower', also known as 'Bear's Lodge', a sacred site for many Indian Americans, and interesting, for later in our story, the constellation of Ursa Major, the Great Bear, will feature. The Tower at Rennes is also referred to as 'the Devil's Tower'! Nick Pope, ex-Secretariat of the Air Staff at the British

Government's Ministry of Defence, and responsible for investigating UFO reports, has shown an interest in our Rennes sighting and told me by email,

> 'It is a fascinating account and clearly no conventional explanation springs to mind. It is interesting to speculate about links between some of these issues, particularly in relation to close encounters and even abductions, where dreams, synchronicities and psychic phenomena do seem to feature quite a bit.'

I feel reasonably comfortable in describing what we saw as the phoenix, in mythology the bird that is immersed in flames only to be reborn from its ashes every 500 years. For a brief moment, I think back to the dramatic end scene of Ayesha, in the movie *She*, when she invites her lover Leo Vincey (!) to step into the mystical blue flame which burns only for a few moments in order that he will be made immortal and join her in life forever. The blue flame precisely hits the designated area like a comet strike from the heavens, its life span before dwindling similar to that moment, or hour of 'heat' prior to female fertilisation. Why I say this is because I have my suspicions about the firebird phoenix, and feel it is a metaphor for pregnancy and birth. The mythological phoenix resurrects every 500 years. If instead, we think in terms of 500 hours, then we have a time scale of approximately 20.8 days. Looking at the word 'hour', we find the origin to be Old French 'hore' and French 'heure'. 'Heure' sounds too much like 'year', and so we may be onto something with our idea that we are talking 500 hours and not years. Greek gives the origin as 'hora' sounding akin to the Old French, and both are unmistakably the same sounding as 'whore', the unfortunate word attributed to those who may be expected to be involved in a more contrived act of sex. Are we onto something here? Is the fire of the phoenix the 'heat' in which a female is most conducive to becoming pregnant?

With the direction of the Collective Unconscious and the Mother Tongue, I would like to now reveal how the Tarot pack is based on the female reproductive system and the process of birth. To look into the word 'tarot', originally a card game developed in 14th Century Italy, then called tarok – tarot, French, from Italian tarocco. It is not coincidental that the long history of these picture cards eventually settled in Italy, the (Gen)Italia – the reproductive organs especially the external sex organs – of the cosmic portrayal of the living earth Gaia. A gentle re-arrangement of 'tarot' affords us the word 'rota' from the Latin meaning 'wheel' which is closest in approximation to a European version of the Tibetan Wheel of Life. The tarot Major Arcana conceals the 28-day continuing cycle in the uterus, the 22 trump cards follow the monthly development of the developing follicle in the ovary to the growing, onto the release of the egg from the follicle during ovulation, to the development of corpus luteum, which secretes the hormone progesterone which maintains pregnancy. Within 'progesterone' we find the word 'gester', the Jester which is the unnumbered 'The Fool' card of the pack, which can occur anywhere, usually to start the pack or end it. Let us look at the word 'fool'. It emanates from Middle English as fol(e), a fool, foolish, from Old French 'fol', from Latin 'follis', meaning bellows, windbag. Paper chasing onto bellows, we locate Middle English 'belwes', belows, plural of 'belu', below from Old English 'belga', plural of 'bel(ig)', 'boelig'; bag, purse, bellows; from Middle English 'bely', 'baly' or 'belly'. Investigating 'belly' to find, firstly, the stomach, secondly, appetite for food and, archaically, known as the womb, the uterus.

The first card in the pack is The Magician, stood at a table. The 'belly' is also known as the front part of the body of a stringed instrument, also called 'table'. Both cards one and two, the Magician and The High Priestess, allude to the magical properties ascribed in superstition and myth to menstrual blood notably as an antidote to infertility. The first two days of the 28-day cycle begins with bleeding, then the uterine starts building up to receive the fertilising egg. The 14th day in the female calendar is the most fertile day for ovulation, requiring sexual abstinence as a natural method for family planning. Card 14 of the tarot pack happens to be Temperance, a word meaning moderation, especially in the indulgence of the natural appetites and passion; self-restraint, abstinence. Although the entire pack is too detailed a task for me to continue here, I will mention two others, card 12 The Hanged Man – representing difficult foetal presentation, and Card 16 The Tower where we can see the fertilised egg divide into two new cells. Was Sauniere aware of this when he built the Tower Magdala dedicated to Mary Magdalene? Did the Collective Unconscious provide it?

Either way, I think we can now begin to see some sort of connection with the Chateau, Mary and our time and date encounter with the firebird of birth. Was the strange 'biological cell' image that Avril had managed to pick up on film rising up at the Poussin tomb exactly that – a biological cell? Again I ask, will those 'UFOs' ever stay out of things? Probably not, but thus ended as much as I care to say about our peculiarly destined 1986 voyage. Having left the world stage in this mystery that fateful April, mission apparently having been accomplished in some undetermined way, I was quite content to leave the mystery of pregnancy and Rennes-le-Chateau behind. But it wouldn't leave me, returning for a rematch in the form of Lincoln Cathedral in 2005....

CHAPTER FOUR
INDUCTION INTO THE SEARCH FOR A SAINT

Having found myself involved in the French mystery of Rennes-le-Chateau, and being led by a series of synchronicities afforded me by the strange machinations of the Collective Unconscious to a conclusion at Lincoln Cathedral, England, I thought it worthwhile to present before those as equally fascinated as myself by this 'treasure' hunting tool, an earlier adventure I embarked upon whilst living in Northern England, as it is a wondrous example of how the puzzle of synchronicity can invite itself into any drama. Naturally, at the time I was unaware that this rather short adventure, by virtue of what would follow later in the city of Lincoln, would serve as a 'dummy run' or a try-out for pursuing a historical figure of status...and with a conclusion that would almost parallel, in some ways, the effort.

I apologise at the onset that many precise details that I usually prefer to present have been mislaid by my imperfect memory, as we must return to 1989, and documents, photos and clippings that I once had in my possession have long since left my safekeeping. However, I will relive and share the story as best I can! I had always had an interest in Durham Cathedral, with its strange chevron-shaped lozenge pillars for which no agreed upon explanation can be confirmed. Durham Cathedral is allegedly the final resting place of St Cuthbert...one of the most important medieval saints, but what interested me the most about him was 'The Cuthbert Code' told me by a retired Benedictine called Walter. Walter brought me up to speed about how, after having originally been buried at Lindisfarne, in 1104 Cuthbert, after much moving about by his protective adherents, was found a resting place within Durham Cathedral, only to be disturbed in 1503 during the Reformation by Henry VIII's marauding commissioners, looting for treasure. Whilst orthodoxy tells us that he was reburied at this shrine in 1542, the Cuthbert Code assures us that his loyal monks, to safeguard against any other attempts of sacrilege, reburied him in a secret location, a substitute skeleton being placed in the tomb.

According to a tradition that will simply never go away, it is maintained that the secret of Cuthbert's reburial location is closely guarded by the English Benedictine Congregation - and the bit that will appeal to fans of *The Da Vinci Code,* with no more than three monks knowing the true location at any one time. Having seen a small article in the local newspaper of the town, I recalled Cuthbert being mentioned in a local legend involving a treasure belonging to the small coastal town of South Shields, located at the mouth of the River Tyne, 19 miles away from Durham Cathedral. This was the legend of 'The Fairies Kettle'. It seemed a good place to start, so I approached the vicar of the ancient St Hilda's Church in the town, one of the oldest churches in the UK, who was custodian of the only copy of a document chronicling the tale, kept in the church safe. With some persuasion, he allowed me a copy of his 1897 original, which I assume may still be in this archive today. To get straight to the point, the fairy guardians of Trow Rocks had a golden cup stolen from their keeping, it being whisked away to stay a short while at Westoe in South Shields, and then onto Durham Cathedral to be buried alongside Cuthbert. It soon became apparent to me that this ancient tale was the origin of the Trow Rock place name and that it should actually be 'Trove' Rocks on account of the magical treasure. Furthermore, I became suspicious that it was, in fact, a deliberate allegory relating to a memory of a 'treasure' that was linking to St Cuthbert, and that the item had not gone to Westoe and then onto his tomb at Durham, but - in actual fact - was telling us that it had stayed there and was joined by Cuthbert himself. During medieval times, the monks of Durham owned Westoe Village, as they did the surrounding area, thus making it truly easy to sneak the Saint onto their own turf. But where?

In Westoe Village during 1989 stood a long, derelict Nunnery once belonging to (something like, forgive my ailing memory) The Order of the Little Sisters of Mercy, and knowing how objects of a religious significance have a habit (pun intended!) of finding their way to religious buildings, I wondered if the innocent placing of the Nunnery may have found its way via that mysterious agent of the Collective Unconscious, with a buried Cuthbert awaiting, unbeknown to all. Another synchronicity in this case would be the placing of the contrived Fairies Kettle document at St Hilda's, which was built in 1100 where a nunnery once stood. At the time of my interest, the nunnery had just started to be disturbed and turned into part of a new block of flats, and so I was allowed access inside having explained my interest to the unconcerned builders. On a stone floor, under inches of dust, was the centerpiece - a mosaic five-point star! I felt that if only I could explore this tumbledown nunnery a little further, particularly underground, I might just come across something interesting. In the meanwhile, I had approached the then controversial Bishop of Durham, David Jenkins, through the Dean and Chapter, asking him if he thought I could have a case for Cuthbert being at Westoe. To be honest, I thought he'd play the whole thing down, or show little interest, but instead he was kind enough to refer me to a particular monk at Ampleforth Abbey, York, whom he said he knew had studied the Cuthbert Code for most of his life! Eagerly I wrote to this brother - whose name I fear I have now also forgotten - and he replied in a letter saying that he was too old now to pursue his interest - he was in his nineties - but urged me that I should continue my work!

By this time I had managed a full page feature in the South Shields local newspaper 'The Gazette' headlined 'Is Cuthbert buried at Shields?' and it had caused immense interest, so much so that I felt I would have to write a follow-up, and with this understanding the Editor promised he would run it. I had a lot of evidence collated from numerous sources and from within the village, one being an old plaque high up a wall curiously stating 'Follow the paths of the Lord and you will find him.' Was this hinting at follow subterranean paths, or tunnels, under the nunnery and you would find Cuthbert? Things suddenly got better when the initial stages of demolishing the nunnery exposed a level of structure under natural floor level with a convenient point of entry. The initial article had interested the new owner of the land, who was about to build a number of plush flats there, and so when I asked him if it was okay for us to nosey about below the site, as best we could, he was quite happy to let us, but adding that we only had a few days, as after that everything would be filled in and levelled over once and for all.

Accompanied by a team of two burly ex-Westoe Colliery miners and a stonemason friend of one of them, we all entered the darkened mazy passageway that led to another sealed off passage. I may have asked short-term permission from the owner to be in there, but what I hadn't told him was that my crew were armed with lump hammers borrowed from the Colliery and so I watched as they actually smashed a hole in the passage wall in no time at all! I also took an imprint of what was a mason's mark on one brick of this wall, using Plasticine. We were now under a stairwell and what turned out to be a small hollow cavity. Our stonemason friend did what he does and informed us that there should be something below...the perfect place to hide something of value!

Frustratingly, our short-term permission was now up, and with no time for us to investigate further, our being on the scent of the Saint was over. Armed with the stonemason's independent report, photographs taken at every step of the way and even the Masonic mark on the brick, I wrote a very intriguing and honest sequel for the newspaper editor, whose public could hardly wait. But they would, and still do today, for the editor at the time was a Catholic, and found the evidence a rather bit overwhelming suggesting that a Catholic Saint was not, after all, resident at Durham Cathedral, and so he refused to run the second article. In the meanwhile, I had taken the story to the Town Council who were interested in a potential tourist attraction, but asked me if I would move my location some 100yards away so that they could fence the area off and not aggravate private homeowners! They even set me up for an interview in *The Times* newspaper, which was conducted, but – and I don't know why - never printed.

My Cuthbert Code involvement next moves ahead to 1997, when new evidence again cast doubt on the final resting place of the Catholic Saint, Thomas Beckett, being at Canterbury Cathedral. This resonated so strongly with my own adventure that I thought I should strike whilst the iron was hot, and so arranged to meet up with the latest editor of the *South Shields Gazette*, and try again to see if what was originally my second and follow up article could at last be presented to the town. The original editor who had thwarted me had since left, and so with the prospect of starting afresh, and with the Canterbury Beckett controversy current, I could see no reason why this time I should fail. Gathering up all my evidence of eight years earlier, I compiled a formidable dossier and took it to the meeting. He was happy to see me and sat studying the work only to eventually break his silence to ask 'Is this a wind up?' Although offended, I was used to these sorts of inferences; it's the usual initial response before people settle down to consider the seriousness of the evidence before them. I assured him not, and we sat talking for some time, but I couldn't help detecting his uncomfortable feeling. He concluded saying he'd think about a feature – which again surprised me as readers love this stuff - and he'd be in contact in a few days. The few days elapsed and he rang to say that he wasn't going to run the article after all. When I pressed him for why, he went one step further – he *couldn't* run it. Why, I asked? 'Because I live in the flat above your location', he replied. And that was that. South Shields has a population of about 90,000, but circumstances presented me a synchronicity that, for once, left me cold rather than amazed. There were more to follow, for as I left the North East for good I would find them wherever I would be – or be 'taken'.

CHAPTER FIVE
AS SILENT AS THE GRAVE

To say that Lincoln Cathedral is a most splendid building would still be an understatement. Dominating the Lincoln skyline, it can be seen as far away as thirty miles, its 271' central tower being England's second most tallest. It may even be compared, in a fashion, with the Tor at Glastonbury, itself visible for miles, for when it is enshrouded in mist it will completely vanish, as if wrapped up in the misty shroud of the Vale of Avalon. The Cathedral was the tallest building in the world from just after 1300 until 1549, and was the first building on the planet to exceed the height of the Great Pyramid of Giza, until the spire that afforded it this accolade was blown down. Before we embark on our Grail trail, let us realise a little of the history of this Gothic Cathedral. The spot that now occupies Lincoln Cathedral pre-dates the Saxon and Angles' arrival, with a settlement that provided the area with the name Lincoln from 'Lindum Colonia', Colonia from the Roman occupation of Britain. Ancient Britons dwelling on this hill named it 'Llin-dun' from the 'Llin' or mere at its foot, the modern day Brayford Harbour, and 'dun' meaning hill.

Massive quadrangle shaped walls, some of which can still be seen today, marked the limits of the Roman city on the hill summit, pierced with four gates. When Lincoln fell into the hands of invaders, it became the chief of the 'Five Boroughs' of the Danish Confederation. When the Saxons gave way to the Normans, William the Conqueror brought with him many prelates, most prominently Remigius who took on episcopate and considered, in the light of a Windsor council decreeing that bishops should fix their Sees (official seats) in walled towns in preference of villages, Lincoln more worthy as being the seat of a Bishop. Following in the footsteps of his predecessors, and turning his attention to the district of Lindsey, Remigius chose Lincoln where William, worried about any rebellions, had set about building what was to become Lincoln Castle. Only a few hundred yards to the east of William's castle, he set about the building of a church dedicated to the Virgin of Virgins, having been given the bishopric of Dorchester, a post which was the largest in England and stretching from the Thames, where it initially situated, right up to the Humber, Lincoln then becoming a mammoth centre diocese.

The Gothic Cathedral of Lincoln sits high up a hill

The counties of Lincoln, Northampton, Rutland, Leicester, Cambridge, Huntingdon, Bedford, Buckingham, Oxford and Hertford were inclusive. This was bad news for the parishioners of the original Saxon parish church of St Mary Magdalene whose early church had to be demolished to make way for William's Romanesque cathedral. Small compensation for them was in the form of the right to assemble to hold services in the Cathedral, traditionally in the Morning Chapel dedicated to the Magdalene, the Minster's font thought to have been constructed from original stone from Mary's church. Presently, the parishioners of Mary's new church, at a site granted to them in 1280, continued exercising this ancient right, and do so on Patronal Festival Day, when the Great West Doors of the Cathedral open, allowing the procession of parishioners right of way to walk from their church to hold Festival Evensong in Mary's Chapel. Owing to the sizeable numbers in attendance in this small Morning Chapel, the service now has to be held in the main Cathedral Choir with a visitation to the Chapel made in procession before a return to the new church at Castle Square. The Minster, therefore, had something of a double life for the following 250 years catering for Mary's parishioners, whose parish united with that of All Saints. It may well be, that in reality this 'double life' extended far beyond the 1300-20 date we are given, and secretly it was maintained with the Magdalene given the majority preference, when we learn from the Lincoln Cathedral Code that the actual body of Mary may have found its way into the county.

Remigius' cruciform church was intended to resemble those of Jumieges, St George de Boscherville, and St Albans with the likelihood of Westminster's Norman Choir thrown in, although it was not his destiny to witness its eventual consecration scheduled for May 9th 1092. He died three days before and was buried before the Altar of the Holy Cross, to be replaced by Alexander the Magnificent. In 1141, when a fire destroyed the Cathedral roof, falling burning beams from the roof shattered the slab of its founder member's tomb ... the very first in a series of curious events that have troubled the Minster which was garrisoned as a fortress when war between Stephen and Matilda brought bloodshed throughout the land. It was at this point in Lincoln Cathedral's history that we first hear of omens of evil, for when the King offered a wax candle in the Minster, it reportedly broke when Bishop Alexander reached for it. For further effect, the chains supporting the suspended pyx, in which the host is kept after consecration, snapped, the holy vessel falling in the Bishop's presence! In 1146, at Christmas time, King Stephen appeared crowned within the city and by doing so defied an ancient superstition which warned that evil would pursue any English sovereign who would do so. The Minster suffered a great earthquake on 15th April 1185 as recorded by Roger de Hoveden, cleaved from top to bottom by a quake thought to have been unrivalled in severity and felt throughout most of England. If this had been some sort of Cecil B. DeMille effect directed from the Creator, then it was some fanfare to announce the arrival of a figure whose name became as famous as any figure in England's vast ecclesiastical history. Enter the personality most associated with Lincoln Cathedral, and clearly the most loved, St Hugh.

Born at the château of Avalon, Burgundy – which is quite ironic when we will later hope to associate Lincoln Cathedral and Castle with the Arthurian version of this name – his mother passed away when he was eight, leaving his father to take Hugh with him as he retired to a nearby priory near Grenoble. Here he took to a monastic religious life, and by the age of nineteen had aspired to deacon. After being dispatched to become prior of the nearby monastery of Saint-Maximin, around 1159, and at the height of its reputation for rigid austerity of both rules and earnest piety of its members, Hugh then entered the Grand Chartreuse. Ascending to Procurator, in 1179 he next moved to the first English Carthusian House at Witham in Somerset, becoming prior. 'Witham' would later be a synchronicity for Hugh, the river with the same name flowing below the Cathedral where he would be destined to make his name. Henry II had established a Carthusian monastery some time earlier, and was experiencing difficulties in advancing building works, and so sent a persuasive embassy to twist the arm of the Witham House and to acquire his services. Upon arrival, Hugh found the monks rather like the building: in a state of disrepair and soon after, an intercession with the King for royal patronage of the monastery soon turned things around. Having attracted many to the new improved version, Hugh found himself on the move again in 1186 when a vacant bishopric was available in Lincoln, whereby the Canons were ordered to elect a new Bishop, electing Hugh, whereby he insisted on a second private election by the Cathedral Chapter, which confirmed the result. Consecrated Bishop of Lincoln on 21st September 1186 at Westminster, Hugh soon became an exemplary bishop who was constant in his residence or travel within his diocese. He was generous with his charity, scrupulous in his appointments, raising levels of quality education within the Cathedral School. Hugh was a protectorate of the Jews, who were facing ferocious persecution during Richard I's early reign, responsible for de-esculation of what was a popular violence against them in many places. This may well be a key to our mystery, when we are speaking in terms of a Jewish figure that would also be in need of clemency and a safe haven.

After Lincoln Cathedral was badly damaged by the 1185 earthquake, Bishop Hugh - as second Founder of the Church - had the role of rebuilding and greatly enlarging it. He met the responsibility of making it the first English structure in the new Gothic style, the earliest building of that style in the world. However, he was only to see as far as the Choir Well begun, having been struck down by an unnamed ailment after a trip that had ruined his health, only to pass away in November 1200.

Hugh's veneration is remembered in the primary emblem of a white swan in reference to the story of the swan of Stowe, which had a deep, lasting friendship for the saint. As his constant companion it would follow him about, and even guarded him whilst he slept. This too, is of great interest in the sense of Arthurian connections, as it was the swan boat that took the slain King Arthur to Avalon under the influence of the Lady of the Lake, and the mysterious Swan Knight best known as Lohengrin, son of the Grail Knight Percival. The tale was originally attached to the family of Godroi of Bouillan, the first conqueror of Jerusalem in 1099. According to Jung, the Swan Knight's real home was always 'the mountain where Venus lives in the Grail.' It was not until 6th October 1280 that the saint of Lincoln was eventually and finally translated to his costly shrine central to the finished Angel Choir. In attendance within this unique gathering, at what has been described as the proudest day in the history of the city, was King Edward and his Queen Eleanor, whose effigy, too, would soon be placed under the same roof. Eleanor is a key figure in our Lincoln Cathedral Code, and so she, too, will be on our growing list of re-visits!

After six years of accruing materials for the rebuilding of his Cathedral, at last the foundations for a new choir were built in 1192, marking a new architectural epoch - not only in the history of the Cathedral - but in English and Gothic architecture. He was the first designer of a building to allow the pointed arch - recognised as the third great form of architecture, that being free expression. The Rose Window of the north transept, constructed between 1190-1200, drew a lot of attention with regard to the characteristic differences between French and English Gothic. There was not a Rose Window of that period divided into four compartments, and the centre of the window did not resemble any French arrangement, the decoration with small roses covering the mouldings being a very English characteristic. We will be returning to this fascinating Rose Window later in our quest, as its purpose extends beyond simply being a window! Hugh carried on his re-designing of the Cathedral for eight years, having finished the apse, eastern transept, the choir and part of the western transept, often carrying stones on his own shoulders as an example to his workmen. And having set this example and given the pattern, his successors continued to produce a building entire.

The following Bishop of Lincoln is second only to Hugh in the history of the diocese. The honour fell to Robert Grosseteste, one of the greatest scholars of his day, and a man who had more influence than any other over the next two centuries concerning English thought and literature. Soon after Grosseteste's appointment a cathedral tower fell ... another interesting baptism! We are told that in 1239, when a rebel canon of the Minster - who did not agree with the actions of Grosseteste - spoke his remonstrations from the pulpit, uttering the very words, 'If we were to be silent, the very stones would cry out for us,' the new central tower crashed down on those below, burying them in the ruins. Grosseteste will also appear later in our story, as we have reason to believe he was in possession of a rather interesting item!

Let us take a wander about this wondrous Cathedral so distinguished for its rare combination of architecture and sculpture. Our first port of call is the 'stone beam' of which relatively little is known and is, therefore, the subject of much conjecture. It is apparent between the walls of the two western towers, a little above the stone vault of the nave. Although of uniform depth and breadth, it is composed of twenty-three stones of unequal length, with an arch of very slight curvature. The number twenty-three will be of interest to us later in our Cathedral Code. If one jumps on this beam, it will appreciably vibrate. Although the suggestion is that its construction was as a tester to see if the towers would be able to support any upper storey additional weight, no satisfactory purpose for it can be agreed. A peculiarity concerning the base of the nave piers being higher on the north side than on the south is noticed, and reported again in both St Hugh's Choir and the Angel Choir, both in the western transept. It is found again in the north at the 'Dean's Eye' Rose Window, which is higher than its counterpart the 'Bishop's Eye' opposite it in the south. On the west front of the Minster, arcading on the lower rows on the north side is at a height above its corresponding southern rows. Is there an explanation for this? The official view is that it is due to an inequality of the ground. Surely, if it had been a capricious error on behalf of Hugh's architect, the succeeding architects wouldn't have carried it on during another century. One wonders if it has to do with what is now known to be 'sacred geometry', and a precise deliberation in order to allow for certain required measurements, for as we will see later, precise geometrical placing of area will provide interesting and equally precise astronomical and optical phenomenon.

We return to the two large round windows in the end walls of the western transept. The 'Dean's Eye' Rose Window was placed around 1220, the tracery of the 'Bishop's Eye' being much later, suspected after the middle of the 14th Century. It is thought that the row of quatrefoils outside the window are what may have been left of an earlier tracery. The near proximity of it to John de Dalderby's shrine, he being Chancellor of Lincoln and one of the Commissioners in proceedings against the Templars. Admirers of this Bishop were struggling to accumulate enough reports of his alleged numerous miracles to warrant a papal court canonization. However, he was still revered as a saint consequent offerings at his shrine thought to have supplied the means to insert the tracery her at the window and the higher one highlighting the roof, and can only be seen from outside. This round window had, in the past, also been known as the 'Prentice Window' – a clear reference to freemasonry.

The Metrical Life of St Hugh, written some time between 1220 and 1235, mentions both round windows. Why the 'Dean's Eye' and the 'Bishop's Eye' are so called? It is thought to be no mystery as one faces the Deanery and the other the Bishop's Palace. But there are others who think there may be something more deeper to these nominations, and it borders on occultism, and there is also a great discrepancy when we learn that the Rose Window in Gothic Cathedrals always faces the west. To the Church, and to some occultists today, the north is the darkened region of Lucifer and the 'Dean's Eye, representing the Church on earth and in Heaven,' is a kind of look-out to ward off the approach of evil. By contrast, staring out at the sunny south, is the 'Bishop's Eye', the direction favoured by the Holy Spirit, whose influence is at hand to repel and overcome any impending evil that may try to penetrate from the evil north. With a potential impending collision of forces prepared for by these ominous round windows and their symbolism, it will come as no surprise, then, when later we hear of one person's thoughts that the Cathedral is a battleground of good and evil. However, who calmly made this stark announcement may surprise you … we will see later! The centre of the 'Dean's Eye' portrays a seated Jesus amidst the Blessed of Heaven. We can speak with less certainty about the four larger compartments with portions of differing subjects, as they do not

The Rose Window - Covert Heavenly Planisphere

The Great East Window - 64 roundels and Chessboard of the Mind

appear to belong to where they now appear. There follows sixteen outer circles.

The 'Bishop's Eye' over at the south is an entirely different picture resembling the fibres of a leaf, filled with delicate, beautiful flowing tracer. Glass fragments collected from other windows have been placed randomly, forming no subject whatever and the effect is dramatically dazzling when viewed from a respectable distance.

Moving along to the oaken series of Choir stalls that were originally in two rows of 62 upper seats and 46 lower, but now 68 and 48 respectively, both rows of stalls given a provision of 'misereres'. The purpose of these hinged seats is of a supportive nature when the occupants of the stands were required to stand during long services; the seats, elbow rests and finials are all decorated with richly carved grotesque subjects, and not all relating to scriptural themes. One can only think that here, amidst all this daring medieval artistry, certain symbols and intimations are being chanced. There is a fox preaching to bird and beasts before running riot in their midst, playful monkeys who go on to bury one of their own, having hanged it. We find men and wild animals warring and can see kings, knights, ladies, dragons, - all very Arthurian - griffins, lions, hogs and wyverns. To lift the misereres is to witness the unique diversity of its subjects although some in the lower row are now missing and have been replaced by a plain block. The upper row contains the following carvings under the misereres, the numbers counted along from the precentor's stall; (2) a fine head and two roses, (4) foliage, (5) a man beating down acorns and pigs feeding, (8) the gateway of a castle and the heads of two warriors in armour, (10) grotesque winged monsters, (12) a boy riding on the back of a bird, (18) a mermaid with comb and mirror, (22) two men with a plough, drawn by two bullocks and two horses, a man with a barrow to the left, sacks of corn to the right, (31) an ascension, with two angels swinging censers.

On the south side, numbering from the Dean's Stall to the west, here are some highlights: (1)The resurrection of Christ, (2) a knight on horseback, (4) the coronation of the Virgin with angels and musical instruments, (9) the adoration of the Magi, (16) two monkeys - one riding a lion, the other a unicorn, (26) a king enthroned under a canopy, (28) a lion fights a winged monster.

Amidst all those discussed, there is one carving that we have just passed over. And it is perhaps the most crucial clue in our Lincoln Cathedral Code that will lead to our final destination. Pause for a few moments and guess which one it will transpire to be! It is a suspicion of mine that some of these random carvings, at least, may well be hiding symbology of an astrological nature and containing stonemason understanding of hermetical principles; some may also be the in the manner of 'say what you see' style visual punning, which we will investigate later in the Templar cave at Royston in Hertfordshire. Certainly, it is known that in gothic cathedrals, where the Templars were involved in the building, that alchemical symbolism was sprinkled about. The appearance of the 'mystic rose', or two to be precise, under one of the miseres, is certainly enough to hint at things spoken 'sub rosa' – 'under

Who defaced the Devil? Lincoln Cathedral East wall exterior

the rose' – associated with the mysteries of the Magdalene.

Today, if we visit the south transept within the cathedral, we will find its Patronal Banner, an embroidered tapestry showing the Virgin Mary complete with a rose on her apron, although I will argue later that this is the symbol of another Mary. Next, we wander over a little to visit the unison of the highest excellence in architecture and sculpture in one single production, and find ourselves at the Angel Choir, referred to as the most beautiful presbytery in England. The geometry is splendidly magnificent with a primitive simplicity; five bays eastward carrying with uniformity in height and breadth with St Hugh's Choir, Lincoln stone relieved with Purbeck marble shafts and capitals. In contrast with elsewhere within, the great arch spandrels decorate with sunken geometrical forms, the triforium bays dividing into two arches enclosing two sub-arches. And then, there is The Great East Window, from where our Lincoln Cathedral Code will first be discovered, but for now we will simply look at it through exoteric vision. Considered to be the finest example of its style in the kingdom, it boasts eight lights formed by doubling the our-light, a great circle within its head filling with a six-foil with half a dozen quatrefoils surrounding. With fully developed bar tracery this great window's appearance decorates more than early English, with mouldings belonging to an earlier style. The Great East Window is now filled with modern glass, originally believed to have contained the arms of English nobility. The firm Peckitt of York had the task of re-glazing it in 1762 with the design of that time being of geometrical forms. The subjects in the present window owe an arrangement to Dean Ward – interesting when we realise that the word 'ward' means 'an act of watching or guarding', for this window surely watches and guards over the secret of Lincoln Cathedral – its Code. Compartments contain subjects illustrating the life of Jesus with a variety of Old Testament scenes. Ward and Hughes, the London based stained glass company who were clearly Freemasons, executed the window in 1855 at a cost of one thousand five hundred pounds.

A stone monument tomb of Queen Eleanor was placed under the Great East Window in 1891. Eleanor was the daughter of Ferdinand III of Castile, and became the wife of Edward I. The monument is as near a copy as one could get of an original monument. This Queen, like the piece in chess, is the most prominent figure in our own Masonic chess game that is going on, and we will find ourselves constantly returning to events concerning her. A short distance away, at the south-east corner of the choir, is a marble monument to William Hilton and Peter De Wint, his brother-in-law (1784-1849), a famed watercolour painter responsible for numerous paintings of Lincoln Cathedral from different points. It is not owing to the marble reliefs taken from pictures by Hilton and showing on its west side that I include this item of interest, but it is for the four kneeling angels at the corner of it. They are all identical to the kneeling Magdalene figure that Sauniere painted at his bas-relief in the Rennes-le-Chateau church! Visiting the Angel choir, we are graced by 28 angels carved high up the walls. The significance of this figure 28 will become apparent later in our mystery.

On the north side of our Angel Choir, there is one solitary figure who stands out, that is if you can locate him! On a spandrel squatting under a corbel above the easternmost pier he sits, wearing a broad grin. A mere foot in height, the Lincoln Imp has the classic devilish archetypal appearance, two short horns behind his ears, a hairy body and cloven hooves. How he has arrived sitting up there is told as thus; Satan himself sent the imp to Lincoln Cathedral to cause trouble in the form of attempting to destroy the Angel Choir of St Hugh. As he was setting about his task, and apparently making a good job of it, an angel appeared to intervene. The imp, feeling less confident than his usual brash self, jumped up onto a pillar and began to throw rocks from the debris at the angel. Having none of this, the angel turned the imp into stone and that is how we find him today. Simple as that. There are variations on this general and most popularly held story, although all appear to have the same basic background. Another is almost identical but with more detail, going back to the 14th Century, when Satan sends two imps down to earth to do a smattering of evil work. Initially, we are told in this version that the terrible two went to Chesterfield and sat on the church spire there and decided to twist it! That's why, if you visit today, you will see the famous crooked spire. Having satisfied themselves with this act of vandalism, our two twisters headed off to Lincoln Cathedral.

I deliberately employ the irony in the term 'twisters' for the word is now designated to refer to a tornado, a very violent whirling wind- storm that affects a narrow strip of country; loosely, a hurricane, for the story of the imp in Lincoln is all to do with the wind. Arriving in Lincoln, the imps are further instructed by the Devil to cause as much mayhem as they can and so they start their spree by smashing up tables and chairs and tripping up the poor Bishop before moving on to start destroying the Angel Choir. As an angel appears he tells them to stop and suffers the bravery of one of the imps who throws some rocks at him, whilst the other imp displays less courage and cowers under the broken tables and chairs. The angel turns the first imp into stone and as he does so, the second takes his opportunity to escape. Yet another version tells us that the imp was blown into the Cathedral by strong winds, and began his mischief by dancing on the altar and annoying all present in the Angel Choir until the angels could tolerate it no more, and turned him into stone where he sits at the top of a column with a grin of mischief on his face.

Another version involving two imps is that, having been sent into the Cathedral to cause trouble, they set about annoying the angels who told them to leave. As before in other versions, one imp started hurling rocks whilst the other hid. The angels, turning the first into stone, gave the second a chance to escape whereupon he so did with the help of a witch. I imagine this slightly differing version, with its introduction of a witch, was to help along the persecution at a time when innocent women were accused of being followers of the Devil when - in reality - all they were doing was being close to Nature. In passing, I will recall an account highlighting this point involving Anne Askew, a lady from an old Lincolnshire family. In the year 1546 we are told how, daily, she would be seen reading her bible in the Cathedral challenging the clergy there on the meaning of particular text, which ones I cannot say. Next we hear that her bold opinions brought brave free-thinking Anne, at the tender age of

25, to burn at the stake. Given how often irony and/or synchronicity puts in an appearance, we can only marvel at the almost mocking tragedy of this lady's surname, Askew – she couldn't resist that; if she saw you she'd ask you.

One more, then. The imp travelled all over the country blown by the wind looking for places to plague. Coming upon the cathedral at Lincoln, the object of his planned destruction became the Angel Choir. As he went up to the top of the nearest pillar to admire his evil handiwork, an appearing angel turned him to stone and rooted him to the spot, leaving him frozen as he was moments before, sitting cross-legged with an evil grin on his face.

Did a bored mason with his tools at hand decide to sculpt the Lincoln Imp out of sheer mischief, hoping that his work would demonstrate his presence? Or did a bored mason find himself the unwitting   tool of the Collective Unconscious working through him as an agency to plant a very precise tool in our chess game of hidden moves? Either way, the imp sits there, and his relevance will be explained later. Passing along the outside of the cathedral, on the buttress at the south-western corner of the Transept, we come across two sundials. The one we call the Dial is one of the most crucial features in respect of the Lincoln Cathedral Code, as it will appear later as a veiled mention in a Rennes-le-Chateau parchment.

We are now outside at what has been spoken of as the finest example of the best period of English Gothic at the eastern limb of Lincoln Cathedral, the Presbytery, a Choir dividing into five bays with bold projecting buttresses crowned with slender crocketed gables with grotesque figures projecting at their bases. The sculptured doorway here is the way into this east porch or, as it also known, 'The Judgement Porch'. This door leads to the Angel Choir, but it was once used as the exit for prisoners who had just had judgement passed upon them and who were on their way to the castle prison or gallows. In the tympanum is the relief of the Last Judgement, the central space occupied by Jesus the Judge flanked on either side by censer-swinging angels, and surrounded by angels supporting a quatrefoiled aureole. Below the feet of the Lord, opens the jaws of Hell, and to his right demons drag them down and to the left dead rise from their tombs. In the inner band, a row of niches shows twelve seated figures thought to be kings and queens, although I will remind the reader that the Holy Grail is often linked with twelve knights and a ruling King (symbolized by Jesus above?); the same configuration as the Christian symbol of the Last Supper. Below the central canopy is a statue of the Virgin Mary and child. Both buttresses on either side of the doorway total four headless statues. To the right of this porch we see, on the corner eastern buttress and on the corner of the Cathedral, statues of King Edward and with him Eleanor, which to the untrained eye could be thought of as Jesus and Mary!

Eleanor will play a major part in our Lincoln Cathedral Code. Upon her death at Harby, near Lincoln, in 1290 her body was carried to and embalmed at the Gilbertine Priory of St Catherine at the south of the city. Although her body was sent on the twelve-day journey to Westminster Abbey, her viscera were sent for burial in Lincoln Cathedral's Angel Choir, where they remain today. The famous Eleanor Crosses were erected at all twelve places where her funeral procession stopped overnight.

We will bring to a close our tour of Lincoln Cathedral for now, but later we will return to the key places we have mentioned, and turn those keys to unlock their hidden aspects.

CHAPTER SIX
LAUDING THE LORD

A poet is variously described as anything from the following: the author of a poem or (formerly) of any work of literary art, a verse writer or one skilled in making poetry, or one with a poetical imagination - a poem being a composition in verse or composition of high beauty of thought or language and artistic form, typically - although not necessarily - in verse. We are now going to look at one in particular, who, at one point in his own day was said to be, along with Queen Victoria and Gladstone, one of the three most recognised living persons, a reputation no other poet in England has ever had. That he is a key figure in our Lincoln Cathedral Code is the reason we must put him under our microscope.

Born on August 6th 1809 at The Rectory in Somersby, Lincolnshire, the third surviving child of Reverend George Clayton and Elizabeth Tennyson, Alfred was taught by his father and his vast collection of books, and began writing poetry at an early age. A contrast in his own family's circumstances, with the great wealth of his uncle and aunt who lived in castles, left him feeling impoverished by comparison and with a worry about money that lasted all his life. Another fear in the young Tennyson's life was fostered by a legacy of epilepsy in the males in his family, a disease thought at the time shameful and to have been caused by excess masturbation! His father and brother were excessive drinkers, and as Alfred reached his late twenties, his father's physical and mental condition worsened, making him become paranoid, abusive and violent. And Edward, his brother, was confined to a mental institution after 1833.

In 1827, few could blame Tennyson escaping the atmosphere of his troubled environment as he followed his elder two brothers to Cambridge and Trinity College. Although he found it hard to mix, he befriended Arthur Henry Hallam, who was a son of an eminent historian. Hallam later became engaged to Emily Tennyson, a friendship destined only to last for four years when, in 1833, Hallam died from a stroke at the age of 22, leaving Tennyson in a profound state of shock. The resultant grief arguably inspired some of his greatest work. By this time he had a collection of poems published, although criticism from the harsh critics of the day - who would prevent him from publishing for a further nine years – instilled in him a hatred of publishing new work. There is little doubt Tennyson was a fragile and unsure person, and in the late 1830s, concerned about his mental health, he visited a sanatorium. His 1842 two-volume collection *Poems*, of which fifty percent was new work, established him as an outstanding poet gaining favourable reviews, and by 1850 he was appointed Poet Laureate, and recognised as the most popular poet of his era.

In the midst of all this, Tennyson had been assured that his own fear of having epilepsy was unwarranted. His father, having also been suspected of being an epileptic, was informed instead that he had gout! Apparently, the onset of this form of arthritis with swelling of the joints would stimulate Alfred's brain so that it would emulate the aura associated with the neurological disorder! There are approximately forty types of epilepsy; so many that neurologists today who specialise in the subject are still updating their thoughts about classification, the condition being difficult in some cases to diagnose. Biographers of Tennyson, and researchers like me, are not convinced about the gout prognosis, and I feel that - like Carl Gustav Jung - he was susceptible to psychic awareness of an altered state of consciousness. He would describe these moments as 'the clearest of the clearest, the surest of the surest, the weirdest of the weirdest, utterly beyond words'. Doesn't sound much like gout to me! Tennyson's 'seizures' involved him in losing the sense of self, indeed a mystic state in the making, and very Buddhist in nature. Decide for yourself as he attempts describing this condition as, 'All at once, out of the intensity of the consciousness of individuality, the individuality itself seemed to dissolve and fade away into boundless being, and this is not a confused state.'

The most common serious neurological disorder, a prevalence rate of 1 in 200 is usually quoted for minimum prevalence in the UK. Epilepsy is any of various brain disorders characterised by recurring attacks of motor, sensory or psychic malfunction with or without consciousness or convulsive moments. The highly complex structure of the brain composes millions of neurons (brain cells), the activity of which are organisational, possessing self-regulating mechanisms. Their responsibilities include the functions of consciousness, awareness, movement and bodily posture. Any sudden temporary interruption in one, or all, of these functions is termed an epileptic 'fit' or seizure, caused by an intrinsic cause giving disturbance arising within the brain. Although there are a number of recognised types, the most dramatic form of generalised seizure in which the whole of the brain is involved, and consciousness lost in an interval, is called a clonic-tonic convulsive seizure; muscles after rigidity began to relax and tighten rhythmically, causing a convulsion. A general stiffening of muscles without rhythmically jerking is called a tonic seizure.

Let us look at the word 'epilepsy'; Old French 'epilepsie', from Late Latin 'epilepsia', from Greek, 'epilambanein'. From the matrices of the word 'epilepsy' the key section is 'e pile psy'. Brain cells working together communicate by means of electric signals. On occasion, an abnormal electrical charge from a group of cells results in seizure, the type depending upon the part of the brain where the abnormal charge arose. In 1929, the

German psychiatrist Hans Berger first demonstrated that the electrical impulse of the brain could be recorded, the brain continuously generating electrical current. Let us consider voltaic pile; a source of direct current consisting of a number of alternating discs of two different metals separated by acid-moistened pads forming primary cells (generating electricity) connected in the series. 'Pile' = 'Pyl', and onto 'pylon' a word from Greek 'pulon', meaning 'a gateway', from 'pule', a gate.

'Gateway' in the world of computing = a link that enables information to be exchanged between one computer network and another. In the scenario of a poet, it is a gateway into the cosmos, to unite deep space and a cosmic unity – a transmission, a communication between the moments of epileptic loss of consciousness – an alteration – of the brain of Tennyson during seizure, at the lambda (epilambanein) the meeting of the sagittal and lamboid sutures of the skull, the brain's outer layer, the cerebral cortex, qualifying how once epilepsy was known as a sacred disease.

Wave forms, a disturbance or oscillation propagated from point to point in a medium space, described in general mathematical specification of its amplitude, velocity, frequency and phase, projected millions of miles into space bouncing off planets and stars, returning to earth, The Lambda is used as a symbol for wavelength. Suture parts of the skull, by their appearance, resemble river terrain, cracked open fissures affected by earthquake – the simulated brain 'tremors' felt during epileptic seizure. Epi lep sy, lep = leap, an abrupt or precipitous passage (the shift of consciousness) or transition. Critics will be sharp to point out that epilepsy, the oldest known brain disorder, was mentioned more than 2000BC, with references found in ancient Greek texts, and in the Bible. Hippocrates, in the third century BC, was the first person to recognise it as an organic process of the brain. It is now known that photosensitive epileptic fits can be triggered by flashing lights, as in stroboscope light, or in sudden changes from dark to light, and vice versa.

Many years ago, ships at sea would use flashing lights to signal messages, a code, to a visual system of semaphore, to each other. Returning to the generalised terms of seizure and Tonic Clonic, the true origin reveals as 'Diatonic'; the tones and intervals of the natural scale in music – epilepsy can be relieved through music therapy – the interval of loss of consciousness, as all music is constructed of vibration, frequency and wavelength. Dropping a stone into a pool of water produces a number of concentric circles that decrease in size until appearing to die away. All vibrations take wave forms. 'Clonic' = 'Cyclonic' from 'cyclone'; a stormy often destructive weather; a kind of centrifuge – centrifugal in physiology = transmitting impulses away from the central nervous system. The seizures, of course, can be cyclic, or recurring. The original religion of Tibet was the belief known as Bon, of which there are still isolated monasteries existing. A major god in the Bon pantheon of deities was Za, with his stormy and destructive weather, replete with lightning bolts and hailstones, who was responsible for causing epilepsy. Although monks today educate a very similar understanding in Buddhist teaching, there is one very significant difference in ritual – Buddhists will walk clockwise around a sanctuary, stupa or mani wall, the Bon adherent will walk anticlockwise. In meteorology, the cyclone – a tropical atmospheric disturbance (our Tonic Conic seizure) – is characterised by air masses circulating rapidly – clockwise in the Southern and anti-clockwise in the Northern.

Tennyson had the disadvantage of suffering from extreme short-sightedness, and so reading and writing was a great difficulty. It is thought this drawback actually accounted for the manner in which he created his poetry, composing the majority in his head. In 1859, Tennyson published four of the *Idylls of the King*, it being his epic story and series of narrative poems of King Arthur and Camelot as thematically suggested by Malory's earlier tales. When completed it was again abused by critics, despite being warmly received by the public. In 1869 he produced his masterpiece *The Holy Grail* – clearly, Arthurian themes and the tale of the Grail were important in his life. I feel Tennyson had, in some way - perhaps through his psychic turmoil - attracted the archetype of Merlin to himself. In fact, in 1889 as an octogenarian, summarising his position through the assumed voice of the Magician, he related how Merlin said that, as a youth, he was taken in hand by a mighty wizard who advised him to 'follow the gleam'.

Tennyson became a Lord in 1884, and after blessing his wife and son when a simple cold evolved into a more serious condition, Tennyson died peacefully with the room filled with light from the full moon at 1.35am, on October 6th 1892. Tennyson clearly had a yearning to write about all things Arthurian, and in his poem 'Merlin and the Gleam' (1889) he declares in the first paragraph, 'I am Merlin, And I am dying, I am Merlin, who follow the gleam'.

Perhaps Tennyson identified with this figure, and the plaque on his statue - within the precincts of Lincoln Cathedral - continues a line from his 'Holy Grail' poem mentioning the magician. The advice to follow this gleam also has interesting possibilities, the poem becoming a Christian hymn celebrating Christian crusades in the Holy Land – very Knights Templar. The poem is directed at the knights in the days of old receiving a vision of the Grail, and being told to follow the gleam of the chalice that is the Grail. In honour of Tennyson, when his statue was first erected a huge crowd gathered to sing his preferred choice and poem of 'Crossing the Bar', so preferred that he stipulated it be placed at the end of all editions of his poems. It starts, 'Sunset and evening star, and one clear call for me!' This, we will see later, appears to be a reference to the star Sirius.

Another integral star connection with Alfred Lord Tennyson is that in his natal birth and horoscope chart, compiled eruditely by Michael D. Robbins in 2002, he had a highlight of Venus parallel to Arcturus, and we will see the importance of this star later on. Robbins writes of it,

'A potent star (Arcturus) prompting the taking of a different path, a different way. Tennyson, as an advanced Leo subject would always be true to his individuality. To be a professional poet is no conventional path and he followed it faithfully for his entire life. The star is called by the intriguing names: The Keeper of Heaven, The Patriarch of the Train, The Guardian Messenger, The Lofty One. As the 'mentor' it looks out for the deportment of its lesser companions – a function which Tennyson, as aesthetic custodian of the values of his society, subtly upheld. The star is said to bring riches and honour to those born under it. The Venus parallel to Arcturus is exactly exact. Venus, already maximally important in his chart, is further dignified by its contact with this great star.'

I will settle for Tennyson as 'The Guardian Messenger', as we will see later in our own Arthurian-tinged Quest, the Lincoln Cathedral Code.

MARY·HATH·CHOSEN·THAT·GOOD·PART·WHICH
SHALL·NOT·BE·TAKEN·AWAY·FROM·HER

Erected to the glory of God, in loving memory of
Mary Forrest of Ardow, Died 23rd October, 1904,
by her affectionate sister, Isabella D. Forrest.
Wolsden Designer

CHAPTER SEVEN
BATTLEGROUND OF LIGHT AND DARK

I n 2005 I began an exhaustive investigation into an area of research that hitherto had been completely unknown to me, the wondrous edifice of the Gothic Cathedral of Lincoln, England. To say that the cathedral is a most splendid building would still be an understatement, rivalling Glastonbury Tor's alleged Isle of Avalon, and made all the more curious by the fact that its patron saint, Hugh, arrived from the village of Avalon in Eastern France. The cathedral was the tallest building in the world from just after 1300 until 1549, and the first building on the planet to exceed the height of the Great Pyramid of Giza, until the spire that afforded it this accolade was blown down. My own research led me to the startling and unexpected discovery of the 'Lincoln Cathedral Code' involving the mystery of Rennes-le-Chateau, Mary Magdalene and the Knights Templar, and I could have been forgiven for thinking that unearthing an occult and mystical side to the cathedral was a unique find. However, as we are about to see, I am now forced to think again, for the cathedral at Lincoln has drawn many a strange notion to itself, long before I came on the scene to publicise my own work.

The first mention I came across linking the minster with the Devil was taken from the *Lindsey and Lincolnshire Star* dated May 21st 1898, and it is possible that the stories were genuine, uninfluenced folk tales, directly or remotely influenced by books. An article 'Lincoln Minster and the Devil' quotes, 'The connection between the Prince of Evil and Lincoln has long been proverbial.' The very erudite 1928 publication *The Cathedral Church of Lincoln* by A.F. Kendrick, BA informs us that at the head of the tall, central lancet of gable of the chapel used as the Consistory Court is a grotesque figure - not to be confused with the Lincoln Imp found elsewhere - known as 'the devil looking over Lincoln'. It quotes, 'There appears to be no satisfactory solution of the origin of this phrase' and 'the most curious legend is that which describes the devil as still inside the Minster and afraid to come out for fear of being blown away!' How completely and utterly bizarre! Do we know of any other religious building anywhere in the world where it has been said that the devil resides within?

And, in our current scientific world, how serious can we take this suggestion? In this day and age, how are we to interpret 'Devil'? What can it seriously be hinting at, or sustaining?

The 13th Century legend of the Lincoln Imp, now symbol of the City of Lincoln, (which I will announce to be a deliberately placed Masonic carving, key to a concluding location opposite the SE corner of the cathedral concealing a Templar 'treasure' of great significance) tells of how the Devil sent an imp to cause destruction within the building, and was eventually turned to stone by an angel – no mention of the Devil himself deigning to put in an appearance! Although there is clearly conflict here in what memory lore is being retained, what we can ask is why do we have this consistent association of Satan with the cathedral? In the south-east Nottinghamshire village of Kinoulton, we hear of the legend of a stone that once stood in the old churchyard, although now neither stone nor church remain. The stone was told to be a diabolic missile hurled at the church, thrown from Lincoln Cathedral. It is accepted that similar stories throughout Europe simply reflect conflict between the early Christian church and paganism, so why in this instance - if the offending rock was considered diabolical - was it hurled FROM Lincoln Cathedral? Even the most respected of accounts do the cathedral no favour when we learn of the title of its beautiful Rose Window, found on the north side of the cathedral, even though the norm is for Rose Windows always to be found on the west of Gothic Cathedrals. Although preferably known as 'The Dean's Eye', it also bears the lesser known title of 'Lucifer's Eye', and has been placed at the north referred to as the darkened region of Lucifer as a kind of look-out to ward off the approach of evil, in contrast to 'The Bishop's Eye' round window staring out at the sunny south, the direction favoured by the Holy Spirit.

The mention of Lucifer brings me to the strangest and most fabulous of tales I have come across involving Lincoln Cathedral. Found circulating on the internet, it appears to have emanated originally from an alleged Templar in Rome and speaks of 'The Ark of Lucifer', an artifact said to control the lifespan of humans, no less! Placed in the cathedral, it is alleged to work on a vibratory frequency affecting changes at the molecular level of living tissue, or the key of the DNA. We are asked to believe that during the 1920s, of 144 people knowing of its existence and issued with a key, only 12 held the real key to opening a vault in the cathedral where the Ark was, and - presumably - is still housed. This occult tale goes on to say that the Ark was originally at St Mary's Church in Lincoln, and that Bishop Alexander's attempt to retrieve it caused the devastating fire that ravaged the building in 1141. After it was rebuilt, another attempt - this time by unknown persons - precipitated the Ark to cause the earthquake that cleaved the edifice in two, this tremor factually recorded in 1185.

The opening of the Ark is a precise and dramatic procedure. If we are to believe it, there is a Master Key held somewhere within the cathedral, described as a corkscrew with the representation of the cathedral as a handle. The functioning valid 12 keys are to be inserted into a metallic 4x4, with holes placed at a varying distance to each other. Inserting the 12 keys into the 4x4 allows the head of the corkscrew to protrude on the side of the door of the vault of the Ark. There are a number of rectangular holes, from the ground to the ceiling with only one correct spot where the Master Key will open the door. The remaining other keys do serve a purpose, but only after the opening of the vault.

And so we have just learned of the 'Ark of Lucifer' hidden somewhere in a vault within the cathedral and with no end of occultists seeking the key to open it and unleash its consequences. The pure *Indiana Jones* aspect of the tale is appealing, but we have to accept that - here again - we have at least a re-occurring theme concerning Lincoln Cathedral, this time wrapped up in a titular Lucifer, and with an already established 'Eye of Lucifer' Rose Window we must ponder over what kernel of truth is being contained within this Gothic temple. In Latin, the name Lucifer means 'morning star', and interestingly enough, just a few minutes walking distance away from the east of the cathedral, is the public house *Morning Star*, dating back to 1781, which is the very year that the once-standing church containing the crypt with my hidden 'Cathedral Code' Templars' treasure was demolished. This is in addition to the fact that, in the same year, French noblewoman Marie De Negre, who held the secret of Rennes-le-Chateau, also died.

Another mention of Lincoln Cathedral and esotericism caught my eye in the heavily theosophical article 'A Precis of Albion' by author Richard Leviton in 1991, where he postulates the layout of a giant cosmic 'being' occupying the land mass of Britain and France, and whose second chakra – or energy field – is at Lincoln Cathedral and its environs. Intrigued by his placing geographical emphasis on Lincoln Cathedral to do with anything, I contacted Richard, now an editor of a metaphysical magazine in Virginia, USA, to see if he would elucidate, and I found his reply quite surprising. Richard had written more about the cathedral since his 'Albion' article, in a book entitled *The Emerald Modem*. In it he describes in detail an event in which he participated, together with a small group of people, concerning a celestial being 'imprisoned' under the cathedral. He alludes to the structure of the building being a perpetual black magic ritual intended to keep the being imprisoned, with ultimately the cathedral opposing the positive energy that is there.

At this point, having learned of an 'Ark of Lucifer', and now an imprisoned spiritual energy within the cathedral, I can imagine the average person in the street would choose to dismiss these assertions as simply fanciful, and of no importance. But I'm not so sure, and cannot dismiss them without asking the question, 'Why Lincoln Cathedral?' especially as they are drawn from unrelated sources.

The common denominator of a hinted dark force receives a most unexpected recommendation nationally announced in 1995, and from the then Dean of the Cathedral himself, the Rev. Brandon Jackson. Within my personal files, I hold a copy of *The Sunday Times*, the crème-de-la-crème of British newspaper journalism, dated 23rd July 1995. The two-page headline reads, 'Where Angels fear to tread', sub-headed 'Is the dispute between the Dean of Lincoln Cathedral and his Bishop mere human frailty or is it the work of an evil force many believe haunts the Minster?' The Rev. Jackson, acquitted by an ecclesiastical court over accusations of sexual misdeeds, announced that he believed he was caught up in a battle of good and evil that centres on the ancient minster, and asked to have the cathedral closed for three months to have it exorcised. Upon his arrival and stay lasting six years, he had first been alerted to this dark aura by a monk working at the cathedral who said, 'There are currents of conflict, hate and evil that have been swirling around your cathedral for centuries.' Jackson went on to say to *The Times* reporter Stuart Wavell that this 'swirling evil' theory had been repeated by Deans and Provosts at their annual conference in April of that year. 'One of them, a Dean of a cathedral, came up to me and said that Lincoln Cathedral was one of the most evil places he had ever been in. Another Dean said that he believed the building sat on the junction of ley-lines.' Mighty strange talk coming from the clergy! Would they dare say such things and risk credibility and reputation if there were no unified belief?

The opening paragraph of *The Times'* article reads, 'Is there seething inherently evil lurking in Lincoln Cathedral? Is a malign force in the ancient stonework making the clergy behave like demented marionettes?' Strong stuff from a quality newspaper not known for its sensationalism!

The Devil still being inside the cathedral, a hidden vault containing an Ark attributed to Lucifer, and a spiritual being held captive within the minster - so what can we deduce from this mixed bag of inferences? My own feelings are that the story of the Lucifer Ark may well be a memory tool to highlight the numbers 12 and 144 and could have a value concerning sacred geometry within the cathedral, and 'ark' may actually refer to 'arc', part of the circumference of a circle or other curve. Richard Leviton's thoughts on there being a figure of some importance held captive may well be an unconscious tapping in, and offshoot, of my own work, in which I have announced the stashed and most sought after Templar treasure of Rennes-le-Chateau residing opposite the SE corner of the cathedral at the St Margaret's burial grounds, involving the revered figure of Mary Magdalene. Of these stories, more than that I cannot say or be sure, but at least I now know I do not stand alone in finding my way to Lincoln Cathedral, and into a labyrinth of mystique.

I will end these findings as I started with that of my own work, and an anecdote that found its way to me in 2000. Circumstances found me in discussion with a woman in her fifties whom I will refer to as 'Sylvia'. Her maiden name and relations placed her within the family D'Arques and she had relatives living at the chateau of D'Arques at Rennes-le-Chateau. Sylvia introduced the conversation, and yet at the same time was reluctant to go into great detail as it clearly bears a scarring, traumatic effect, and so I do not know what year she and a female friend where spending some days at the Bishops Palace, facing Lincoln Cathedral, during a spiritual retreat. Things couldn't have gotten further desperate and unwelcome, when apparently the two were visited at night by an appearance from the Devil himself, bent on destroying their sanity. Sylvia told me how in the midst of this psychic onslaught, and the most dreadful stench one could imagine as the prominent feature of the presence, the females resorted to furious and unrelenting prayer throughout the night and into the welcome arrival of morning, their only shield against the intense harrowing and vile assault. The incident succeeded in as much as it destroyed their friendship after such an ordeal with no seeming rationale as to what had brought it on. She refuses to speak further of it even today, as does Brandon Jackson about his troubled days in office. Assuming there is some validity in her story – and I see no reason to disbelieve her account on whatever level it manifested – could it be that it was simply confirmation of what Jackson stated as being the conviction held by many senior clerics in the Church of England – Lincoln Cathedral, for whatever conclusion, IS a battlefield between Good and Evil ?

MARY·HATH·CHOSEN·THAT·GOOD·PART·WHICH
SHALL·NOT·BE·TAKEN·AWAY·FROM·HER

CHAPTER EIGHT
THE LINCOLN DA VINCI CODE

There is a suspicion of true irony in the fact that Hollywood came to film scenes of Dan Brown's *The Da Vinci Code*, written as fiction but considered by some as partly fact, at Lincoln Cathedral, England during the summer of 2005, when it now appears that the cathedral may well have revealed its own 'Da Vinci Code' starting with the discovery of a strange depiction at the scene of The Last Supper – a dog on Christ's plate instead of bread or the Holy Grail cup. I can remember thinking, that day of May 20th 2005, when I collected my copy of the local *Lincolnshire Echo*, and the front page headline 'Da Vinci Code to be filmed at Lincoln Cathedral', just how mad life can often be with unexpected circumstances catching us fully on the hop. Hollywood coming to duplicate Westminster Abbey, as Westminster had refused to allow them permission to film there, disgruntled with the general tone and implications of the book, whilst Lincoln Cathedral were relatively happy to accept the one hundred thousand pound 'blood money', as some local would later put it. Filming on the day even brought a protest to the west front door entrance by a local 61-year-old Roman Catholic nun kneeling outside the west front in prayer for twelve hours, the story reverberating and carried that day by most press agencies, and national TV bulletins. I was left thinking to myself, how mad is all this? The Echo set me off on the trail with their breaking story in April, the month before the Hollywood surprise, headlined 'The riddle of Jesus, the Last Supper and Lincoln's own Da Vinci Code' by reporter Paul Whitelam (ironic name 'Whitelam' for such a story, 'white lamb' being Jesus, of course!). And just as I'm beginning to compile my evidence for an unsuspected factual coded trail, having scoured the cathedral for other anomalies, along comes the world's most famous film crew in my own backyard – as I live in the shadow of the cathedral – to promote a storyline about a treasure and coded clues on how to find it, although their revelations are only a fiction. A natural magician having invoked Hollywood through ritual couldn't have done better! I'd better not laugh out too loud at that thought, as by the time you have finished this book you may just want to believe that I had possibly played a role with the insistence of what is referred to as the Collective Unconscious – definitely more on that later.

The Masonic Dog on the Platter, Scene of The Last Supper

Anyway, I wrote a letter replying to their interesting article and suggested that if they wanted Lincoln's own Da Vinci Code, I'd offer myself up to write it – and I prophetically did!

Having had the 'dog on the platter' find brought to my attention, I soon busied myself searching the cathedral for any other anomalies and as you will learn, I found them all. With such a project thrust on me so hurriedly and unexpectedly, I felt it would be worth a visit to Glastonbury, which claims so much of the Arthurian and now Magdalene credibility for itself. I wasn't concerned that those in Glastonbury pride themselves as being the seat of spirituality in the British Isles (which unfortunately makes them quite aloof I have found), for what I was seeking was that very real spiritual vibe that is within the area independent of its residents. And, of course, any old excuse to get myself up my favourite place on earth, Glastonbury Tor, for a heartfelt one to one, our relationship having blossomed and remained stable since my first visit in 1984. My objective was to instill some sort of strength and any 'assistance' to help me prepare for the task that lay ahead – cracking the Lincoln Cathedral Code. Just as Hollywood's arrival had come out of the blue, so did another surprise element awaiting me at the Tor! Now, you must realize that I have visited this energy point many, many times since '84 - and that weird shower of 'ping pong' balls - at all times of the year, in all seasons, weather conditions and times of the day, and it had been a port of call for me to summon strength before visiting any anticipated danger at Rennes-le-Chateau in 1986. In passing, there is a carving of a phoenix on the Michael Tower at the Tor and given what I would be about to witness at Rennes on April 24th '86 in April - a visit from a fiery 'phoenix' - I wonder if there was more significance in this paying of a call than I imagined. In June 2005 I set off up the winding trail to the summit in the same fashion as all those previous visits – there are two optional path ways to ascend – the only difference being that after twenty years this was the very first actual time I had gone up there with a camera at the ready. With my old days of being able to pick up phenomenon on photos well behind me, I was wondering if I could have a partial resurrection of success, and had made this well known in my thoughts as I approached my old friend. Then, at about two-thirds of the ascension, I suddenly became filled with an instant and irrational fear, what I imagine people describe as a panic attack! My thoughts, incredibly, having came all the way from Lincoln to Somerset just to do this, was to run off back down the Tor and call it all off! Doing 'a runner' is not my style and never has been, so what was going on?

I sat down for some time and although not managing to compose myself at all, did slowly make it all the way to the summit and take some pictures. The fear never completely left me all the while up there, and I really was glad to go. So much for seeking composure for my Quest! When the photos were developed, taken in a silent blue sky, a peculiar cross-shaped object had appeared to the right of the St Michael's Tower. Only I know there was nothing in the sky at the time, and certainly not any aircraft or birds that skeptics could claim I had captured. The following year I was back at the Tor again, and as I started the steep climb I had even managed to have misplaced the experience of the previous visit. I received a sharp reminder when, at exactly the same point as before, I again became filled with that wash of terror...I was experiencing a repeat performance. So, for the second time, I just about overcame the impulse to run off, sat down and eventually and slowly made my way up there again taking some photographs, and feeling relieved to be away. Some interesting blips appeared on this series of shots but the most impressive find was the reappearance of the aerial cross...and in exactly the same place! They say things come in threes don't they? The following summer I ventured back to Glastonbury, poised for Round Three. At the expense of boring you I will tell that, yes, at that same point of ascension – only this time I was ready for it – that overwhelming, overpowering fear gripped me again, only this time it was worse than the previous occasions put together, and I was definitely going to do a runner, no messing! It was horrendous, but somehow after sitting down in a fearful state I finally reached the archway to Michael's Church...and this time, unlike the other two ventures, the fear began to subside and I actually did feel quite composed, after three years of trying.

I continued the photographic experiment, but this time nothing to report. And so, what that was all about, my most favourite place on the planet giving me so much grief, I don't know, and I'll continue visiting the Tor as often as I can. Nothing has altered my relish for reaching its peak . Being me, I can't help but have at least one theory. Maybe trying to recreate my success in elemental photography from the '80s in which I believe the Collective Unconscious obliged with its ability to impress images on sensitive photographic film has also brought about the re-emergence of that other archetype I was experiencing at the time. Had the archetype of the god Pan sat there at the top of the Tor awaiting me, and with his presence, his unequalled natural and expected ability to unleash the fear of panic? Who can say?

Dan Brown's *The Da Vinci Code* sold 25 million copies in just over a year, earning Dan somewhere in the region of 77 million pounds, propounding the theory that Christ married Mary Magdalene and had a child. Sony Pictures bought the rights for a 53 million pound screen version to this fastest-ever selling book for, by comparison, a mere 3.1 million, with the filming in Lincoln to take part over five days as scenes shot in the Chapter House, ironically where the Knights Templar were historically tried and sentenced, would double up for Westminster. As the cast and crew of 200, and 400 extras, set to work, my own Lincoln Cathedral Code, still in its infancy at that time, gained its first press mention in *The Independent* whilst the cathedral, having upset most of their regular flock by accepting a huge rental pay out, were dramatically inviting controversy back on their stone doorstep again. One small satisfaction for me was presenting movie producer Ron Howard with a proof copy of my original 'Lincoln Da Vinci Code' book, having waited for him to leave the *White Hart Hotel* at six in the morning to, unlike the rest of the visitors, walk the three minutes to the cathedral for that day's filming. Co-star Ian McKellan actually mentioned this interchange on his website, having seen the book on Ron's desk. Wonder what he thought of it? Lincoln Cathedral has a long history of dramatic events heading its way. Built in 1097, having knocked down the church of Mary Magdalene to do so, it was damaged by fire in 1141 with the roof burning down, Alexander rebuilding it in 1145. In 1185 on May 1st there

The Dog looking up - Station of the Cross, Cathedral Nave

Grail Poet Lord Alfred Tennyson and his dog

was an eclipse of the sun over northern Europe. Whether this somehow played a part in what was to come – earth tremors on August 1st that damaged Lincoln Cathedral beyond repair – we cannot be sure. What we do know is that the earthquake must have been powerful, as it was said to have been felt throughout the country. Only the west face survived in good shape and the rest of the building had to be demolished. The year of 1237 saw another drama when, during a sermon by one of the Canons, the newly finished Central Tower collapsed, burying some of the congregation. Next, the wind thought it would have a turn in wreaking some cathedral havoc, and in the 16th Century a wooden spire was blown down by a gale. Even the Lincoln Imp notoriety for misfortune was blamed for one of the worst football disasters in British football, when Lincoln were playing at Bradford in 1985 and a stadium fire breaking out caused 56 deaths (disturbingly, the number 56 is involved in our mystery) and more than 260 injured.

A sex scandal in the 1930s was totally eclipsed by the events of 1995, when the Dean Brandon Jackson, caught up in a sex scandal of his own, in July made a most puzzling and unexplained public announcement, declaring that he believed a battle of good and evil may centre on the ancient minster and then went on to ask that he close the cathedral for six months for it to be exorcised with prayers. A startling thing to say, indeed, by any standards, or by anybody come to that. After the furore subsided and he resigned from his post and just about made himself publically unavailable, I managed to track him down by a forwarded email in 2006 to ask him if he would like to clarify exactly what he meant, but he declined to make any comment. To suggest that the cathedral could possibly be embroiled in any 'battle between good and evil' made me think. Was there somewhere within her a suggestion based on some knowledge in the past that had best been kept within the confines of the cathedral? Could it even be, perhaps, that the minster held some sort of age old lost or forgotten secret, frozen in stone and time in its ancient architecture What if there was a secret hiding place of some great religious consequence? and occasionally aided and abetted by those who passed on the information covertly?

From such musings, the Lincoln Cathedral Code was born. The most prominent clue had been placed as far back as the 13th Century and it was in the form of the Lincoln Imp, a symbol barely investigated, and overlooked as being of no significance. This despite the Dean of Lincoln stating in his message to the people of the city, by way of an explanation to the cathedral's acceptance of *The Da Vinci Code* filming, to quote his Bishop to say 'People have been coming to Lincoln Cathedral for centuries in search of the Lincoln Imp...', even though it has gone on to be the actual emblem of the city. That a secret was meant to be maintained could have been dismissed so easily, and might have indicated that here a game of chess was being played out. A battle or game of strategy involving some who would guard the secret and keep it alive, and those who would prefer it never to be learned as it would completely re-write key teachings that had been deliberately withheld within the Church for centuries.

This game of chess consideration need not feel it is without support, for in connection with the cathedral we are not short of a bishop, a castle, a knight, a king or a queen, as we shall see. Connoisseurs, and collectors alike of coincidences, would note that on the final scheduled day of *The Da Vinci Code* filming, the Circular Chess Championship – with a board shaped like King Arthur's Round Table – was also being held in the cathedral, the first time it had ever been in such an environment. If the 'Lincoln Cathedral Code', with its numerous interlocking clues happens to be real, then it is reasonable to assume that it may well lead us to a key location where the greatest of all, and longest sought, complex treasure hunt concludes once and for all. Let us go see!

A circulated story from the 1970s was hard to miss. It was of Berenger Sauniere and the inexplicable unfolding of his almost sudden wealth at his small church at Rennes-le-Chateau at the foothills of the the the Pyrenees in the South of France. Some have said it was the equivalent in total of approximately thirty million pounds throughout the saga, starting in 1887! Spawning many, many books about what has been popularised as the 'Mystery of Rennes-le-Chateau', there is now a complete industry that has seen the area steadily ascend to almost the level of a theme park, and there has still been no satisfactory, or conclusive, explanation or resolution to date. What is clear though, is that the fellow decorated his church dedicated to Mary Magdalene, built high up a hill, in a most bizarre fashion, with commentators and researchers readily recognising his perhaps over-contrived contents as clues to either a treasure, or secret he discovered himself. A 'something', it is reasoned, that would allow him to blackmail his peers. The story is long, and the 'clues' vast, but I would prefer to keep it short, and in the true fashion of a knight 'cut to the quick'!

In reality, the church is not such a puzzle, for its decorations and adornments are clearly Masonic as suggested by its very basic foundation, a black and white chessboard floor and a blue ceiling with gold stars. Most Rennes investigations feel the church, under the careful eye of a shadowy and powerful organisation known as the 'Priory of Sion', affords clues to lead one to a great discovery in the Rennes-le-Chateau area, and yet despite years of fruitless searching by thousands of intrepid, in all manners of fashion - and even with official excavations in 2004 - nothing that could meet the promise of a great discovery has ever been found. A simple explanation would be that, yes, the famed Mary Magdalene Church at the top of the hill does harbour a repository of clues leading to some great find, but that its location is not even France let alone Rennes, but instead some other geographical point in another country. Just because the clues were deposited at Rennes does not automatically ensure that the solution is nearby. There has to be some starting point wherever it may be, and it could just be that a Magdalene connection did - at one point - reside within the Rennes Valley, but is no longer there, removed for safer keeping.

Most adventurers who abide by the law that seek out South American tombs usually discover to their dismay that unscrupulous looters have gotten there first. If we are willing to accept that there may indeed be a 'something' to find, let us go and see if we can decide what it might be and then even, where it might be! Dan Brown, in his book *The Da Vinci Code*, which suggests that the Grail is to be found in England, visits St

Sulpice in France, and Chartres Cathedral as scenes for his dramatic element of what he describes as fiction, whilst cheekily turning a blind eye to any reference or remark about the actual church at Rennes-le-Chateau, an actual place that gave birth to an actual mystery that he has picked up on, and enlarged to a conclusion. One of his fictional prime characters is even called Sauniere! It is widely accepted, that in modern times, Rennes is the building block for the contemporary search for the Holy Grail, and what it may actually be. Incidentally, it is fair to say that very little interest was even aroused by the French, even though the centre of all this media attention was in their own backyard! As I have said, I have neither time, space nor inclination to wade through a close scrutiny of analysis of the literally hundreds of clues left lying about (some almost certainly red herrings), and so with haste and alacrity I will begin the Quest for the uniquely original Lincoln 'Da Vinci Code'. Let us begin to think in a fashion like nobody else before us.

Like all before me, all I need to sieve and sift to avoid being led astray lies literally before my eyes and right in front of my nose, for as we enter this French church dedicated to the Magdalene, high up a hill, we are greeted by a statue. Not a gargoyle, common in churches, but a demon or devil, usually held to be Asmodeus, Guardian of Treasure. I am immediately reminded at this point of Dan Brown's 'draconian devil' in one of his clues, the word 'draconian' originating from the Latin 'draco', a dragon or snake, and also a constellation that can only be viewed from the Northern Hemisphere. This demon guardian has a contrived arrangement whereby his left right leg crosses over his left. Above him preside a group of angels who collectively etch out the sign of the cross, and above the scene is a design of a cross also, which could be described as a 'rosy cross'. Above the demon is a French quote:

PAR CE SIGNE TU LE VAINCRAS
...which has, amongst other versions, been translated as:
BY THIS SIGN YOU WILL WIN/CONQUER

The next statue, beside him, is one of St Roch, who also draws attention to himself by virtue of him showing us his right knee exposed to the top of his thigh. As patron saint of invalids, I wonder, could this be a reference to Dan Brown's clue that accompanies his draconian devil, and to whom he refers to as the 'lame saint'? Either way, I am going to suggest that it is not hard to see the parallel here – a church dedicated to Mary Magdalene high up a hill that keenly draws our attention to a carved devil statue with clues that wishes to lead us to another place of worship high up a hill, built on the demolished site of a church dedicated to Mary Magdalene and containing a carved devil statue...Lincoln Cathedral, England.

BY THIS SIGN YOU WILL WIN/CONQUER = 'LINCOLN' (wI LL wi N CON quer, all the letters contained within)

Let us re-trace and re-cap the initial steps of our journey so far. Thanks to the publication of two global best sellers in recent times: *The Holy Blood and the Holy Grail* (a historical detective story in 1982) and the further controversial work of fiction ... although not completely, as some think otherwise, *The Da Vinci Code* in 2004, the concept of the Holy Grail has now taken on a whole new meaning and symbology. No longer the cup or chalice partaken of Jesus at The Last Supper, the Grail is now redefined as being synonymous with the figure of Mary Magdalene whose name was forbidden in the church, and so became secretly known as the Grail, the Chalice or the Rose. There are those who believe implicitly that there is an actual secretive Masonic-related shadowy organisation known as the Priory of Sion who guard, and have guarded, the Grail because of a hinted at marriage of Mary to Jesus, and the continuance of a bloodline or 'Rose Line'. This redefined search for the ever-elusive Grail therefore translates into a hunt for the bones of Mary and accompanying documents that offer proof or validate this alternative history. Or so we are told. To date, she has been placed at Rosslyn Chapel five miles out of Edinburgh, Scotland, somewhere in the region of Rennes-le-Chateau in Southern France, and also at Glastonbury, Somerset, England. Like King Arthur and his many resting places, obviously, she can't be at all three. What if she isn't at any?

Meanwhile, back in Lincoln, a good place to start would surely be within the cathedral precincts at the statue of Alfred Lord Tennyson, Poet Laureate and most famed of the Grail commentators. There are only two statues of Tennyson, the other being at the Isle of Wight. The 1903 statue in Lincoln is the work of George Frederick Watts. Tennyson (1809-1892) was born at Somersby, Lincolnshire, an Arthurian poet whose lifelong interest was in re-working the medieval legend of King Arthur and the Round Table for the 19th Century readers, and whose own personal life was one of conflict between faith and doubt. His 1869 masterpiece epic poem *The Holy Grail* is considered the finest amongst critics.

Let us take a closer look at this bronze statue, for it appears to be laden with Grail clues awaiting discovery, as one might expect. There is a plaque on both front and back of the casting. Firstly, at the front, the plate or plaque bearing his name, as with the plate directly below it, has a five-petalled dog rose design on either side, the five-petalled rose known to be a symbol of Mary Magdalene. The significance of the dog, we will catch up with later! The plate on the front of the plinth of the statue contains a poem entitled 'Flower in the crannied wall'. Now, it is well-known also that the great poets, akin to artists like Da Vinci, and architectural masons, would conceal hidden information or clues in their work for fears of orthodox reprisal. It is likely that Tennyson's 'Flower in the cranny' was the rose, symbol for Mary, and the cranny, as the dictionary definition explains, meaning 'secret place' from the French 'cran', a notch – a notch being a 'v' shaped cut. Now, the slightly odd thing about the verse is that the double 'o's in the word 'root', that appears twice, are presented as interlocking to create the symbol of the *vesica piscis*, of which much of the symbolism to emerge at the beginning of the Christian era had its origins in the geometric motif, associated with Jesus and also explained as a female symbol. The subject of mystical speculation throughout several periods of history, the vesica *piscis* can be seen in an artistic rendition upon the lid at Chalice Well at Glastonbury. We will return to the

FLOWER IN THE CRANNIED WALL,
I PLUCK YOU OUT OF THE CRANNIES,
I HOLD YOU HERE, ROT AND ALL, IN MY HAND,
LITTLE FLOWER-BUT IF I COULD UNDERSTAND
WHAT YOU ARE, ROT AND ALL, AND ALL IN ALL,
I SHOULD KNOW WHAT GOD AND MAN IS.

Vesica Piscis and the Root and offspring of David - the Bright and Morning Star

ROI and SION - to whom the treasure belongs.

significance of the word 'root' soon.

Another glaring anomaly is on the fourth line down where the word 'could' has its 'o' merging at a slight height to the 'C' giving the appearance and indication of a numerical zero degrees. This is our own 'Zero Meridian' that turns up in the Rennes-le-Chateau mystery as being the Paris Meridian in association with the Rose Line. Now, turning to the plate which is at the back of the statue, we read a line from Tennyson's lauded *Holy Grail* poem which says: 'Over all one statue in the mould of Arthur, made by Merlin' followed by an epitaph to its composer. If we dig out a full copy of this poem in its entire length and look up the very next line that follows on, it will read: 'With a crown, and peak wings pointed to the Northern Star..' Let us put that on hold, too, if we may!

Now, in the true spirit of concealment and cryptic style we are expecting from Masons, if we look at the third line of this plate at the back – the name TENNYSON – and then look at the line directly below it at the date of his death in 1892, we will notice that the number '1' is placed rather conveniently and precisely below the 'O' in Tennyson, which when we care to encapsulate in a 'v' shaped notch, will then involve the 'S' and final 'N' in his name, to hint at a reference to the word 'SION' – the overseers of the Grail secret. Equally as precise is when we start at the 'R' in Merlin on line two and come straight down through this 'Sion' passing through the 'O' again in Tennyson and the 'I' in 1892. It reveals 'ROI' which in French means 'King', and this is referring to the King in the second Rennes Parchment 'For Dagobert II King and for Sion is this treasure and it is death'. We have located both the King and Sion encoded in this plaque! Next, I must ask you to return to take another peek at Tennyson's *Holy Grail* poem, this time at the very last four lines of his epic, lengthy masterwork for it reads: 'Nor the high god a vision nor that one who rose again'.

As before, I implore you to consider what may be deliberately hidden in this crucial ending, in the style we expect, for as a Masonic cryptogram it reads: 'Nor the high god a (vi)SION NORTH (at) one who ROSE again.' North..Sion..Rose..what could it imply? Actually, 'imply' is rather a good choice of word, for now it is high time to take a much closer look at an interpretation of Lincoln Cathedral's most infamous attraction and uninvited guest, the Lincoln Imp, flippantly considered to be no more than a Mason's joke, high up between two arches on the NORTH side of the Angel Choir (one of the more celebrated achievement of Gothic arch is named after thirty angels decorating the triforium arches) seen on a spandrel squatting under the corbel above the easternmost pier. If you didn't have any idea where to locate the imp in the cathedral, it's unlikely you'd ever find this twelve inch figure, and the cathedral now has him illuminated by a light to help you. Significantly, as we will see, this 13th Century demon is said to have been blown into the cathedral by the wind. If attention is being drawn to this imp, then maybe it is time to ask, what is an imp? Do we really know? Generally speaking, an imp is a small demon that has such a restricted power that it relishes in creating havoc by spreading untrue tales and lies amongst the gullible. The word originates from Old English 'impa' meaning 'shoot', 'offspring', 'graft'. In Masonic architect a graft is 'the place of junction of stock and scion' ... 'scion' a word from Old French 'sion, scion', meaning a young member of a family, a descendant, an offshoot. Is this a reference to what Dan Brown in his *The Da Vinci Code* refers to as the alleged fathered child of Jesus and Mary, and the Priory of Sion who keep the secret? The imp is clearly of Masonic handiwork, nobody argues this, but if we look closer at his deliberately exposed left leg (with his right above it just as is the demon's in the church at Rennes) – the bare left leg being an early stage in Masonic initiation – you will see what is of even more interest, a clearly defined notch or 'v' shape which on page 321 of *The Da Vinci Code* informs us is called the 'chalice' (one and the same that encapsulates 'SION' on Tennyson's plate), a metaphor used throughout the Grail lore for female, and the Grail. What are we being told here?

Now, if we take a walk along Eastgate alongside the cathedral, about 12' up a wall, a little to the left of the Rose Window far behind it, we will see a baffling scene. There is a figure popping, or peering, out of a stone wall block, as far through as his breast level, looking down to his left! The carving is known to be 13th Century. It has no meaning or explanation, but I will suggest this. If we 'say what we see', we see a head that peers, by virtue of a standard orientation, to its east. Head – Peer - East. In masonry and architecture an identically sounding 'pier' is the support of an arch, and at the head of the easternmost pier is...the imp! It seems our mystery peering figure is to draw

The Demon Guardian with Masonic 'V' on exposed left leg.

attention to our imp! The imp looks down the Angel Choir where it is located, a similar arrangement of having angels above it as in the Chateau church.

Lincoln Cathedral is in the form of a cross. Is this 'cross' the sign by which you will win/conquer? On the north-side of the Choir, further long to the right of our demon guardian, we can see the carving of an angel with a sword in his right hand, expelling

Adam and Eve from Eden. It is referred to as the 'Angel of Expulsion' or should that be 'ExpulSION' – as the Magdalene was also expulsed from biblical text? What is rather quite interesting is that back at *The Da Vinci Code* we learn from a Grail poem on page 573 a reference to a 'blade' and 'chalice' guarding over the secret location of Mary. Have we, during our search in the Angel Choir, located both the blade and the chalice – the blade held by the sword-wielding angel and the symbol of the chalice on the Imp's exposed leg? This blade and chalice, we learn, guards over her gates, (page 573) 'gate' coming from the Old English meaning ' a way, path or narrow opening'. A cranny perhaps? Or maybe we refer to the cathedral's Choir Screen, or gate, at the Crossing of the North and South Transept, flanked on either side by beautifully carved roses. Or maybe the place names Bailgate, Eastgate, or West Gate that surround the cathedral? Is this the 'Crossing' meant by the angels above the demon back over in France?

For the next 'clue', we return briefly to the Tennyson statue outside for the last, but not least, time. Looking up at the root in his hand as Tennyson looks down at it, is a DOG, albeit Tennyson's own Irish wolfhound Karenina. It looks up in much the same way as the dog that accompanies St Roch in the Rennes church. If you search within the cathedral, along the aisle leading down to the Great East Window, you will come across a carving of Jesus being accosted prior to the scene of the crucifixion. It is the third of four 15th Century German woodcuts of select Stations of the Cross. In this particular carving there is a glaring anomaly. Underneath the main gathering of the figures in the scene, and yet a part of it, there is - as if meant to be hidden from view - a dog looking directly up at Jesus. Why? There is certainly no such mention in any biblical account, and no obvious reason why there should be. Unless Masons are trying to tell us something, yet again. It is exactly one and the same dog as our canine friend highlighted in the *Lincolnshire Echo* article. And so let us turn our attention to this unusual scene at The Last Supper – very Da Vinci territory, wouldn't you agree – at this Great East Window, made in 1855. For instead of seeing a loaf of bread on the plate as we'd expect to, there is this dog again. The Jesus figure in this magnificent stained glass depiction holds his hands above plate and dog in the same way or gesture that our Grail poet friend Tennyson is holding and inspecting the root. Again, what can it mean? I am reminded of the passage in the book of Revelations 16:22. The passage reads: 'I, Jesus, have sent mine angels to testify unto you these things in the churches, I am the ROOT and OFFSPRING of David, and the bright and morning star..' Have we discovered the meaning of Tennyson's root, at last? A reference to an offspring, or child, and something else. Those of you who paid attention in the classroom at your astronomy lessons will no doubt recognise the significance of this bright and morning star, resisting comparisons with the planet Venus, as being one and the same as Sirius, known as the Dog Star, synonymous with the Egyptian Mother Goddess Isis. The dog looking up at Jesus at the Stations of the Cross...the dog on the plate at The Last Supper...Tennyson's dog looking back up at the root. Is attention seriously being drawn to the nearest star after our own sun? Sirius, so called by the Greeks from the adjective 'seiros' (anagram 'is rose') meaning 'hot and scorching'. Sexual heat?

On July 23rd each year, noticeably the day directly after the celebrated Feast Day of

Mary Magdalene, this star Sirius is in conjunction; it meets, or joins, with our own sun. The ancients named this period of time from 20 days before the conjunction to 20 days after, the 'Dog Days', named after the dog star Sirius. These dog days, most accept, commence on July 3rd and finish on August 11th. However, if we count 3rd July as day one, then the 20th day after then becomes the 22nd, the date associated with the Magdalene. Thirty foot up the buttress of the south east corner of the Transept, we find two sundials, the South and the East Dial. The East Dial bears the motto: *'Pereunt et Imputantur'*, or, translated, 'They (the hours) are consumed and will be charged to our account', and is unusual owing to the oddity of its numerals – no hour lines are marked earlier than 6am, presumably because the cathedral itself blocks out the sun at such times. The numerals shown are: 6 7 8 9 10 ... the 10 is further spaced away than the others. If we add 6, 8 and 9, we arrive at 23, leaving us with the 7. If the 7 represents the 7th month and 23 the day, then we have discovered 23rd July, the day of the earth-Sirius conjunction! What are we to make of the then solitary standing 10? It is the Roman numeral 'X', as an abbreviation, used to represent the word 'Christ'. Today, it is more commonly used as to represent an unknown or unnamed person. There may be an alternative reason to the accepted as to why no hour lines are marked earlier than 6am...and this reason is to draw our attention to the very issue. As seen in Lincoln, it is earlier than 6am that we see the sunrise during the Dog Days in conjunction with the star Sirius. It is not until late September that the sun resumes rising after 6am. Is the East Dial suggesting itself as a Dog Day marker? Let us look again at the translated motto; 'They (the hours) are consumed and will be charged to our account' – the completeness of the merging of Sirius with our sun...charged to our – our sun's – account. There are 64 roundels and illustrations at the Great East Window, the number of a chess board, and if we consider a standard number grid system, you would find the scene of the dog at The Last Supper at exactly 5 down and 4 across: 5 x 4 = 20, the exact number of days before and after the Earth-Sirius conjunction...the number of the Dog Days!

A short distance away, the East Dial faces the splendour of the East Porch, known as the Judgement Porch. Underneath a dog rose-shaped detail, we see Jesus high above Mary and child. I find it strange that we are being asked to accept the adult Jesus above Mary who is already cradling the infant Jesus in her arms. To gain entry to heaven we must be as children, and so is it totally unreasonable to suggest, that seen through a child's eyes, one might think it was in fact looking at the adult Jesus, or father, above the mother and child - the child of that father and mother, Jesus and Mary Magdalene? Why is this statue of Mary the Virgin outside of her cathedral? Is it because she is actually Mary Magdalene upon whom the early Church passed judgement and cast out? Here she is cast out at the Judgement Porch? The figure of Jesus above wears a robe and sash that clearly shows a specific tied knot. Are the Masons telling us that he has 'tied the knot', a phrase that goes back to the Roman days and means 'to be married'?

If we visit the South Transept, we will find the embroidered tapestry that is the Patronal banner of the cathedral purporting to show the Virgin Mary. However, I'm not so sure. The figure stands with a crescent moon to her right as she holds a staff and is greeted by the swan that was the constant companion of St Hugh. The floodlit cathedral sits behind her head like a crown, and we can see the castle, King Edward House and Lincoln Prison. What I find may be the work of the Collective Unconscious in the production of this wonderful tapestry is the following: if it is the Virgin Mary, then why is she wearing a scarlet scarf? The scarf has real shells placed as the brooch actually picked from the shores of Lake Galilee. Wasn't scalloped engrailing at all times connected with love goddesses and fertility, cult females associated with the sea, from Aphrodite to the modern day interpretation of Mary Magdalene who came from Magdala on the northwest shore of the Sea of Galilee? There is more to be concerned about, for there are drops of blood on the staff below its cruciform head. If you say what you see, you will say you are seeing blood dripping down a line – the centre of the staff – or a 'bloodline'! There is further blood on this Mary's left hand as if displaying a bleeding spot or stigmata, the signs of wounds associated with Jesus' crucifixion. This would suggest to me not only a reference to this person being associated with the crucifixion, and we must remember how Mary was the first person to visit the tomb, but also that the blood is a common bond between Jesus and this Mary. It can therefore only be Mary Magdalene we can see in her colour scarlet, this vibrant red being also much of the remainder of her dress. Why is the prison included in the background? Did it have to be? A Collective Unconscious metaphor for the confinement and restraint the Gospels reserved for her? The Patronal banner tells us of the appearance of the rose that is on her apron that this indicates her title of 'Mystic Rose'. I would argue that Mary Magdalene's association with a rose is far, far stronger – she IS the Rose, the code word for the Grail, and that coupled with her scarlet decoration and the drops of blood on the line of the staff, these are the major clues provided through the creator of this banner by the Collective Unconscious Magdalene archetype, telling us that is not Mary the Virgin.

French poet Robert De Boron (1215) who, in his 'Joseph d'Arimathie ou Le saint Graal', first definitely attached the history of the Grail to the Arthurian cycle, was first to mention the Grail as a chalice containing Christ's blood. De Boron forges a link between the table of the Last Supper and a 'grail table' in the 2nd poem in his Grail trilogy, Perceval. There, Joseph of Arithamea is given guidance to search for a table that resembles the table of the Last Supper. Once he finds the table, he places the Holy Grail on it. The Grail table has thirteen seats, one of which is kept vacant in memory of Judas who betrayed Christ. Having established this link, de Boron goes on to then forge a link between the grail table and Arthur's Round Table in the 3rd poem in his trilogy, Merlin. Near the beginning of the poem, Merlin creates the Round Table with fifty-two places, one of which is a vacant seat called the Judas seat. 52 places = 52 weeks in a year = a calendar, an almanac or 'table' of months, days and seasons.

The visual highlight along the southern side of the cathedral is the delicate leaf-like tracery of round window known as the 'Bishop's Eye', not correctly a Rose Window unlike the 'Dean's Eye' that faces it opposite to the north, and in doing so becomes one of the major mysteries of Lincoln Cathedral. It is a simple fact that all Gothic cathedrals feature Rose Windows to their west! If one phonetically rearranges 'Dean's Eye' to

'Deaseyne', pronounced as 'design' – meaning 'to contrive', 'to set apart or destine', and 'a plot or an intention' (French 'designer', Latin 'designare', 'de' meaning 'off' and 'signum', a mark), we may well begin to understand why the Rose Window proper has been deliberately misplaced. Another strange feature about this Rose Window is that it is somewhat spoilt, by not being completely visible until approached very closely. Along to its right are glass panes containing the Seal of Solomon!

Perhaps I can cast some light, not through the glass pane of the Rose Window, but more importantly on its very mystery. This 13th Century 'Dean's Eye' is a Wind or Compass Rose, the latter earning a mention in Dan Brown's *The Da Vinci Code* on page 148 in association with the 'Rose Line'. It has appeared on charts and maps since the 13th Century. The term 'Rose' springs from the figure's compass points, and how it resembles the petals of this world famous flower. A Compass Rose is a figure displaying the orientation of the north, south, east and west cardinal directions, a term for the traditional magnetic compass graduated markings. Arabian navigators were responsible for the earliest 32 point Compass Rose during the Middle Ages. In the days of its origin, this device was employed in indicating the directions of the wind, then known as the Wind Rose, but the 32 points of the Compass Rose originate from the direction of the 8 major winds, the 8 half winds and the 16 quarter winds. Let us remind ourselves that in the story of our Lincoln Imp it is the wind that blew him into the cathedral. The north is traditionally indicated with a fleur de lis symbol – the Arms of the Crest of Lincoln and the symbol of the French monarchy. In occult, the north is traditionally associated with dark forces. There is alleged circumstantial evidence that once upon a time, medieval churches remembered the use of a 'Star Clock' and that remaining evidence of this is reflected and contained, no less, by the Masons in their stone architecture of Lincoln Cathedral. A possible further possible reference to 'I, Jesus, have sent mine angels to testify unto you these things in churches'? The Rose Window, named after the navigational Compass Rose measuring the wind in ancient portolans, faces north (in the middle of a compass we find a star..) Long ago, Masons guarded the information that if the window of the beautifully stained glass decorated Rose Window be removed, and if one were to stand in a certain acknowledged position within the cathedral at the dark of night, the revolving constellations of the Northern Star Clock could be seen to revolve through the stone circles in all their beauty. It would of course highlight the 'Northern star' alluded to in Tennyson's 'Holy Grail' poem...SION...NORTH...ROSE. Which star could it be? We will discover the identity of this star later!

Geoff Clinton, Engineer for both cathedrals of Lincoln and Wells had the job of piecing back, restoring and conserving the condition of the Rose Window in 2004. He had this to say about our hidden star Clock: 'The Dean's Eye is unusual. It has relatively thin spokes in correspondence to most other Rose Windows and it has a quatrefoil instead of a central circular panel which has complicated load paths through the structure.' But that pales in comparison with what also occurred in 2004 – a classic example of the Collective Unconscious rearing its head, literally! The Dean of the Cathedral, the Very Reverend Alec Knight, for reasons only known to himself, had a winking figurehead of himself carved and placed around the Rose Window Tracery, 85 feet above the ground and around the Dean's Eye stained glass, where it remains! There is no escape from the understanding and symbology that a wink is an informal mode of communication indicating shared, secret knowledge. In Alec's case, of what? What was he giving us the wink about? The Rose Window being a Star Clock? The cathedral's equally hidden connection with the Magdalene? In any case scenario, what was he thinking about? It is also psychologically interesting that at this critical time in the minster's evolution – the revelation of its code and with unavoidably Arthurian links – here we had in its charge a Dean with the surname of 'Knight'!

According to *The Da Vinci Code*, the Grail waited underneath ancient Roslin. Could this possibly allude to the Rose Window at Lincoln, adorned in the architecture of a cathedral built by Master Mason's loving art? May we announce this Rose Window as a planisphere, the Round Table given to Guinevere (correctly pronounced as 'Queen-of-air'), a map of the atlas of the Northern Constellations, a portal to our elusive star? *The Da Vinci Code* assures us that She, Mary, the Grail, rests at last beneath the starry skies. Could that read 'rests at last beneath the starry skies of the Rose Window, atlas of the Northern Heavens? Radio astronomy has proven to us that the iron content of the star Sirius is the same as the iron in our blood and the iron of the earth and of our solar system. Sirius is our blood...the blood and the Grail ?

Initially, at this point, my Quest for the Lincoln Cathedral Code was now at its end. I was quite confident the cathedral had some sort of inference with the star Sirius, and that the many number of anomalies both within and about the giant structure did contain a secret that belonged with the tale of the Grail and consequently Mary Magdalene. Over many years my feet had taken me to many a cathedral visit in the British Isles, and many a spotted anomaly from the chevron shaped lozenge pillar within Durham Cathedral, to the peculiar broken inscription in English at the stain glass window crucifixion scene in the South Transept at wonderful Wells Cathedral in Somerset – the word 'passion' in 'By thy cross and passion' is strangely broken into two, to leave the word 'SION' at the bottom left. I had never seen this sort of thing ever happen before. Was it deliberate? Is there really a hidden secret society known as the Priory of Sion? Perhaps they have always existed throughout history, perhaps changing their name periodically when necessary. One thinks of such underground organisations such as the Rosicrucians and the Order of the Illuminati, and of course the Knights Templar who, in order to continue, would have been forced underground. Perhaps Dan Brown's coded explanation of Da Vinci's Mona Lisa is not quite correct after all, for it has not escaped my attention that if we were to encode 'Mona Lisa' as a simple phonetic, we would discover 'anomalis'... 'anomalies'...something which is irregular or different from what is normal.

As I was just about to dismiss any reality of the Grail being buried below the Rose Window as being in tandem with Dan Brown's *The Da Vinci Code*, I took one last look back at the blood and the Grail, and that strange classic example of what is called 'serendipity', the faculty of making chance finds, or what you are looking for finds you first. The name of the man who started all this, with his historical role in the writing of the 1982 best seller *The Holy Blood and the Holy Grail* – the solitary inspiration behind Dan Brown's even more phenomenal best seller *The Da Vinci Code* – chose the name Lincoln. This was the Collective Unconscious working at its best. My 'Lincoln Cathedral Code' simply had to go on…it had been handed to me on a plate…a plate with a dog on it! My individual Quest hadn't ended at the Rose Window - it had just started. Perhaps Alec Knight was winking at me.

CHAPTER NINE
TEMPLECOMBE AND THE TEMPLARS' HEAD

It's only very recently that I remembered how I stood in the ruins of the churchyard at Coustaussa way back in 1986, and in a private moment of reflection at this, my first stop off point in my only visit to Rennes-le-Chateau, asking aloud if the spirits of the Templars both past and present would assist me in my Quest. My memory had totally misplaced that solemnity having happened, and looking back now, I wonder if they, in some way, have. The previous year, sacred geometrist and fellow Rennes author David Wood had shown me his discovery in the valley – the Temple of Solomon etched out on the ground, and strongly resembling, to my mind, a giant camera! No surprise we are dealing with Light, then!

Back in England, Lincolnshire is one of the most important Templar counties due to the Bishop of Lincoln's power extending over most of England at the time, for nearly 500 years the Seat of the Holy See was held at the Bishop's Palace – only a few hundred yards away from my Lincoln Cathedral Code final location – from the Humber to the Thames. The Patron Saint of Lincoln Cathedral, St Hugh, had bought the original Temple in London from the Templars, who then went on to build the second one which stands today. (It's believed Hugh died in the original, of which nothing now remains). Yet it is well within the bounds of possibility that the Templars hid treasures in Lincolnshire because of its largest and most efficient Orders were concentrated in different parts of the county, having built Preceptories at Temple Bruer and Willoughton near Gainsborough, South Witham and Aslackby, near Sleaford. Bruer being one of the only Templar sites never to have been properly excavated as it was waterlogged at the time raids were made on most Templar properties. Although not full Preceptories, other Templar related buildings can be found at Eagle and Mere, near Lincoln, and the *Angel Inn* was built by them at Grantham. The Templars owned investment property throughout Lincolnshire and in Lincoln, the Jew's House, leased to Aaron the Jew in 1158. During their persecution, Templars were imprisoned in Lincoln Castle, where even today you can see their graffiti on stone walls, including a scene of the crucifixion, and according to Lionel Fanthorpe commenting on the Lincoln Cathedral Code, 'With their architectural knowledge they may even have helped to build the Cathedral and plant these clues'. In 2006, after 800 years absence, the Templars met up for the first time in Lincolnshire at Ashby Hall near Sleaford, thereby puzzling many by breaking tradition as their earlier historical meetings had always been held in the cathedral. Why not this time? Had my Cathedral Code drawn too much attention to the sacred geometry of this majestic stone womb?

Seeking further evidence of the Templars' involvement in the Rennes mystery leading me to Lincoln, my Templar peregrinations had taken off all within 2006-7, during which time I had visited Temple Bruer (where an excavation in 1833 had provoked tales of underground vaults being found, another in 1907 failing to find them, instead discovering two flights of stairs leading down to an underground crypt that is still there today), a church of St Helens, South Scarle, a church at Eagle, and inspired by Juliet Faith's article in Oddvar Olsen's 'Temple Booklet' publication, the church of St James, Cameley and of St Mary's, Templecombe in Somerset. Bruer had interested me as I had made a most interesting find – on the west face of the Preceptory wall, which we will read about later indicating that a treasure did arrive here from Rennes. Did this treasure stay temporarily at the Bruer crypt before moving the few miles to the cathedral corner? It is accepted that freemasonry originated from a Templar legacy, and it is equally well known that these freemasons have as their own cherished Lodge symbol, the blazing star that is Sirius. We must also include that at the time Bruer was alive and well with Templars, the church of St Margaret had already been built and was in use, and there was a strong Jewish community within Lincoln. Could Bruer have forwarded the Templar treasure, removed for safety from Rennes-le-Chateau, to St Margaret's in the knowledge that ancestors relating to its race were nearby?

The last time I visited Bruer was on July 12th 2008. I had been surprised that there wasn't a single Youtube video uploaded on the Internet and so thought I'd be the first to do the honours. A synchronicity awaited, for at a certain number of steps up the winding staircase somebody had taken it upon themselves to expertly and perfectly remove one stone slab from the wall to reveal a hiding place behind the block. Had there been anything there when they removed it, or had it already gone? Whoever had been responsible had done it recently, as everything had been as usual when I visited only weeks before, leaving the now loose slab pushed back in. What a bonus for my Youtube film! You cannot visit Bruer without noticing how the arched entrance to the tower has been chipped away to make it bow unusually, as if widening the entrance for something larger to be carried in, or out.

The church at St Helen's (or St Helena, to give its proper title) at Scarle was built in the 13th Century but could be even earlier. The church was enlarged perhaps due to its connection with the neighbouring Preceptory of the Templars at Eagle, the Knights holding the Manor of Eagle by gift of King Stephen. Interestingly enough for me, there is a knight in armour, with dog, dated 1510. The Templars of Eagle are thought to have visited the church a number of times, although it didn't belong to them. The 'carved pew' of the knight at Eagle Hall was on the north side of the chancel, occupied until it was removed in 1871 by the tenants of Eagle Hall. Whereas most visitors to St Helens will not miss the stone slab knight, will they discover the 22 or so strange letter etching, scratched almost deliberately high up a pillar? Who is responsible for this most difficult to spot handiwork, and when it was etched is impossible to know. Is it telling us something? I next visited the archway at Eagle, Lincoln. The Templars had a hospital there (one of two in the UK) and other buildings. After the Order was suppressed, it was given to the Hospitallers (they had properties there themselves) and they rebuilt the old All Saints Church there that the archway leads to. This magnificent archway has a Templar on the left, a Hospitaller on the right, and a Maltese Cross presiding at the top. People mistook the Hospitallers for Templars due to them having a similar cross on their mantles apart from it being white on black for the knights and white on red for others, Temple sergeants had red crosses on black or brown habits, hence the confusion, and owing to rule 141 from 'The Rule of The Templars': 'The surcoat of the sergeant brothers should be completely black with a red cross on the front and back, and they may have either black or brown mantles, and they may have everything that the knight brothers have except the horses' equipment, the tent and the cauldron which they will not have, and they may have a sleeveless coat of mail, hose without feet, and a chapeau de fer, and all these aforementioned things they may have according to the means of the house'. This explains their later connection to John the Baptist, even though it was the Hospitallers who had the Baptist as their Patron Saint.

I can't leave Bruer behind without mentioning the appearance of a strange anomalous aerial object to the right of the Tower deciding to include itself on some photos – in a clear blue sky – taken during my first visit there. It was snapped in the presence of two attendant members and premier members of the Lincolnshire Paranormal Research team – Garry Ross and his lovely ex-partner Sarah Greenway. Garry is a splendidly accurate Templar historian with his feet firmly planted on the ground; if I feel I'm drifting too far off he'll bring me back to earth with a realistic thud!! Mind, sometimes, as I have conclusively discovered, the way in is through the 'way out'. The Templars, we are told, were well versed in the ancient esoteric and alchemy, something that today often translates into that puzzling world of what we call 'unidentified flying objects'. These objects have a habit of appearing at places where I specifically visit, maybe they should stop peeking in my diary! When I was at Bruer in October 2007, I was showing two French Templars inspired by my work and on a visit from America especially to see Lincoln Cathedral Code and Bruer, psychic Gloria Amendola (who has a commanderie at Rennes-le-Chateau) and her travelling companion Jane. Just as we were leaving we all saw a weird elongated orb high up in the sky to our right...it just appeared and hung there, pulsating! As if that wasn't enough, at the same time high up to the right of the Tower appeared a blob of rainbow colours, also just hanging! Sadly, that day we simply marvelled watched this dual phenomenon, as if treating my guests as they were leaving, with no attempts at snapping pics. Two weeks earlier, in my own garden at about eight in the morning, a strange 'sun dog' phenomenon appeared up in the clouds – three bright lights – although unlike any other supposed 'sun dog' phenomenon that I have seen or been acquainted with. My wife brought it to my attention, and by the time I managed to find and take a hurried photo, they had started fading, but I did manage some photographic evidence. (Gloria, incidentally, took the opportunity whilst at my Cathedral Code Marker tomb, to dowse at the spot. Her crystal pendulum started circling immediately from a still start, and then began to revolve anticlockwise!)

Well, although I am not advocating spaceships piloted by aliens, I do find this object worthy inclusion as it – or others similar to it – have popped up on my Questing upon Glastonbury Tor (twice) and above Lincoln Cathedral, all on different days. The objects that appeared above the cathedral showed half an hour before the key time and date of mid-day 22nd July, Feast of the Magdalene 2006...maybe they had their own diary! Perhaps all these places are situated on earth energy ley lines, providing strange natural geophysical phenomenon? Or do they just follow me about? Scientific, if at least sober, evidence, suggests that it is the planet itself that produces these UFOs. The earth lights such as observed upon the Tor at Glastonbury, where significant ley lines cross, behave as if intelligent, seeming to have the properties of electrical and magnetic attributes. Combined magnetic fields may well affect parts of the brain to produce hallucinatory experiences, but also physical encounters in the shape of plasma, a type of gas sharing the approximate equal number of positive ions and electrons. Observed study of created laboratory plasma has shown it to behave in the same fashion as living cells, and I think this is because that is what they are – living biological cells exuding from the body of Mother Earth, one in particular picked up on camera at the Poussin tomb photographed by my wife! (Plasma in the human body, is the liquid portion of the blood). When the unprepared human brain has an encounter with one of these sudden manifestations, it scrambles the information in order to keep the viewing person sane, presenting the picture as something they are more likely to cope with, and the current archetype is that of the UFO or 'alien spaceship', just as mysterious to the daily functioning level of consciousness, but at least providing an image with something that has a label.

Next, I left Lincoln behind to visit Templecloud and the St James Church at Cameley with its odd wooden head – a mould perhaps? Finally onto Templecombe where I have no doubt that the wood panel is a Templar artifact, one of a series that gives rise to the 'Baphomet' head worshipping allegations, the one charge against the Order that may have had some substance. More, however, on this panel shortly, as we now return to the subject of heads. There have been numerous accounts and associations involving various heads allegedly kept by the Templars, many different shapes, styles, figures etc., so much that one wonders why there can't be just the one definite account. John de Dorrington's account during the trial in England asserted that the Order possessed four principal idols, one of which was kept at Temple Bruer. On the basis that there is no smoke without fire, I am going to suggest that there was something to all these Templar affiliations with heads – maybe a singular one or maybe many – and my suggestion may not be as unlikely as one would first like to imagine.

We must remember that in dealing with Templarism, alchemy appears to be a complicity, as was their involvement with those of a magical penchant – and we must remember that there are two types of 'magic', one involving the art of producing marvellous results by using the secret forces within Nature, the other the art of the stage magician who produces illusions by legerdemain. I am going to suggest that the Templars did own a head, but that it was an automaton, a self-operating machine that were in evidence as far back as Ancient Greece in one form or another. It is quite possible that they did, as the chronology of these heads accommodates our requirements. A brazen head, or Brass or Bronze, are recorded in history as being a prophetic device attributed to many medieval scholars believed to be wizards. Always in the form of a man's head they could correctly answer any question asked of it, answering freely, variations restricted to a simple 'yes' or 'no'. Those who are thought to have owned such a device are as follows: Pope Sylvester II (950-1003AD) who was a prolific scholar of the tenth century, a scientist ahead (no pun intended!) of his time who introduced Arab knowledge of arithmetic, astronomy and astrology to Europe. The first French pope, he was reputed to have studied magic and astrology at Islamic cities. Sylvester was supposed to have built his brazen head or to have acquired it from a Buddhist secret society called 'The Nine Unknown Men', a robotic head answering yes or no.

The nine unknown men are described as a two-millennia old secret society founded by Indian Emperor Asoka 270BC with the purpose of preserving and developing knowledge that would be dangerous to humanity if it were in the wrong hands. Echoes here of a prototype 'Priory of Sion', but we must seriously consider that our own secretive society of Templars also started with nine men in 1118. Another owner of a head was the important Arab Muslim scholar, inventor and mechanical engineer Al-Jazari (1136-1206BC), celebrated during the Islamic Golden Age and credited with first recording designs of a programmable humanoid robot in 1206. (Leonardo Da Vinci sketched more complex automatons around 1495). Let us not forget that the Templars did involve themselves with the Muslim world, a world they so often opposed only on the battlefield. Now it begins to get a tad more interesting. Robert Grosseteste (1175-1253) was another reputed owner of one of these magical heads. Grosseteste being a philosopher, theologian and Bishop of Lincoln in 1235 – the Lincoln connection, at last! His most famous student was Robert Bacon (1214-1294) who surfaces in Umberto Eco's novel *Foucault's Pendulum* described as a rogue magician. Bacon is said to have created a brazen talking head that could answer any question. One of the most famous Franciscan friars of his time, Bacon advocated a modern scientific method, although studies at a later date revelling him to place a reliance on occult and astrological traditions and alchemy. Albertus Magus (1193-1206) was acknowledged as being Germany's greatest philosopher and theologian, a Dominican friar achieving fame for a comprehensive knowledge advocating peaceful co-existence of both science and religion. Like Grosseteste, after his death, stories present Magus as a magician-alchemist, and he too, is recorded as the creator of a brass head mechanical automaton capable of providing any answer asked of it.

And so it appears that the Templars are in good company when it comes to being custodians of a talking head! Maybe this theory – and it appears I have now joined the legions of theorists – is correct, but without the evidence of a discovery we cannot be sure. Maybe an automaton connected with Grosseteste awaits us with other artefacts in a cache buried deep below the Marker Tomb of the Cathedral Code? I have tried to build up a case for the Templars involvement with alchemists and varying degrees of magician. Before I present one last rabbit out of the hat, involving the Templecombe panel painting, we must first tarry a short while with the phenomenon of synchronicity. My Lincoln Cathedral Code is a complex, yet simple, series of network involving these experiences of two or more events that consistently occur meaningfully, casually inexplicable to the person who has the experience of them. One of my more obvious Cathedral Code ones is that my 'Grail' searching led me to the city of Lincoln, and the name of the chap who instigated the UK's interest in Rennes-le-Chateau and the Grail is Henry Lincoln! Not to mention Hollywood choosing to film scenes for *The Da Vinci Code* within the cathedral when the cathedral has its own 'Last Supper' code! Such is this, our phenomenon known as synchronicity, Jung describing it wonderfully aptly as 'meaningful coincidence' and 'acausal parallelism'. Jung announced synchronicity as a governing dynamic underlaying the whole human experience and its social, emotional, psychological and spiritual history. I would think the Templars figure in that spiritual history.

And so this marvel we call synchronicity is quite a bit of a sleuth, clue hunter and provider, which is just as well as we now return to Templecombe and its very own treasure, the puzzling panel painting which some say represents Jesus, others arguing John the Baptist. It is placed near the Baptisimal Font. Templecombe was given to the Hospitallers after the Templar suppression and it was rumoured to be an old Hospitaller painting of John the Baptist who was the Patron Saint of the Order of the Hospitallers of St John, more so than the Templars. The Hospitallers were said to have unearthed the Baptist's tomb and burnt his bones to prevent relic hunters' success, keeping only the head. Our head, as most of us know, a life-size painting carbon dated as 1280, was discovered hidden under plaster upon the ceiling of an outhouse in the small Templecombe village, owned by Mrs Topp. I would like to point out, in support of those who claim it represents the Baptist (given that the Templars are said to have given special homage to John) that the geometric shape that frames the panel head can be found identical to the one that can be seen on the South Doors of the Florence Baptistery, which shows a presentation of the head of John to Salome – by Andrea Pisano 1330-36. By employing the same John related design, is this telling us that the Templecombe head is of John?

I would like to take it all a step further, but first I must appear to take a very strange and unexpected digression! In the mid 1950s a set of cards called 'Foldees' were produced by America's top bubblegum card company (although an earlier set had been made as early as 1949) – an innovative and original set of 44 'metamorphic' cards, nine different pictures being able to be made from every card by mixing and matching tops and bottoms of each card. A similar set in 1976 enabled 33

Foldees containing three images to produce 297 combinations of changing faces and bodies. So why do I tell you this? Well, it is the best example I can provide whilst I continue scouring the stage magician's set of 'visual conundrums' to demonstrate that this is EXACTLY what the Templecombe panel head actually is! A hidden image that can be sought by altering the arrangement of the wooden panels as they stand.

Stage magicians from earlier centuries had a similar presentation with wooden slats that, with a pull of string down the sides, would spin the strings around so that they would land randomly and show a different picture from the original. By inverting the 3rd panel, placing the first below it, and below that inverting the second panel, the head of a talking automation appears! A face represented on a 14th Century 6 foot stone coffin lid at the 13th Century Church of St John the Baptist, the only remains of the site of the Templar Preceptory at South Witham, shows a near identical representation of this Templecombe revision, particularly with the same noticeable hairstyle, and a representation of the tracheal rings of the windpipe, mistakenly thought on the slab to be a beard. Is this what the Templecombe panel finally reveals? I save the best revelation in this little particular episode, until last. Remember synchronicity, the clue hunter and provider? Well, the name of that bubblegum company that invented the Foldees card and who still trade in the USA today is none other than 'Topp's', one and the same as Mrs Topp, in whose outhouse the painting and its meaning was hidden, and who donated it to the St Mary's Church..!

MARY·HATH·CHOSEN·THAT·GOOD·PART·WHICH·
SHALL·NOT·BE·TAKEN·AWAY·FROM·HER

Erected to the Glory of God in loving memory of
Mary Forrest of Ardow. Died 23rd October, 1904,
by her affectionate sister Isabella D. Forrest.

CHAPTER TEN
ROYSTON CAVE GRAPEVINE

Given that the Knights Templar were in receipt of the knowledge of Mary and a child and assuming this responsibility in Lincolnshire, I wondered if I could investigate any allegations outside of the county of any visual evidence that they knew this secret. Hearing whispers that at Royston was a cave with a Templars riddle only solvable by employing the device of the elusive 'Rabbit Language', or lost Mother Tongue, I found myself heading off to this small town situated slightly west of the Greenwich Meridian, one sunny Saturday autumnal morning in October 2008. In the small town of Royston, Hertfordshire, there stands a stone that signifies the intersection of two straight roads orientated to the cardinal directions. This 'Roi Stone' or 'Rose Stone' has been moved a short distance to rectify hindering traffic, but what remains in the same place is the artificial cave below it, a circular bee hive shaped chamber some 26' high with a 17' diameter discovered accidently in 1742 by workmen who dug around the curious stone and discovered a shaft leading below into the chalk. It was more than half buried beneath soil, similar one might say to a time capsule, and when emptied revealed medieval carvings of the Knights Templar, who founded nearby Baldock. To this day the carvings, suspected to tell a story best kept secret, remain open to interpretation, apart from a singular and reservedly conventional attempt. More excited devotees of the KT, who prefer to view the Order as one who were custodians and guardians of a great secret and who had somehow gained an access to knowledge way ahead of their time - 'a complete and absolute knowledge' (obviously related and allied to the explosive secret they kept) - still await an induction into the ancient hieroglyphic language of the 'Rabbit' and how Druids and the Templars used this veiled and coded language to communicate. Perhaps, employing what amount I do know of this codex, the time to brave a wider scope attempt to have the story of this well-preserved frieze at the Royston cave, is now. We are going to see how the Templars code hid the very thing that the Roman Catholic Church feared discovery of the most - the workings of the female body, and a sacred marriage of Jesus and Mary Magdalene, the woman they character assassinated to paint as a 'whore', and in doing so desecrate the concept of the sacred feminine and the spiritual act of the Heiros Gamos.

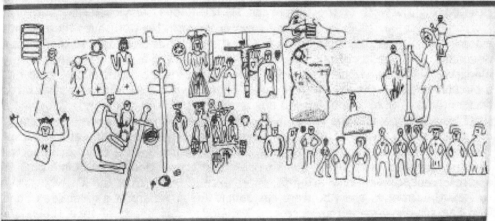

ABOVE: The Collective Unconscious conceals gynaecology and pregnancy.
BELOW: *Corpus Luteum* and a pregnant Mary Magdalene.

To initiate us into how the Rabbit language works, we shall look at the symbol of the Templars, two knights sharing one horse. If we resort to the code, and 'say what you see', this will transform into 'Knights (2) on a horse' and furthermore into 'Knights to honour whores'....in an ironic statement to play the Church at their own game by returning what they had instigated as a negative term, and desecration of women in general. In more nobler terminology, the Templars were to honour females, and in particular keep the secret of the Magdalene and the Grail. Hoping that nobody will be too offended if I bypass most of the orthodox assertion regarding the carvings, I will move straight into the Rabbit language of visual puns and play-on words (similar to the popular British TV programme 'Catchphrase').

The pictorial record starts at the right hand side where we see some figures involving a crucifixion, and leads us into a figure seemingly holding a sword pointing to a further twelve figures above. The interesting feature here is that the ninth 'figure' along squeezes in, unlike all the fairly regularly spaced others. The reason is because we are not looking at a figure or person at all. I have no doubt that the Templars were openly receptive to the manifestations arising deeply from the Collective Unconscious, and in this respect they were innocently unaware of their freedoms from the fetters of conventional time and space, perhaps explaining how they were allegedly worshipped a head. Could that be 'ahead' a futuristic term? This would allow for their clear presentations of microscopic biology and anatomical workings, for the shape of the ninth representation is that of a biological spermatozoa, and it is situated in 9th position to draw attention to the illustration not being of twelve people, but twelve months, and with the sperm being drawn attention to at the 9th month we are here discussing gynaecology and pregnancy. The figure is not holding a sword as one would automatically think. It is intended to be perceived as a beam .. a ray .. a shaft of light ... the origin of the word 'beam' coming from the Anglo-Saxon and meaning 'tree' 'stock of a tree'...' a 'stock' from Old English stocc, a stick, is the rooted trunk that receives a graft, and also means family, ancestry, descent. Recall, a 'graft' is the place of junction of stock and scion .. 'scion' a word from Old French 'sion', 'scion', meaning a young member of a family, a descendant, an offshoot.

To the right of the figure holding the beam is a defaced circle which upon closer inspection resembles a biological cell. Alongside the twelve-month calendar we see a two rowed section with 15 along the top and 16 below it. The total designates a calendar month of 31 days. The bottom line shows us scored vertical marks in sections number 17-22, both numbers key to the mystery of Rennes-le-Chateau. In pregnancy the corpus luteum begins to develop on the 22nd day. (When a woman ovulates, the egg bursts from the follicle, and what is left becomes corpus luteum. The luteul phase is the 2nd half of the menstrual cycle). There is a figure at the bottom left of this monthly calendar, allegedly Templar Grand Master Jacques Molay being burned at the stake, or on fire. However, what we are meant to see is a figure 'on heat', the phase when a female is sexually receptive 'in heat' or 'on heat'. The puzzling illustration below this is another table with five graduations – with more to the right than the left and with a period or interval between - which shows us that the fertile period starts 4-5 days before (more) ovulation and ends 1-2 days after (less).

We move next onto a figure associated with a grid, and it is St Lawrence who is said to have martyred on a gridiron. The story goes that Lawrence was dispatched with the Holy Grail, amongst other treasures of the Roman Catholic Church, and that he sent it to his parents in Spain where it lay hidden and unregarded for centuries before finally arriving at a monastery for safe keeping. The figure below Lawrence is an example of 'say what you see', it has its hands up in the air, or is a figure 'up in arms' at the above suggestion of Lawrence being Grail custodian. Alongside Lawrence are the Holy Family, but not as we regularly know them. The secret of the Templars prefers Jesus, Mary Magdalene and child. Below them we see not a horse as some think, but a dog, the symbol of the dog star Sirius, which stares over at the centre of the cross of a presumed sword in the same way as Mary Magdalene stares at the centre of the cross in the bas-relief in the RLC church. Between them is a figure with exaggerated vulva. This figure is Sheela Na gig, a Celtic figurative carving of naked women displaying exaggerative vulva, who is associated to Caillech Bhaerra who was blinded in one eye. The tribe neighbouring the Dogon, the Bozo, called Sirius B, 'the Eye Star', and if we look closely at the only other scored out and defaced circle in the vision of the dog, we can see it duplicates the orbit of Sirius and Sirius B. The apparent sword, as there is no scale to go by, is a dagger, and a dagger, in printing, is also a 'mark of reference', to draw attention to the Sirius connection. The appearance of a dagger here within the Royston carvings, also has a vital importance in connection with the Holy family, as we will see later.

The next illustration shows us a bud, a knob-like shoot, or offspring. Alongside the Holy Family to their right is a female figure. Her left arm and hand, we are told, holds a wheel, but instead we can see a representation of a fallopian tube, also known as an oviduct, which leads from the ovaries into the uterus. To her right there is a crucifixion scene with a hand containing a heart on either side. The hand is to be seen as being on the heart, to reveal the idiom 'hand on heart' for if you put your hand on your heart and say something you say it knowing it is the truth. With Jesus responsible for fathering a child with an impregnated Mary, we are being informed that he survived the crucifixion, and this is the truth known and kept secret by the Templars. Below this scene we see a gathering and a figure being taken down from the cross. To the right of the main crucifixion scene there is the sepulchre with Mary Magdalene sitting on a rock. Above the sepulchre there is a hand appearing to release a dove and a falling object. The 'hand releasing dove' is a common wedding release ceremony in which bride and groom hold two doves which are then released together. The object falling appears to be an egg or yolk (the non-living material contained by the ovum) again indicating that Jesus and Mary were married and that there was the expectancy of a child resulting from their union....the corpus luteum we learned of earlier in the calendar section of the frieze, or, as Rabbit Language would have it... 'corpse....loot...tomb' - corpus luteum - as Jesus' body was removed from the tomb by his bride. Next to this amazing pictorial representation we see a woman carrying a child. Those who would prefer the conventional argument that it is the traditional representation of St Christopher should know that his Templar carving predates that particular Christopher image. There is an even greater irony here and little wonder what the imagery is interchangeable - many of Christopher's earliest images, show him as having the head of a dog again hinting at a Sirius connection. The staff she holds can be viewed as testicles with erect penis. Below this sepulchre and Mary with child scene is a larger gathering of people which is telling us that there many people who are aware of this story, the marriage of Jesus to Mary and a resulting child....the secret held by the Knights Templar and recorded for posterity in a once concealed beehive shaped cave 26' below the ground at Royston, the symbol of the bee, we learn, being one of the two most common Dogon symbols. Whether the Templars carved out Royston using their own knowledge or whether the Collective Unconscious was the tool that guided the hand - within this remarkable cave was the proof I had set out to find.

MARY·HATH·CHOSEN·THAT·GOOD·PART·WHICH
·SHALL·NOT·BE·TAKEN·AWAY·FROM·HER·

Erected to the Glory of God in loving memory of
Mary Forrest of Ardow, Died 23rd October, 1904,
by her affectionate sister, Isabella D. Forrest,
Mistress of Ardow

CHAPTER ELEVEN
HAVE WE FOUND THE TREASURE?

I had reluctantly left the imaginative Lincoln Cathedral Code at the Rose Window, on the north side of the cathedral, after a year of research that had left me wondering all manner of things, with a modicum of healthy doubt, and although I was happy to leave all followers of my Quest suspended there, as shared through local media and brochures that had sold well with the Tourist Board within the City, there was no doubt that the numerous coincidences and synchronicities we had previously encountered, did not! They kept coming as if forcibly moving the paper chase onward, begging or beguiling me to take notice of their presence.

From the moment we entered the cathedral, the puzzling word 'Fricabon', followed by its strange elliptical platter-shaped design upon the ceiling in the Nave – mistakenly thought to be an untraceable name – revealed itself, in the fashion that we have become accustomed to - to alternatively read: 'Freak, up on', referring to the dog found on the platter at the scene of The Last Supper at the Great East Window, for who can deny that a dog and not a cup, or a loaf, on the plate is indeed a freak (Old English; frician) meaning something markedly odd or unusual, this anomaly the starting point from where my Cathedral Code initiates. On the opposite side of the Nave to the Mary Magdalene's Morning Chapel, there was once a South Chapel later used as the Consistory Court or Church, with two windows facing south and east, possibly to draw our attention to the SE of the Cathedral where coded clues gather aplenty and congest. The gable of this South Chapel is worthy of notice for at the head of its lancet was the unexpected figure referred to as 'The Devil looking over Lincoln'. What? There is no satisfactory explanation for the origin of this rather unnerving phrase. The most curious legend is that which describes the Devil as still being inside the Minster – not to be confused with his servile demon the imp – and afraid to come out for fear of being blown away! Today, the slang term 'blown away' is a phrasal verb meaning 'to defeat decisively'.

With the lost secret of Lincoln Cathedral having been discovered by its code and brought out into the open by virtue of my own humble efforts, the Devil has well and truly been blown away. With the fear of finally being conquered, maybe the subservient Lincoln

ÉTPACTUMESTCUMIN
sabbaTOSECUNdePRIMO à
bIREPERSCCETEsaisGIPULIAUTEMILLIRISCOE
PERUNTUELLERESPICASETFRICANTESMANTbUS + MANdU
CabANTquIdAMAUTEMdEFARISAEISAT
CEbANTEIECCEqUIaFACIUNTdTSCIPULITVISab
baTIS + qUOdNONLICETRESPONdeNSAUTEMINS
SETXTTAdEQSNUMquàmboC
LECISTISquOdFECITdAUTdqUàNdO
ÉSURUTIPSEETqUICUMEOERAI + INTROIbITINdEmUM
dÉIETPANESPROPOSITIONIS   REdIS
MANdUCAUITÉTdEdITETqUI   bIES
CUMERANTUXÚ8 qUIbUSNO
NLICEbàTMANdVCAKESINON   SÓLIS SACERdQTIbVS

Rennes-le-Chateau Parchment with dog in a manger design.

Imp did try to sneak out undetected as you would expect; a coward's machinations behind his Master's scaly back, when we learn a little about a connection with Lincoln College. This is not found in Lincoln, but situated in the centre of Oxford some 105 miles away. Oxford is where, in 1224, our Bishop Grosseteste became Chancellor of the University, a Master of students, teaching the newly found order of Friars. The college, one of the constituent colleges of the University of Oxford, was founded by the then Bishop of Lincoln, Richard Fleming, in 1427, and for a very sound reason indeed. Fleming wished for it to be 'a little college of true students of theology who would defend the mysteries of Scripture against those ignorant laymen who profaned with swinish snouts its most holy pearls'!   Sounds like a man after my own heart! The mysteries of Scripture? What aspects of mystery, I wonder? Magdalene? If we go to the front quad at the college we will meet up with an old friend (or enemy!), for we will be greeted above the entrance to the Hall by a replica imp based on the original back at the cathedral's Angel Choir. This version was placed there in 1899 as a successor to the famous Devil carving at the western end of the north gable that used to overlook the college, and which was taken down on Sept 15th 1731 having lost its head two years earlier in a storm. This resonates with the original demon statue at Rennes-le-Chateau,

The Collective Unconscious at work - West Wall of the Templar Tower.

who incidentally, had his head stolen in 2004! The original Oxford College statue was responsible for the proverb: 'To look on one as the Devil looks over Lincoln'. Clearly, there is no getting away from this 'devil' connection with the city of Lincoln, but in a scientific world today, what could it mean to us now? Yet another devil was erected at the college in 2003 to replace the earlier weathered one, he just isn't going to go away!

Unexpectedly, Lincoln College has something else in common with Rennes-le-Chateau – a denial of espionage! Whereby Rennes is often associated with rumours of involvement with agencies such as the French freemasons, British Intelligence and the American CIA, (David Wood once laughed down the telephone to me when he said 'Didn't you know the Valley was run by the CIA?' - Whether he was simply joking or had greater insight I can't say) the Cold War spy novelist, and once spy himself, John le Carre - who had been a Lincoln graduate - confessed that the character George Smiley, his own fictional spymaster creation, had been modelled on Vivian H. Green, a former Lincoln Rector. It is, however, a recorded fact that Sir Maurice Shock, another Lincoln Rector, had been working for British Intelligence, which probably goes some way to promoting a reputation for the college being a recruiting ground for spies. In 1882, the college also broke new ground by being the first in Oxford or Cambridge to admit a Jewish fellow, Samuel Alexander the Austrian born philosopher. The Chapel, also contains an anomaly at its stain glass 'Last Supper', it being the appearance of the Virgin Mary! What is it with these Lincoln 'Last Supper's'? A Mary Magdalene connection is reinforced as we learn that Bishop Hugh rebuilt the final incarnation of her ancient Oxford church in 1194.

A wooden church dedicated to Mary had stood in Oxford over a thousand years ago, and at the time it would have been situated outside the northern wall of the city. It transpires that this humble offering went up in flames some time between 1010-1013, when Viking raiders torched much of Oxford, with a single aisle chapel built by Robert d'Oilli, the Norman Constable of Oxford, replacing the original Saxon foundation. There are two other tenuous connections involving the city of Oxford with Lincoln Cathedral and Rennes. Alexander of Salisbury, the Bishop of Lincoln, commissioned Geoffrey of Monmouth, whom at the time was clerk in Oxford, to investigate the story of immortals, *Prophetiae Merlin Vita Merlin*, translating as 'The prophecies of Merlin'. The work was a series of ancient Celtic prophecies, which - at his request - Geoffrey translated into Latin. We can only raise an eyebrow whilst wondering why the Bishop of Lincoln would want to study the prophecies of this Arthurian wizard-magician. After, Geoffrey went away to write *Historia Regum Brittaniae* - 'History of Kings of Britain' in which the myth of King Arthur featured, and there was an adaption of the figure Merlini to Merlin, the personality that was of such interest to our poet Tennyson that his name features on a plaque at his statue at the cathedral precincts. The other connection was first noted in the 1990s by authors Andrews and Schellingberger, author of the Rennes *The Tomb of God*. Both realised that Abbe Boudet, (who many believe was the real prime mover of the mystery using Sauniere as a front), the neighbouring priest of Rennes-le-Bains, had dispatched an original edition of his strange book, *La Vraie Langue Celtique,* and an accompanying letter to Sauniere's grandfather, the Rector of Oxford University, and had inscribed the cover himself. The letter remains in the Bodleian Library in Oxford.

It never surprises me when we find how all things Lincoln connect up...all is encompassed within that spider's web, that finest of structures whereby some criss-crossings are only a hair's breadth away, whilst others may be great distances away, but all are still on that one spider's web and can lead to any other area or part of it - the original labyrinth. Have you ever had the good fortune and keen eye to espy a spider's web high up in the air resting upon trees or telegraph poles? At first they may as well be invisible, but when you do see one you will realise how far they extend, great distances in fact, and yet when the topic of a web is discussed we only ever seem to think of a web being isolated and small. Let us tightrope along such a strand, and return to Lincoln Cathedral where there is a story that whilst upon a visit to a French Monastery, such was the desperation of Bishop Hugh of Lincoln, that he reputedly gnawed away two fingers from the hand of what was supposed to be the bones of Mary Magdalene in an attempt to fetch a relic of Mary to Lincoln. Rather ironically the one - and numerical - clue he needed to find the actual Mary, or something of most value to her, was already waiting etched in wood at the Mercy seats within the Choir Stalls named in his honour, having literally sat there since the 14th Century. It would be left to the guardians and overseers of this treasure, the Priory of Sion, or the working of the Collective Unconscious with human agency as an innocent agency, to ensure that where this number could be found, so would Mary, her treasure or both. In 1890, this was achieved and a fresh clue leading to the resting place of her trove placed at Rennes in France - to match one already catered for within Lincoln forty years earlier – left in a bas-relief at the altar of the Rennes-le-Chateau church, further accompanying clues followed back at the cathedral with the 1855 'dog on the platter', and, lastly, the placing of the Tennyson statue in 1903.

In the South of France, those who held a belief contrary to the authorised teaching of Christianity and Catholicism suffered the merciless persecution of a Crusade after 1220, and it was both safer and wiser for it to seem that the Grail Romances were fading from favour. It is, still, curious that the Church never did actually challenge them in a direct fashion, but even so, both literary and political imagery and symbolism had faded by the middle 13th Century. Nevertheless, they did live on, replaced by and within the

Why has the Bruer entrance been widened?

permanency of the stone engravings, at the onset of Gothic Cathedral architecture, initially found only in porch and nave, and here within the Gothic splendour of Lincoln Cathedral it is no different, except here we find the most searched for clues to the concluding mystery of a fabulous and forgotten treasure, a treasure that the Collective Unconscious of the human race insists we pursue. Respected researchers of the Rennes-le-Chateau mystery agree on at least one thing, that being that parish priest Sauniere's affiliation with Masons, confirmed by diocese records in the archives, was to a tradition claimed as descendants and preservationists from the 'warrior monks', the Knights Templar, a form of Scottish rite Masonry called Rectified Scottish Rite. As instigators of the building of great Gothic Cathedrals, the Knights Templar would transmit secrets in their architectural knowledge, thus explaining some perplexing stone decorations within old cathedrals.

In our story, the Lincoln Imp is one example of paramount importance, passed off simply as being a joke or the handiwork of a bored Mason. It may well be that it was also at the behest and insistence of the sculptor's subconscious, for after all, did it have to be an imp, placed exactly and crucially where it ended up as a key marker in the chess game? The dog, instead of cup or loaf, at the scene of the Last Supper at the Great East Window is given a similar fate, written off as nothing other than the meaningless product of a Masonic sense of humour. In both operative and speculative Freemasonry, there are certain rituals in the placing of cornerstones of Masonic monuments and edifices. Hardly surprising then, that we are going to find the major and final clues to our Lincoln Cathedral Code mystery at the very south-eastern corner of Lincoln Cathedral.

Rene Grousette, who was the greatest French historian on the Crusades, made a comment that the throne of Godfroi was founded on 'The Rock of Sion'. He elaborated only a little by indicating that this was a reference to some royal tradition that was on equal status to the reigning European dynasties. He fails, however, to elaborate on his original comment which leaves an open interpretation and speculation regarding its meaning. If we skip forward now some centuries, we learn that in 18th Century Masonic Rites there are repeated references to 'The Rock of Sion' – the same Rock of Sion that rendered the 'royal tradition' established by Godfroi. It had been previously assumed that the Rock of Sion was simply Mount Sion – the 'high hill' south of Jerusalem on which Godfroi built an abbey to house the order that became the Prieure de Sion. But Masonic sources ascribe an additional significance to the Rock of Sion. Given their preoccupation with the Temple of Jerusalem, it is not surprising that they refer one to specific passages in the Bible, and in these passages the Rock of Sion is something more than just a high hill. It is a particular stone overlooked, or unjustifiably neglected, during the building of the Temple, which must be subsequently retrieved and incorporated as the structure's keystone. It is 'the stone that the builders rejected, that has become the chief cornerstone', and at the south-east corner of the Gothic Lincoln Cathedral, we find it, leading us to the lost and almost forgotten resting place of the Magdalene, and her secret that must be retrieved and incorporated as the cathedral's keystone. Lincoln Cathedral, aligned at 100 degrees, deliberately points to the east, facing the daily rising

Lincoln Castle in the background - identical match with Sauniere's bas-relief.

sun and the direction of Jerusalem, or Sion. Psalm 48:12 reads 'Walk about Sion and go round about her; and tell the towers thereof'. This passage written centuries before the thought that took physical form to lead to the building of Lincoln Cathedral appears to have influenced the placing of Mary, and/or Grail when we consider the Lincoln Imp carving a marker of Sion and of the influence of Sion within the cathedral. 'Go round about her' – you can, for the nearby Mary burial site, as my Lincoln Cathedral Code will show, is at the burial grounds of St Margaret ...('For Sion is this treasure and it is death') ... 'and tell the towers thereof' – the magnificent towers of the cathedral, once the tallest building in the world. The epithet 'Magdala' from the Hebrew has the meaning of 'tower' and 'elevated, great, magnificent'.

Where do we start to account for the possibility that a historical Jewess may have came to be buried in Lincoln? Well, the thought is not really so outlandish, for Lincoln's Jewish connection was cemented and at its height during the early 12th Century, well-established before officially noted in 1154 until their ignominious expulsion in 1290. Lincoln Cathedral, itself, was believed to be in debt to their Jewish moneylenders. It is well recorded how St Hugh, the patron saint of the cathedral, was famed for his defence of the Jews. There is, in local legend, the story of there being a lost well – St Hugh's Well – once noted for its miraculous cures of the ill, and believed to have been located at Jew's House at the bottom of Lincoln's Steep Hill. However, one does not have to be a master of pronunciation to see that in order to articulate the title 'St Hugh's Well' one cannot help but pronounce 'Jew's Well', also. It set my mind wondering, and my brain ticking – what if we were commemorating not a St Hugh's Well, but, simply, a Jew's well? A well in connection with some famous Jew. Or Jewess. Either way, there may be a simple reason why the actual whereabouts of this well is so elusive today. One of the more famous Glastonbury legends is the claim that the Grail is hidden down Chalice Well at the foot of the Tor. Could it be that this Chalice – a code name for Mary – originated from a living memory of a well and its association with the Magdalene, being nothing more than a metaphor for her, now both currently lost? A well is a spring or a source. The word is interchangeable with 'spring'. Maybe we are actually referring to an 'offspring', a child, or issue of 'source', that from which anything rises or originates, or even a book or document serving as authority for history. The lost Rose Line?

Comparisons with Glastonbury do not end there. The cathedral, high up a hill, was damaged by an earthquake in 1185, and St Michael's Church at the top of the Tor was all but destroyed by a similar tremor in 1275. Known public wells in use during the medieval period in Lincoln have numbered around a dozen, at least half located in a 'zone of springs', the only remaining one still visible being the Castle Well which, although not in use, can still be visited today. However, there is one specifically unlocated well, which could be one and the same as the lost Jew or St Hugh's well. First recorded in the 16th Century, and suspected to have been in the Pottergate area of St Margaret, is the offensively and derogatorily titled 'Slutswell'. This unfortunate named well is more than significant when we remind ourselves of the persistent character assassination and biblical enforcement that Mary Magdalene was a prostitute, or 'slut', a word conjured up by males to represent a woman who they say regularly engages in casual sex. There was a recorded well or spring in the Parish of Holy Trinity Greestone Stairs from which sprang (pun intended) its name Trinity Well Street, Slutswell, on the boundary of this parish allegedly, possibly a well on top of the hill. Previously, and its old, faded name plate can still be read today, Greestone Stairs had been known as Grecian stairs. Why, in an area of Roman settlement, should there be a reference to anything Greek? In all leases of the 17th Century, it is referred to as 'Greezen', 'Greycings', 'Greyse head' and 'Greyce foot', 'Grece' or 'Greyce' signifying a 'step'. First things first! Is the reference to Greece telling us that in this area we have a portrayal of Arcadia, the utopian vision of pastoralism and harmony with nature, and the very Arcadia shown by the famous Poussin painting, dating from around 1630 showing a group of three shepherds examining a tomb bearing the inscription '*Et in Arcadia ego*' ('Even in Arcadia am I'), and being watched by a shepherdess. We are certainly in the right area to invoke images of a shepherdess, for St Margaret was one! Is this 'step' the mount upon which we can see both shepherd pointing at the tomb, resting his left foot, as does the Lincoln Imp in the Cathedral also? Is the place name

The tomb of the unnamed woman - a red herring.

'Greetwell' possibly a reference to a 'Great Well' somewhere in the area? Is the Grecian Place or Greestone Place, perhaps referring not to some lost well or underground spring, but, instead, an underground 'grey stone' crypt? If so, could we possibly locate exactly where?

During the years 1824 to 1864, a local Freemason and solicitor Joseph Moore decided to build a garden whereupon once stood the Holy Trinity Church, naming the site Temple Gardens - at its highest point stands a temple styled after, and copied from, the Greek designed Choragic Monument of Thrasyllus. Nobody knows why he made this choice. Situated at the back of the Bishop's Palace, this structure gave birth to the beautiful, restful grounds of the Temple Gardens, approachable from Steep Hill by following Well Lane. These grounds were further bettered by the Usher Art Museum, courtesy of fellow Freemason James Usher (1845-1921) who also gained sole rights to use the Lincoln Imp in his work promoting it as the symbol of the city. Was he aware of the true significance of the imp as a Masonic marker within the cathedral? It is doubtful we can ever know for certain. So why a Grecian temple in what was predominately a Roman area? Just like

'Grecian Stairs', again we find another Greek influence to our hidden representation of Arcadia. If we follow the winding path up to the hilly gardens, we arrive at the Choragic Temple to find a statue of the Greek female Niobe, which adorns the roof. It was she who so offended some of the female goddesses with her pride that she was turned to stone, and from the rock formed a stream from her ceaseless tears. One of the more tragic figures in Greek myth, Niobe - in a supreme moment of arrogance - bragged about her sons and daughters at a ceremony in honour of Leto, mocking her host along with Apollo and Artemis into the bargain. Then the latter pair acted upon Leto's instruction and slayed Niobe's entire family. Fleeing to Mount Siplyon in Asia Minor, she turned to stone and from her ceaseless tears formed a stream. Poor Niobe is the symbol for eternal mourning. Given that the Freemasons so enjoy their use of puns, I wonder if this could also refer to the symbol of 'morning' as in the bright and morning star? The key words in Niobe's tale of woe relevant to our Lincoln Cathedral Code are 'pride' and 'stone', both of which sit well with the Germanic take on the Grail legend, whereby the Grail is a stone that fell from Lucifer's crown when he was thrown out of heaven for his pride. Let us recall also that the only explanation the cathedral offer up for their carving of 'The Falling Knight' is 'Pride before a fall'. The stone's Luciferic heritage originates from Wolfram Von Eschenbach, whose major epic German poem *Parzival*, was an adaptation of the story of the Grail, and his favouring of the German poem *The Wartburg War*, which summarises how - during the heavenly battle fought between Archangel Michael and Lucifer - the stone of heaven fell to earth as an emerald dislodged from Lucifer's crown and descending to earth.

The true origin of Lucifer's' expulsion appears to originate from the fact that the planet Venus – the other bright and morning 'star' after Sirius – orbits between the asteroid belt and the sun, and as an inner planet it is never seen at dark midnight as it never rises high in the sky at night. For this reason Lucifer-Venus has been 'cast out of the heavens'. The statue of Niobe is so placed that it is in direct line with another specific and obscured statue on the cathedral SE wall, with the Bishop's Palace between them. The significance of the stone with Niobe is key, when we know that the winding staircase of GreeSTONE Place leads us to our final destination at the St Margaret burial grounds. Niobe was turned to stone on Mount Sipylon - coincidently hiding 'SION'... SI-pyl-ON – in Asia Minor, home of St Margaret! Also, her ceaseless tears resonate with that of the Magdalene, her weeping giving way to her little used name of Mary Maudlin. Choragic, incidentally, relates to 'choragus' - a leader of chorus in Ancient Greek drama - from chorus we find a choir, and it is in the Angel Choir within the cathedral that the stone imp sits as a marker and 'The Falling Knight' within the Choir Stalls. In Ancient Greece, also, a chorus can mean a person who rules, or guides, or inspires others. Mary?

Now, as if the importance of this temple isn't enough, if we care to travel some twelve miles or so south from the cathedral to our place called Temple Bruer, set within another delightful garden near to farm buildings, we arrive at 'Templum de la Bruere' - the 51 foot high tower or, Temple of the Heath - the remains of a church of the Knights Templar, responsible for the building of the Gothic cathedrals and guardians of the Grail! Here we have one of the most important Templar sites in the UK, and one of the few left where any remains can be seen. This estate of land was given to the Templars around the middle of the 12th Century, whereupon they built a round church and formed the Preceptory of Bruer. An excavation in 1833 provoked tales of an underground vault being found, another in 1907 failing to find them but instead discovering two flights of stairs leading down to an underground crypt that is still there today – a most convenient hiding place to store a treasure en route to Lincoln Cathedral grounds? If this were all to report, an important Templar site so close to Lincoln – in 1308 when trumped up charges of heresy had the Knights arrested, they were imprisoned at Lincoln – all well and good...but there is a more significant and almost incredulous twist! On the west face of the Preceptory wall, caused by the structure of the Chapel that is no longer standing, we can see a huge etched triangle with extended legs, and which encloses a window. Amazingly, this Piscean fish shape can also be found on the Rennes-le-Chateau parchment, as a device at the very top, or start, of the 'Shepherdess no temptation...' coded work – even within it is a small window! In order to match our design left upon the Templar church wall we simply have to re-orientate the parchment by inverting it, and there we now involve a single letter 'w' presumably confirming that this design can be found on the west face of the church! As many Rennes researchers feel that the two French parchments are copies from older originals, this explains how it can include our remnant design on our west face of the church, as once further architecture would have been attached. The triangle on the parchment even encloses the Templar church window identical to how it stands today! This find leaves nothing left to conclude other than this is absolute confirmation that we are being told that there is a connection between Temple Bruer and the Rennes parchment that reveals itself at Lincoln Cathedral. When inverted, the design points, in relation to the text, at its south-eastern corner, the very area where our clues congregate at the cathedral. We will be returning to a further analysis and even deeper explanation of this inverted 'w' later.

What is this triangular design with a window in the middle? I can tell you. The window in the middle refers to the Great East Window of Lincoln Cathedral, the very one where our Lincoln Cathedral Code started with its dog on the plate at the Last Supper, and the design is that of a manger, the Masonic symbolism being that of 'a dog in a manger'. The accepted explanation for the expression means someone who has something of value that they cannot, or will not, use themselves but which they won't let anybody else have either ...the remains of Mary Magdalene? The triangular shape on the wall also reminds me of how the star Sirius, along with Procyon, is one of the two vertices of what is known as the Winter Triangle, an approximately equilateral triangle mostly upon the Northern Hemisphere celestial sphere. I have found that Bruer is related to 'The legend of Briar Rose' by the Pre-Raphaelite English artist Edward Burne-Jones. 'Briar' = French 'Bruyere' and West Saxon 'Braer' = Bruer. His third painting in the series painted between those key Sauniere years of 1885-1890, contains the poem and clue 'The Rose Bower', relating to Bruer. Reading: 'Here lies the hoarded love the key, to all the treasure that shall be, Come fated heart the gift to take, And smite the sleeping world awake', it should, however, be read: 'Here lies the whore dead, love the key to all the treasure that shall be.' An enduring legend, supposedly associated with the Templars, tells of the nearby place, Byards Leap. Take a look closer at this name 'Byards Leap' – it is an anagram... 'bryd asleap'... 'Bride asleep'...Mary Magdalene!

The arched entrance to the tower has been chiselled away at both sides to make it wider, as if to accommodate something of a greater size either coming in or out of the door. A sarcophagus? A little distance away to the left of the tower is a curious folly sculpted during the '90s as part of an art project. It is an 11 foot tall tapering chest of 20 stone drawers. However, the 16th one from the top is metal and open. Is the Collective Unconscious alerting us to something with this bizarre monument? Is the metal chest drawer indicating a real metal chest meant to 'draw' us to Bruer? Tarot card 16 is 'the Tower'! The sculptor also left another strange object inside the tower, a metal chair. Pronounced phonetically, we can reveal 'metal a chair' sounding 'metallurgy' – the alchemical science of transformation, turning base metal into gold and associated with the Templars!   For me, it was no surprise that I would end up one day at this Preceptory, for if we consider its 'Temple of the heath' title, my link to the spot will become clearer. A 'Heath', coming from the Old English heath, is a barren open land covered with low shrubs, is also known as any shrub of the genus Erica, sometimes extended to heather. Heather, consequently the low shrub of the heath family is also known as 'ling', that word that has a habit of re-occurring in my life at crucial points – Samye-Ling...and 'Lincoln' cannot be pronounced without it sounding 'Lingcoln'!   The name of the very helpful lady who is Director of the electronics company I later worked with, regarding a ground penetrating radar scan at Lincoln Cathedral was called Erica! Having been led there by this strange medium, and having deduced there was a link with Rennes was good enough for me at the time, and then an unexpected individual made his stage debut in this unfolding play!

Tony Peart of Digby, Lincolnshire, grabbed the cover of the *Lincolnshire Echo* with what was to him an embarrassing headline during June of 2006. It read 'Tony's Holy Grail Secret', and involved my own contribution as their reporter had contacted me for a quote. Naturally, it caught my eye! Forty-year-old Tony had announced that churches south of Lincoln built hundreds of years ago sit on pagan sites that form a mystical pentacle, and that the Templars had built their Bruer Headquarters as part of it! Tony was looking for an explanation as to why an extended five-pointed pentacle should exist on the Lincolnshire Heath created by church alignments, and how could it be that the physical manifestations in that area, both natural and man-made were affected by the pentacle's dimensions. A good question, or two! I contacted Tony without delay, and it turned out he was an admirer of my own work that had featured heavily in the local and national media. Tony's original pentacle involved churches at Harmston, Nocton, Blankney, Bruer, Ruskington, Cranwell, Leadenham, Fulbeck, Westborough, Carlton-le-Moorland, and Bassingham. Tony made the finer details of his discoveries and extensive work available on his website, Templar Mechanics, explaining that he thought the original pagan sites of worship were thought to be on ley-lines that link sites of ceremonial and cultural interest, or natural earth energy lines that were responsible for creating the geometry. The planetary Collective Unconscious at work!

Tony's work had no interest in seeking a Grail or a holy relic, hence the encumbrance in the local press headline, he was more into solving and demonstrating how the Templars knew where the ley convergences were to build their settlements nearby and that the Order were fully aware of an earth energy grid system, a hypothesis followed up by the makers of the DVD series 'The Quest', Barry Walker and Robert Garofalo, with whom we would later cross paths. The pyramidical roof of the tower appears to owe its re-design to Edwardian times, but Tony points out that when viewed from the vortex point of his geometry it resembles a pyramid sat on the rising mound between church and Preceptory, and further excitement is involved when we learn that court astrologer John Dee, one of the most learned men in Elizabethan England, and whose goal was to communicate with angels through Enochian magic, gave up his Rectorship at his Upton-upon-Severn church, founded by a Templar, to take over at Leadenham. Dee was a noted mathematician, astronomer, astrologer, and occultist studying alchemy, divination and Hermetic philosophy. Did he think by moving in at Leadenham, one of the major churches found by Peart's geometric 'energy' pentacle', that he could finally achieve his angelic communications harnessing Templar natural energies of the earth? Tony has since gone on to demonstrate a definitive link between the Bruer pentacle and a similar geometrical shape at Rennes-le-Chateau, as well as elsewhere, although in Lincolnshire suggesting that the energy of the divine feminine principle is anchored, with the Templars leaving clues in the landscape for those with eyes to see. But naturally it is the evidence of the link with Rennes that interests me...it seems beyond all doubt that I was always on the right path ..the link between Lincoln, Lincolnshire and Rennes was now well and truly exposed, and I am quietly confident that it was the machinations of that Collective Unconscious that led both myself and Tony to make our collective and complementing discoveries.

Now we are going to return to the south east corner of Lincoln Cathedral where, sculpted high up and slightly to the right of the Judgement Porch, and the nearest statue to King Edward and Queen Eleanor, we find a female figure traditionally identified as that of Queen Margaret of France, the second wife of Edward. However, as with the figures of Edward and Eleanor, it has been altered over the centuries and was almost certainly intended to represent something else. I can reveal that something, or rather somebody, else. Whether the mix up of identification is a deliberate one or not, the female figure is clearly identifiable as being Margaret of Anjou (1430-1482), daughter of Rene d'Anjou and a prime player in the War of the Roses, ironically. Not only do we have the appearance of the key word 'rose' and the name Margaret, but most importantly we have the connection with the royal and aristocratic Anjou family and her father Rene who, it is alleged, was a Grand Master of the Priory of Sion 1418-1480. King of Naples and Sicily, Rene was no newcomer to the search for Mary Magdalene, and excavated a crypt at the church Notre-Dame de la Mer searching for her remains, even though his relative Charles d'Anjou had claimed to have them two hundred years previous. Talk about keeping it in the family! However, it is Rene that is most important to our Lincoln Cathedral Code. This renowned Grail intrepid wrote a work *The Heart Smitten with Love*, a Grail Quest, no less, in 1457 of which a part was a famous and cryptic illustration 'La Fountaine de Fortune' in which we see a knight called Cuer or 'Heart' standing by a magic spring and looking at a monument. A translation of the monument warns against 'bitter water'. We will learn later of a strange document that mentions this 'bitter water'! There is also a 'fallen knight' to be seen - who has also fallen asleep – and behind him we can see the sun lazily rising. On the fallen knight's helmet are a heart and a pair of wings. Commentators conclude that the scene is representing the broad esoteric current coined by Rene as the 'underground stream of Lost Arcadia'. In the picture there is much to remind us of our own Lincoln Cathedral Code findings.

Let us take a look.

The Knight is called Heart. In the Rennes Poussin painting 'Shepherds of Arcadia' we can see a heart-shaped shadow on the tomb being inspected by the two main shepherds. The statue of our Queen Eleanor at the south-east corner of the cathedral is now left touching her heart (once she held a trident) and staring diagonally across towards the St Margaret burial grounds. There is the idea of a magic spring, which may well be knowledge of our lost spring at Grecian Place, our own Arcadia. 'The Falling Knight' is a hidden wood carving at the misereres, located at the chorister in the St Hugh Choir. Rene's fallen knight has a wing-shaped helmet...are these the wings that point to the Northern Star from Tennyson's poem *The Holy Grail*? And then there is the suggestion of a Lost Arcadia – the one we have found at Temple Gardens and St Margaret's burial grounds. Not least of all, we have the indication of the sun rise - the dog star Sirius that rises in conjunction with the earth on July 23rd, the cathedral full of telltale Masonic symbolism directed at the significance of the bright and morning star Sirius. Can ALL this be coincidental, or are we looking at a depiction that provides us with a concluding set of clues to what Rene and his dedicated family had always dreamed of - finding the resting place of the Magdalene? Did he already know of it? Why are we told it is Queen Margaret of France alongside Edward and Eleanor when it is, instead, the daughter of this great Grail seeker...and why is the statue of Margaret obscured from comfortable viewing, unlike any other at the Cathedral?

Above the church of Mary Magdalene at Rennes-le-Chateau is the Latin inscription '*Terribilis est locus iste*', translating as 'This is a terrible place'. We know that the quotation is not original, as it is taken from passage 28:17 from the Book of Genesis. Our Lincoln Cathedral Code will make further sense of the passage, and claim its import for England rather than France. 'Grecian Stairs' is a corruption of 'Greesing stairs', Greesing (steps) still survives in the architectural word 'grees', and even more impressively in the compound word 'de-grees', for not only does the word 'degree' mean 'one of a series of steps in a process relating to the thirty-three degree Masonic ladder', but also 'a step in a direct hereditary line of descent or ascent' – the Rose Line! Jacob's angels continually ascend and descend the stepladder in the Genesis passage. To ascend this mysterious ladder is to embark upon a symbolic spiritual journey – our ascending up the steps of this 'Jacob's ladder' begins at the foot of Lincoln's Greestone Stairs, and the steep climb leading up to Greestone Place, both once known as Grecian Stairs and Grecian Place, our lost and hidden Grecian Arcadia. Upon reaching the summit, to our immediate right, we have arrived at the conclusion of our spiritual and

Masonic ascension – the burial grounds of St Margaret and the dreadful secret that this shepherdess keeps. This 'Place' is, indeed, terrible! Venturing one step further, in Shakespeare's *Othello*, Act One, 'greesen' from the early English 'gree; a step', makes its first appearance in the sentence '...which as a grize or step may help these lovers'. Coincidentally (!), during the 19th Century, Auguste de Labouise-Rochefort, a French author who had earlier written a book that linked Rennes-le-Chateau with treasure, wrote the work *The Lovers, to Eleonore*, with the Arcadian shepherds motto '*Et in Arcadia ego*' on its title page. A reference to our Queen Eleanor who stares over at our lost 'Poussin' tomb, and the source of the lost well of Rene d'Anjou's well, not 'Jews Well'?

Inevitably, critics who find it unlikely to accept that there could be an undiscovered, significant tomb or crypt in the vicinity of Lincoln Cathedral are already in for a rude awakening, for 'coincidentally', as we have come to expect, in the same week that Hollywood arrived to shoot scenes for their screen version of *The Da Vinci Code*, a most unlikely event did occur. As workmen were digging electrical cable to provide power for the increase in indoor lighting, in the lawned area in front of the south-east corner of the south-west Transept, between the corporation paving and the cathedral wall, exposed in a deep wide trench lay a coffin containing several small bone fragments of a woman whose skull was missing! Tourist Elona Rogers of Beccles in Norfolk, a stranger to me at the time but now a friend, takes up the story: 'Not having seen Lincoln Cathedral before, we decided to traverse the exterior before going inside. We were in awe of this soaring ecclesiastical building; the sheer might, the shapes and proportions are breathtaking. While we gazed upwards at towering scaffolding on this supreme structure a workman emerged from his van and said, "This might interest you!" He allowed us to look into a deep, wide trench cut around an outside perimeter wall. "We unexpectedly unearthed this 13th Century coffin about ten days ago," he said. "It contained several small bone fragments – no skull but thought to be a woman. They have been taken away by the cathedral archaeologist". My husband thought it unusual for a woman to be buried so near to the outside of the cathedral. It was an intriguing and startling find that we were delighted to be given the chance to view. The workmen said the remains would subsequently be reburied where found.' Not only did the cathedral archaeologist concede that the unexpected find was in a very unusual place, but no further information was coming other than nobody had ever known or had any record of the burial or person and that the tomb dated as 14/15th Century. In fact this had not been the first time the tomb had been unearthed! Apparently, according to the cathedral archaeology department, it had once previously been disturbed some time in the sixties, when a main cable was being installed, but its significance ignored and re-covered over almost immediately without any fuss or investigation. Well, call me old fashioned but isn't that some example of apathy! In the August of 2005, discreet reports only mentioned that no lid had been found and the remains, after examination, put into a small container and reburied where found. And so ends the mystery of the tomb of the unknown woman.

Who had she been? Why was there no cathedral record of her tomb and of her? To have been placed in a tomb within the cathedral grounds is a prestigious honour requiring clerical paperwork and recording, so how come a female burial can go totally unrecorded as if missed? Could records have been removed and in the fullness of time the memory of the burial and tomb forgotten? Why was she left in such an unusual place? How could a tomb with contents have been buried so close to the cathedral without any recognition? Still nobody has a suggestion, let alone an answer. Until now. Amongst the charges levelled at the Templars was that they worshipped the skull of a female, possibly thought to be Mary Magdalene. If there had been some secret knowledge or whispers that Mary was buried somewhere nearby at the cathedral – as we strongly suspect she is – it is reasonable to assume that those who did not want her to be found or for others to seek her, would engineer a 'red herring' or location to suggest that she had already been furtively found and removed, without themselves being in receipt of the genuine location. This would most certainly explain why there were no kept records, as the entombment would have to have been carried out under maximum secrecy. Where the true Mary actually rested most probably had even been forgotten by the Freemasons as modern Masonic constitutions state that their secrets were lost over three centuries ago. The other possibility is that, again, the tomb is a contrivance, but by Guardians of the Grail. The clue here is that the tomb revealed a female with no head. Only a short distance away, we have the burial grounds of St Margaret of Antioch, and where her church once stood. Here, our concluding research will soon take us – to the true resting place of the Magdalene and her secrets. St Margaret was martyred by being beheaded, just like the mysterious female in the tomb! Look not to the tomb of the unnamed woman with no head or name, but to the church and burial grounds of the named Saint who was also without skull! One thing is indisputable. The tomb of the unknown woman was buried without knowledge below ground level in the precincts of Lincoln Cathedral. If this could have happened in the 14/15th Century, who dare say that it could not already have happened once earlier before?

CHAPTER TWELVE
THE ROSE UNFOLDS

For many of the now hundreds of serious researchers involving and inviting themselves into the Rennes-le-Chateau mystery over the last thirty-five years, the Nicolas Poussin painting 'The Shepherds of Arcadia' is still a main attraction. Although a replica construction of the tomb in the painting stood in the Rennes Valley until being dynamited by its owner in 1988, it is still felt that it is the clue to a final location, if only it could be understood correctly. Arguments raging over whether the background in the artwork truly resembles the surrounding area of the valley, thus hinting that a search nearby would accordingly afford reward, are counterbalanced with an equal number who point out that it does not match anywhere near enough to be taken seriously. Whereas I do feel the painting is indeed a valuable clue, again, the mistake interpreters are making is in assuming that the importance is in the immediate area, but like the church high up a hill in France, it, too, needs to transfer its imagery to the East Midlands of England where it can be located in its intended sense.

'The Shepherds of Arcadia' shows us three shepherds and a presiding shepherdess around a stone tomb. In order to inspect the *'Et in Arcadia Ego'* motto on its face, the middle shepherd casts a heart shaped shadow on the tomb. We have already looked at how the shepherd nearest the shepherdess has his left foot resting on a convenient mound, as does the Sion marker that is the Lincoln Cathedral Imp. The shepherdess, unnoticed by many commentators, appears to be pregnant! Although it has been noted that a depiction of this apparent tomb had appeared earlier in a work by Italian Baroque artist Giovanni Guercino in 1618 as a much smaller tomb/focal, the 'Tomb of Arques', as it had popularly been known by - as in the valley - had been constructed there in 1903. If we hastily return to Lincoln Cathedral and its precincts, and to the Tennyson statue that is so crucial in our investigation, we learn that it too was constructed in 1903! British researcher and author David Wood of Kent, recorded in his work on the subject - and having measured and inspected the Arques tomb before its demise - that it displayed 56 face stones. In 1985 a group from The Society for Lincolnshire History and Archaeology recorded 56 inscriptions at the St Margaret burial grounds at the SE corner of the cathedral, dating from 1749-1871. The number 56, if it has any significance at all, is the number of the year 1956, in which the Priory of Sion surfaced

Edward with pregnant Eleanor - Jesus and Mary Magdalene.

from the shadows to announce themselves openly. (Coincidentally, it is also the year in which I was born !)

In our Lincoln Cathedral Code, it is the very area of the St Margaret burial grounds that allusions to Poussin's tomb comfortably settle. If we take a look at the second of the two famous coded parchments thought to have been discovered by Rennes parish priest Berenger Sauniere, and widely published in 1967, it reads:

'For Dagobert II King and for Sion is this treasure and it is death'

Again, many interpretations have tried unsuccessfully to make sense of this statement, and yet if there is a 'treasure' associated with death, where better to find it than at a burial ground? We will now bravely venture a step, and take the second and last coded parchment further. This perplexing code is usually given to read as, translated from the French:

'SHEPHERDESS NO TEMPTATION THAT POUSSIN TENIERS HOLD THE KEY PEACE 681 BY THE CROSS AND THIS HORSE OF GOD I COMPLETE THIS GUARDIAN DEMON AT MIDDAY BLUE APPLES'

What can we do with this? Let us go where no-one else has gone, and see. Would-be code crackers have always had Rennes-le-Chateau as their starting point and so have had no success.

Away we go, then, and let us look at the coded work in sections at a time. Starting with 'Shepherdess no temptation', we can instantly relate to the mention of a shepherdess for we know that St Margaret of Antioch, in whose burial grounds we linger, was represented in art as such. We can say that regards this female there can be no sexual temptation, as we have decided from the Poussin depiction that she is pregnant. 'That Poussin Teniers hold the key peace' is next. Poussin, we know a little of his role through his Arcadia painting, but what of this Teniers? From the Teniers family, a father and two sons, over a dozen similar biblical scenes were committed to canvas carrying the same title, 'The Temptation of St Anthony'. In one alone, he is not being tempted at all, again underlining the emphasis put on NO temptation! Both Poussin and Teniers, the latter in one isolated example, appear to be drawing our attention to NO temptation – can this be because the image of Mary Magdalene had been so tarnished by the untruth that she was ever a prostitute? Not only does the French word 'tenure' meaning 'to hold' sound one and the same as 'Teniers', but it appears that both he and Poussin, who chose to include a pregnant shepherdess in his work, do hold the key peace/piece in the sense of 'hold' meaning 'to aim, to direct' when we again take a close look at what indeed is the key peace/piece in our chess game, the Queen Eleanor high up the SE buttress. Interesting that early reports concerning the Rennes Parchments claim that they bore the seal of Blanche of Castille, when we in our mystery have our Eleanor of Castille. Back to the buttress concerning her and at first, as with the shepherdess in Poussin's painting, it may go undetected, for we are not expecting it - and folk have a habit of only seeing what they do expect - but a further close inspection shows that Eleanor is carved as pregnant. Stand sideways to the left of the statue to witness the telltale bump and there is no doubt. Furthermore, she now has a missing trident, which she once held, as did the demon statue in the church at Rennes, and we can see how her right hand now touches her heart, a reference to the heart clearly shown on the contrived shadow on Poussin's Arcadia tomb. If we follow the gaze held by the slightly turned head of Eleanor, it looks out towards the St Margaret burial grounds in a diagonal line, which is unsurprising as the Queen on a chess board may move in this fashion. Her gaze is being both held and directed! Also, if we take a close look at the shepherd next to the shepherdess, his head is cleverly intersected by his staff, suggesting decapitation, the same fate as St Margaret! There is a bonus to add concerning this 'Teniers hold the key'... if we pop around the SE corner a few hundred yards away to Tennyson's statue and the poem 'Flower in the crannied wall' upon it. The third line in the poem starts, 'I hold you here...'.

It is not possible to pronounce the first six letters of his name Tennyson – 'TENNYS' – without saying the same sound as 'Teniers'! An even more convincing synchronicity is when we familiarise ourselves with a David Teniers painting entitled, 'The Cabinet of Archduke Leopold' painted by him in 1657. It is of over fifty paintings contained within one. The centrepiece of the one overall picture shows a figure looking at a framed portrait of St Margaret with a suspiciously draped green cloth hanging over the top right of the frame. The Collective Unconscious at this point has ensured that the most modern place name for where St Margaret burial grounds is now located opposite Lincoln Cathedral is 'The Green'! This painting went on to become the property of the Hapsburg family, who are often mentioned entwined with the Rennes Mystery.

Next, we study what is perceived to be '681'. We discover these numbers when we look the 30 feet up the buttress of the south-east corner of the Transept at the East Dial. There, the equally spaced numerals clearly show us the 6, 8 and 1. That is the simpler explanation. Now, as consciousness is multi-layered and multi-levelled, there is a deeper one, and so let us treat ourselves to another bonus. The Dial is an important part of the solution of the enigma as the first name of the Tour Magdala, the tower dedicated to Mary in Rennes-le-Chateau was 'Tour de l'Horloge' – 'The tower of the clock'. In Shugborough Hall in England, where we find a sculpture of a mirrored 'Shepherds of Arcadia' painting, we will also see a so-called Horlogium (water clock and wind tower). On many pieces of art concerning Mary Magdalene, her hands present in a fashion whereby they are folded in a strange way, the fingers crossing to form a 'XXX' sign. With the dial of a regular clock, there are three possibilities to make a cross, like an 'X', like this. Let us explore them as we may be about to discover a surprising conclusion and that there is a hidden relationship between the number and the dial of a clock, and the arrangement of hands of Mary Magdalene.

If we take a look at the Roman version of 681, it will read as DCLXXXI, and here again we see those three X's. The most important 'X' we will find is the one where the number 1 and 7 on a clock dial are linked by simply connecting them with a straight

Jesus and Mary stare over at the concluding Marker tomb.

line...the 'X' is completed by joining the numbers 4 and 10 on the same clock face. We have our first 'X'. The 1 linked to the 17 also makes 17 which is referred to as the 'holy' number of Rennes-le-Chateau, a starting point and basis for all other combinations. Back on the Dial at Lincoln Cathedral the only visible numbers are the ones 6,7,8,9 and 10, which means – if we now view these numbers as if on a clock dial – numerically below the 6, the numbers missing are 1, 2, 3, 4 and 5. Adding the total of the sum up we arrive at 15, which is the same as if we add 6,8,1, providing us with a balance. Imagining again the missing numbers on a clock dial, then the missing numbers above the 10 will be 11 and 12, which when added makes 23. So, we have found the number 23. When we compare the Lincoln Dial with this alternative, with the 1 – 7 line, you will see that all that is left out is the number 7, no longer 17 as the 1 is missing. So we have found a number 7. We have now found a number 23 and a number 7, which clearly is referring to the 23rd of the 7th month, 23rd July, the day of the rising Sirius and earth conjunction...as I deduced earlier, a simpler way by adding 6, 8 and 9 arriving at 23 to leave the single 7!

Some may say, though, why not October 23rd? Indeed, another number is left, the 10, since the 4 is missing. Ten in Roman = X. There are more considerations concerning our 681 and a Clock Dial, for if we go on to take the high number and subtract the lower number directly across from it, we are left with a 4 which could stand for a quarter. There is also a quarter left by the hands of the clock that form the 10 and 7. Another inspiration is that if we remove the XXX out of the Roman version of 681 – DCLXXX1 – the remaining 'CILD' could be a reference to 'CHILD'...if only we can go further and locate a hidden 'H'. Let us look! In the original, untranslated 'shepherdess no temptation' coded parchment, we find PAX DCLXXXI. The word 'PAX' is in Latin, however, whilst all the other words excepting 681 are in French. The clue is that if we add 'I" to PAX to make the word 'PAIX' (= peace) in French. This letter 'I' becomes the hidden clue, for when you turn the 'I' a quarter of the clock, you create an 'H' effect! – the 'I' has turned (literally) into an 'H'. Coincidentally, when remarking about the positioning of the hands of Mary Magdalene, we must remind ourselves how casually we refer to as the hands of a clock! Finally, we can now say that 681 is conclusively solved in the following fashion: PAX = Peace, XXX = Mary Magdalene, and CILD = Child...not to forget our 23rd July date with Sirius! Any association or confirmation with pregnancy and birth within our mystery is always most welcome. The word 'Sothis' (Sirius) in Egyptian signifies 'pregnancy' or 'to be pregnant'.

I had a wonderful synchronicity on the actual date and time of the Earth-Sirius conjunction on 23rd July 2006. I thought it would be worthwhile to investigate being at the East Dial at the rising of the sun and Sirius on that date, finding out in advance that it would occur at 5.03am. Would there be any particular sun's rays, beams, shafts falling upon any strategic part of the cathedral architecture at that precise moment? Only one way to find out – be there. It was a very foggy, misty morning and later that day. We had been having thunderstorms in Lincoln the day before. I only live less than a quarter of an hour away from the cathedral and so I set about walking down there at 4.30am, feeling a little bit wary should I be stopped by the police. I wasn't walking a dog, and how could I tell them I was up to witness the conjunction of the earth and Sirius at a specific point at the cathedral? Luckily, I didn't have to worry as I didn't come across a soul on my short journey, neither pedestrian or in the way of road vehicles. I arrived at my destined point and awaited the conjunction time, unfortunately it was very foggy and visibility was poor, so even at that point I wasn't too hopeful, but at least nothing could take away from me the experience of knowing the conjunction was taking place and I was there. At about 5.15am I decided it was time to go, nothing to report, and I could hardly even see the diffused rising sun. I had only left my post a minute or so and came around the corner away from the Dial when a solitary car drove slowly past and away; its licence plate was 681! Surely a consolidatory confirmation that my thoughts and intentions, at least, where synchronised with the Mystery! Needless to say, upon my turn voyage home, still no further encounter with man or animal in any form!

I can also recall one earlier 681 close encounter many years previous, back in the early 90s. I'd arrived at a Doctors' Surgery early for an appointment and so had to wait outside the closed door. To while away my wait I looked over at the adjacent factory car park and at all the car spaces through the wire fencing. I said to myself, 'I wonder if there are any licence plates with a '681' and so spent the next minute or so looking at all the parked cars from my vantage point. The car park was full, apart from one solitary space available. I soon deduced, no, not one car with the 681 sequence. No sooner had I concluded that thought, then along came a car to fill the only available space, and its plate read '681'! These two accounts are the best of my many synchronicities with the number, and when it has produced itself in conjunction with my thoughts.

The solution of the statement 'By the cross and this horse of God' is to be found inside the cathedral at the Choir Stalls where we find a strange depiction entitled 'The Falling Knight', a finely detailed carving of a wounded knight with an arrow shaft through his back. It is extremely difficult to find as you wouldn't know it was there. At first I thought it could be a word pun and that what we were really being shown was a 'Falling Night', as fastenings on the horse look like they could resemble star formations which would then be in the night sky, but I convinced myself this was not so. There is no explanation even for it being here. In this, God's Cathedral, the horse's legs are curiously formed to make a cross shape! And so, here we have the cross and horse, of God! There may even be a reason why there is an arrow in the back of the knight – 'The Arrow' is yet another name for the Star Sirius!

We move on now to 'I complete this demon guardian at midday'. Some translations say it may even read 'complete – or destroy', and so we will look at both options to keep all happy. This Demon Guardian, clearly, is the Lincoln Imp. How do we complete (or destroy) him? It's really quite simple. We must return to the East Dial sundial, for we are involving midday. Looking again at the deliberate motto there: 'Pereunt et Imputantur' we will notice 'Imp' in the word 'Imputantur'. To complete our demon guardian we take the word 'imp' and complete it to read 'imputantur' – we have completed him! To destroy him, we must look to the translation of the motto: 'They are consumed and will be charged to our account'. This time, the imp is consumed, thus destroyed!   Now that the demon guardian has been completed, let us complete decoding the parchment with the final enigmatic 'blue apples'.

When the sun, assuming the sky is clear and there is no cloud, is at its height at noon – hence the attention drawn to the 681 of the East Sun Dial – and strikes down through a red-blue section of the central pane of the cathedral window next to the statues of King Edward and Queen Eleanor, our pregnant shepherdess, on 22nd July, the Feast Day of Mary Magdalene to create an optical phenomenon – the blue apples! Having witnessed this in 2006, I watched how firstly a small blue patch appears on the floor, followed moments later by two red 'apples' approximately two yards away, these red apples then join the blue patch and red and blue 'apples' form, at the foot of the tomb of St Eleanor, our shepherdess. Back at Rennes at their small church, they claim a similar phenomenon, but this occurs on 17[th]January. Lincoln Cathedral displays 'blue apple' phenomenon all the year around when light strikes through the numerous and glorious red-blue panes strewn along its south face, but for it to appear at midday on July 22nd alongside the Eleanor tomb is the meaningful and precise blue apples we are seeking. Now, as if all this isn't enough, it isn't!

Next I am going to explain how, having fulfilled decoding the Rennes Parchments, which confirms we are at Lincoln Cathedral and certainly not in France, we are going to work out how we arrive at our precise and final location in our search. For an exact location of the treasure contained in this coded parchment we must excitedly return to the chess piece of 'The Falling Knight'. We know that, as is generally understood, an arrow is indicative of a direction to follow, but hidden here is the directive. The carving is most deliberate in its presentation. When we look at the number of fastenings on this horse of God, we will see that there are seven to the right side and four to the left. These fastenings are separated by the leg on the knight to show that the numerals have a separate identity. The legs of the horse are crossed. If we then take the 7 and the 4 and multiply – or cross them, 7 X 4 – we arrive at the number 28. Let us take a short breather before we return to this key figure.

At Shugborough Hall, Staffordshire, stands 'the Shepherds' Monument', a marble mirror-image near likeness of Poussin's 'Shepherds of Arcadia', commissioned in 1748 by Earl Thomas Hardy and thought by many to be a map containing the location of the Holy Grail. An enigmatic inscription at the bottom of the tableau has never been successfully deciphered despite intervention by code experts. One major and noticeable difference in the monument concerns the angle of the thumb of the kneeling shepherd who still points at the letter 'R' in 'Et in Arcadia Ego'. To his right, our 'decapitated' shepherd friend, as his head is 'severed' by the angle of the staff he is carrying, points at the area of the tomb above that is a straight line to the head of his kneeling companion. Perhaps this is trying to say to us, here we have the 'head' of the River Humber deduced by combining 'thumb' and the letter 'R' ('t humbR'). The relationship in distance between both shepherd's fingers, in the sense of a map of the British Isles, would reasonably

The 681 Sundial.

suggest that the kneeling shepherd is pointing towards the region of Lincoln. This is not too surprising, as for nearly five hundred years the seat of the Holy See was held at the Bishops Palace, (only 100 yards away from our final location) from the Humber to the Thames. The River Humber – Lincoln – St Margaret's, whose church was still standing in 1748 when Hardy had his monument built. We will return later to study Shugborough Monument again.

St Margaret's burial grounds at The Green is situated at the south-east corner of Lincoln Cathedral. In January 2005 a commemorative tree was planted there in honour of Anne Frank for her enduring courage displayed in the face of such adversity, gaining international fame posthumously following the publication of her diary that documented her experiences hiding during the German occupation of the Netherlands in the Second World War, a sentiment that pretty much sums up the struggle endured by the Jewish race during xenophobic persecution and genocide. Anne Frank, of course, was Jewish. Why should a tribute to such a stalwart Jewish girl have been chosen to be placed here to almost provide a Hebrew 'marker'? Has the Collective Unconscious placed her here? Another irony is that her name is Frank, the name of the tribe that founded France, the original home of our entire mystery.

The church of St Margaret of Antioch once stood here on the green, within the Close. In the 12th Century it stood outside of the Roman city wall and was often known as St Margaret of Pottergate. Drawings that are still in existence show that the church had a squat tower with double belfry openings without a midwall shaft. There is evidence to date this Norman structure as standing in the 11th Century. Another interesting feature is that at the east end of the church there was an early English window and a *vesica piscis*, the symbol cryptically hidden on the Lord Tennyson statue but a short distance away. At the time that the church stood – it was demolished starting in 1778 and culminating in 1781 – there was a strong Jewish settlement in the area that had been established before official records confirmed this in 1154. Both church and grounds were dedicated to St Margaret of Antioch, one of the most popular saints in the 9th Century with two hundred or so early churches dedicated to her in England. She was known in the Christian East as Marina, a virgin saint, portrayed also as a shepherdess. What is the significance of Margaret in our search? It is paramount! Margaret is usually represented carrying a small cross, and part of her story involves her encounter with the Devil in the form of a dragon. Margaret was swallowed by the dragon, but eventually escaped safely by employing her cross to stick it in the dragon's innards forcing it to disgorge her, this accounting for her association with pregnancy. Not only is the dragon symbolic of the constellation Draco, visible from our Lincoln Cathedral Code Northern Star Clock, but in modern times it is seen as a guardian of a cavern filled with vast treasure hoards. Margaret was martyred by beheading.

And now for a strange thing. In 1969, the very same year that Mary Magdalene was canonised, elevated to Sainthood and no longer considered to have been a fallen woman, the worship of the cult of St Margaret was suppressed by the Vatican, declaring that she in fact never existed. How strange. Mary is elevated and Margaret relegated, nevertheless drawing attention to them both that same year.

We have seen how the revealing of the puzzle of the wood carving 'The Falling Knight' at the Choir Stall Mercy Seat leads us from a fallen knight to a once supposed fallen woman, and to a plot in the burial grounds that stands in a place, once under the St Margaret church until its destruction over a period of three years in the 1700s. Although the church that stood there and protected a crypt buried deep below it may no longer stand as shepherdess and protectorate, a crucial synchronicity does. It has been there since 1850, a family tomb innocently enacting the role of Rene d'Anjou's 'La Fountaine de Fortune', the slab at the next plot being so ridiculously close as to be indistinguishable from it, (more a part of it) despite it belonging to another family. This peculiar arrangement echoes the effect of the water-filled trough at the foot of d'Anjou's monument, and the man standing alongside it looks into his hand exactly as does Tennyson at his statue. The statue of Queen Eleanor at the SE corner of the cathedral looks directly over at this marker, and we have been sent, too, by the also beheaded unnamed female, whose nearby and unsuspected tomb was only fully investigated in 2005. There is more! Not only do we have the final clue to the location from within Lincoln Cathedral, but I can now announce that it has always been there, awaiting the person who would find it, at the altar of Berenger Sauniere's church at

'By the Cross and this Horse of God' - 7 x 4 = 28.

Rennes-le-Chateau. A bas-relief of Mary Magdalene sitting in a cave and painted by Sauniere himself, is the one clue nobody has ever been able to solve. To do so, they would have to realise what the Lincoln Cathedral Code alone has done...revealed that we have been wrong all along to seek Mary in France...the clues have been designed to lead us to Lincoln Cathedral, England.

In Sauniere's bas-relief, Mary rests in her hidden underground sanctuary staring up at a cross. This cross is exactly the same as portrayed in history as being carried by St Margaret. There is a skull at her feet. The skull and cross indicate that we are at a place involving death and burial, as indicated in the Rennes Parchment stating '...is this treasure and it is death'... the burial grounds of Margaret. How do we know we are in Lincoln? Outside of the cavern in the distance to the right, we see three indicators. They are, in turn, from right to left, the steep high hill upon which the cathedral was built – the way up is actually called 'Steep Hill' – the west gate of Exchequergate that one passes through to the west front of the cathedral, and finally, Lincoln Castle itself. Returning to the kneeling Mary, and her accompanying treasure of a historical document or book containing evidence of the Rose Line, if we take a close look at what I will describe as a pouch above her clasped hands, we will see there is a right angle removed, or south-east corner, to indicate that we are close to the south-east corner of the cathedral. Her clasped hands deliberately show us a representation of ascending steps, the stone stairway that can be found at Greestone Stairs leading to Greestone Place and into St Margaret's burial grounds, the site of the tomb.

It could not be more descriptive. But how to know which tomb out of the recorded fifty-six that are recorded there? Marvel upon marvel...for if we draw a perfectly straight line through the eye level of Mary and through the centre of her cross, it will continue until it strikes one of the tomb-shaped inner designs that frame the scene. Counting these 'tombs' from where they start at the left, we will find that the line we have drawn through the eyes and cross arrive at tomb number 28! This line, if fully drawn to extend further to the left of the painting also strikes at the top of the hill and at the foot of Exchequergate, as if telling us when we pass through the gate we arrive at the cathedral. If we stand at this Lincoln Cathedral Code marker tomb, and orientate ourselves with the scene in the painting, we will clearly see Lincoln Castle in the distance, exactly where it should be. It is an amazing experience if one is fortunate to be able to stand there and do this. Combined with the revelation of 'The Falling Knight' and the 7 x 4 = 28 clue, we can now feel safe that the evidence for arrival at the point of tomb number 28 is conclusive, with the major clue coming from both France and England equally. Why is Mary buried below the tomb with the number 28? I can also tell you that, for she would always be associated with the number 28; it is the number of the 28-day continuing cycle in the uterus that leads to pregnancy....

According to the novel *The Da Vinci Code*, the final resting place of Mary Magdalene and her Grail secrets lay under a three foot, tiny structured pyramid. According to our Lincoln Cathedral Code, the hidden, or lost Mary, can be located in a crypt at a depth below the existing number 28 plot at the St Margaret burial grounds, our own little version of Arcadia, with the pregnant Queen Eleanor looking over at the tomb revealed to be the pregnant shepherdess who also looks down at a tomb in the famous, Poussin clued 'The Shepherds of Arcadia'. The synchronicities of our Collective Unconscious provides our 1850 marker with its own pyramidical top, and, yes, it is three feet in height! Some forty or so yards away it aligns, by pure 'chance', with a brass door knocker of a lion - Leo the Lion that gave birth to the very name Leo as in our artist friend Leonardo, the lion a symbol of the Israelite tribe of Judah, from which King David originated. A similar distance away, continuing the alignment, is the memorial tree to Anne Frank. The name on the current memorial stone placed under which our Quest has led us, is the family name of Rayner, Thomas and Martha, and was placed in 1850. We may finish our quest as we began, for in hindsight the Tennyson statue at Priory Gate, but a few hundred yards away, always provided us with a precise clue, not only by having the French word for king, 'Roi', and 'Sion' interlock on his plaque to hint at the Rennes-le-Chateau parchment 2, 'For Dagobert II and for Sion is this treasure and it is death', his carefully selected poem 'Flower in the crannied wall' (the flower obviously being the rose known to be Mary) always containing a key word assisting us where to

The Tomb of Shepherdess Queen Eleanor whereupon the 'blue apples' conclude

look nearby. 'Cranny' meaning a secret place, is from the Middle English 'crany'. As it is known in Masonic cryptogram rather than anagram that letters may be used twice, selecting strategic letters from both 'crany' and 'crannied' we can spell the phonetic 'raynr' and 'rainr'! Tennyson's dog accompanying him on the plinth, Karenina, also contains the word 'reina'! Even in the name Marina as St Margaret was favoured in the Christian East, we locate 'Raina'.

Let us look at the name Rayner, variously cited as originating from the French patronymic name from the Anglo-Saxon, Old German, and perhaps of more interest to us, Jewish (Ashkenazic) as an ornamental name from an inflected form of German 'rein' or Central Yiddish 'rein/rayn' meaning 'pure'. And then one is also reminded of the House and Sovereign State of Lorraine, supporters and protectors of the Knights Templar. Rene d'Anjou became Duke of Lorraine, not to ignore Charles de Lorraine, Grand Master of the Priory of Sion 1746-1780, and Maximilian de Lorraine, Grand Master of Sion 1780-1801. A linguist may well argue that it is difficult to pronounce 'Rayner' without it sounding like a blunted 'Rayn'.

The tomb that is so close alongside the Rayner marker as to be part of it is of the family name Jackson. This is synchronicity when we recall the name of Dean Brandon Jackson who caused such an upheaval with his declaration of the cathedral being a battleground of good and evil. The lady who had caused him his own problems was named Verity Freestone, and what might we say we are hoping to achieve by revealing the hidden Magdalene tomb? Could we say we are 'freeing the stone'? We can even add another confirmation of the location from one more source placed in France. Having arrived at tomb 28 at St Margaret's, from our Parchments and Sauniere's bas relief, it was simple working backwards, so to speak, to then decode what is known as the 'De Negre Headstone'. It's easier when you know how, and far easier working out clues when you already have the answer, otherwise I would imagine these enigmatic slabs we are going to look at now would remain unsolved as they have for over a century. Marie de Negre d'Ables was married as a nineteen-year-old orphan to Francois d'Hautoul Rennes in 1732. When Francois died in 1753, Marie lived a further twenty-eight years (!) in the Hautpoul manor, passing away on the famous 17th January date, to be buried in the Rennes-le-Chateau actual cemetery where noble ladies were reserved a special plot, unable to be placed in the church crypt as this was reserved for men only. It is thought that Marie, on her deathbed, confided the Rennes secret known to the Hautpoul family to the priest Antoine Bigou who buried her, and in turn allegedly left specific clues pertaining to what this secret was, and the stones we are about to look at were most likely his handiwork, putting clues in both the horizontal and vertical tombstone.

The story goes that Sauniere, finding Marie's tomb, deciphered it and set about defacing it with hammer and chisel. It was still visible in 1905, but had been discovered by a group of local historians and scientists who compiled a report and included the drawings of the slabs that Sauniere thought he had destroyed for good. Let us look at the two slabs, and the 'answers'. The Headstone is decoded by means of a skip sequence using the total 119 letters. By employing a technique of using two examples of three couplets, (11,12,13...20,24,25), two of two couplets (49,53...54,66) and seven of one letter, (82,86,90,97,98,99,115) or, 4 examples of a gap of 4 spaces...2 examples of a gap of 7...2 examples of a gap of 16...one example of a gap of 12...one example of a gap of 24 with a key number of 4, divisible into 12, 16 and 24, we spell out the code; 'MARGARET AT LINCOLN'. The gravestone is translated as follows; '*Reddis Regis*'...In Latin '*Reddis*' means 'You restore'..and '*Regis*' means 'Royal'. '*Cellis*' means 'Basement/cave' and '*Arcus*' means 'Box/enclosure'. '*Prae-Cum*' translates as 'The time before'. The vertical arrow down the centre of the slab simply denotes measurement, or in this case, depth. The symbol below *Prae-cum* is not a spider, as many have thought, but an eight-legged octopus, 'octopus' from the Greek 'okto' meaning eight and 'pous' meaning 'foot'. Here we are being informed of a depth of eight foot! Also, an octopus is known as a marine mollusk, and St Margaret is known as Marina - the '*Et in Arcadia Ego*' inscription down both sides of the stone is partly in Latin and partly in Greek to remind us, and signify that 'Margaret' in Greece was known as Marina. With its mention of a royal restoration, a basement or cave and a box or enclosure, The Marie de Negre Headstone and Gravestone finally tells us that eight foot down in a cave basement at St Margaret's in Lincoln, there is a restored royal.

Marker tomb 28 - conclusion of the Code.

It appears our chess game has finally come to an end. Have we truly found the most important piece on the board, the Queen, or, in French, REINE, buried deeper under an existing tomb? There is no doubt the Rayner family have their tomb at plot number 28, but is it placed over an already standing crypt that once belonged to the St Margaret Church, guaranteeing that the secret location will never be disturbed? The assurances of the quantum physicists of today tell us that everything in creation is ultimately connected like points on a spider's web, and it therefore comes as no surprise to me that we have fared so well with our Lincoln Cathedral Code. Does the Grail hide deep below our designated site? In October 2005, whilst carrying out routine conservation work, the ancient tomb of Edward the Confessor was discovered by chance under Westminster Abbey (which Lincoln Cathedral doubles for here in *The Da Vinci Code* movie). A crypt and a chamber with a stone vaulted roof was revealed by archaeologists using the latest Ground Penetrating Radar technology, forgotten subterranean chambers of a number of royal tombs dating back to the 13th and 14th Century also being discovered beneath the Abbey. Records show that a Christian church had been on the

The Magdalene stares over at tomb 28.

site since at least 960AD. Perhaps in the same way that St Margaret's Church had once occupied our forgotten crypt? My thoughts were then that perhaps the miracle of science would take a look for us, too, and so I would have to approach Lincoln Cathedral for permission.

My work had naturally captured the imagination of the local and national media, and had a mixed reception across the Internet. For those who had taken the time to review it rather than dismiss it out of hand without as much as studying what I had presented, they were quite interested in the theory that the Rennes treasure may not be in France after all. The response of most of the French die-hards was predictable, but generally the two epithets that kept heading my way were 'fascinating' and 'intriguing', so I must have been doing something right. In Lincoln itself, the implication seemed to fall in and nestle between both the traditional religionists who obviously wouldn't have any of it, and most of the remainder of the city who thought that if it had anything to do with the bible then it must be rubbish!

On July 14th 2006 there I sat on the front page of the *Lincolnshire Echo* alongside my marker tomb, accommodating the front and second page of the edition, the headline on page one reading 'X Marks the Spot'. It quoted the cathedral, stating: 'Librarians at

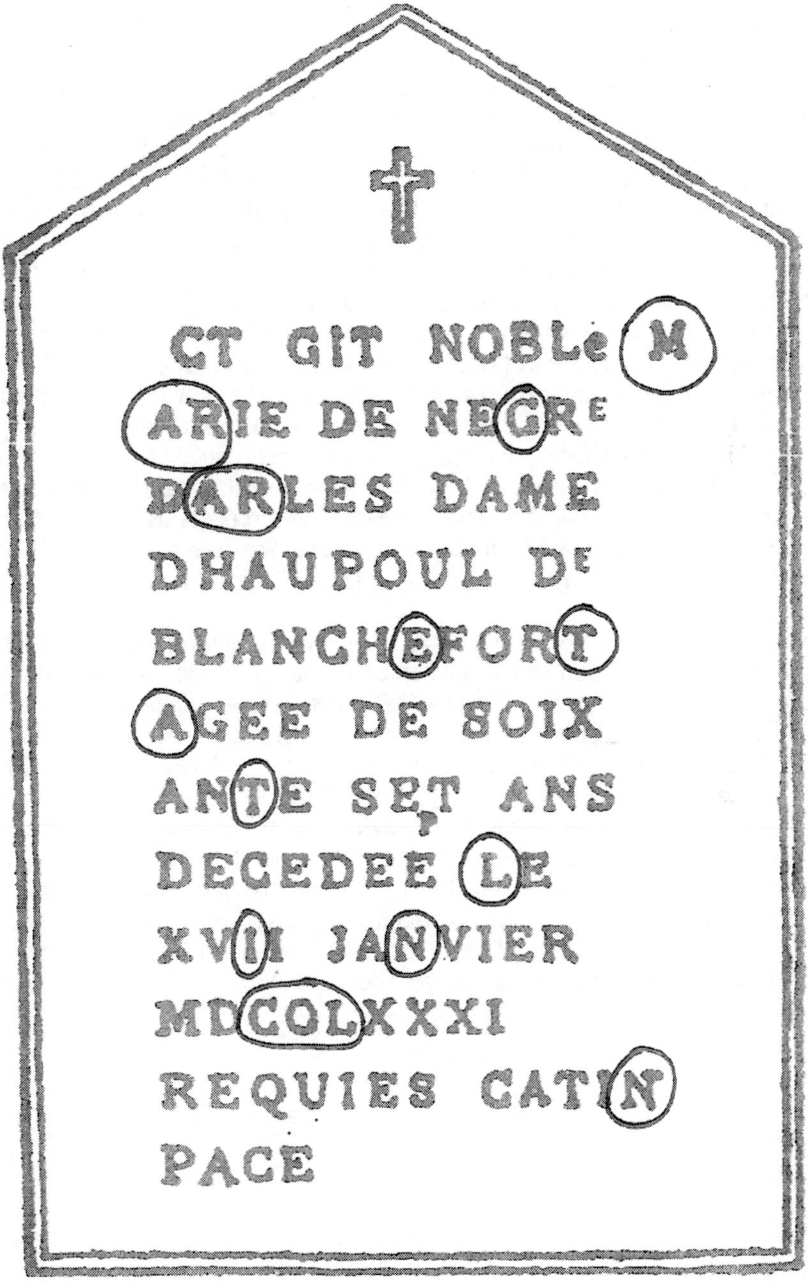

CT GIT NOBLe M
ARIE DE NEGRe
DARLES DAME
DHAUPOUL De
BLANCHEFORT
AGEE DE SOIX
ANTE SET ANS
DECEDEE LE
XVII JANVIER
MDCOLXXXI
REQUIES CATIN
PACE

The Collective Unconscious reveals 'Margaret at Lincoln'.

Lincoln Cathedral say there is no historical evidence a crypt still exists under the site. But cathedral officials say in theory there should be no problem with the research. Roy Bentham, Cathedral Chief executive and Chapter Clerk said; 'If this is just a radar survey that will have no structural impact then I can't see a problem. But if something comes up and we're talking about excavation then things get more complicated.' This looked quite sanguine, as there would certainly not be any structural damage and I had already enlisted the very Company responsible for the finds under Westminster Abbey, the very efficient Utsi Electronics of Ely, Cambridgeshire. I next put the request in writing and submitted it to Roy Bentham, his immediate reply of July 20th reading: 'I have consulted those involved and, whilst they are confident that it can be done, they feel it needs to go through our normal permissions procedure. So I'll put it to Masters' Committee on 19th September and to Chapter on 3rd October. I'll then contact you.' And when naughty Roy didn't, I knew something had gone off. After waiting for what I thought was more than a respectful time facing a wall of silence, I next approached the cathedral in February 2007. First of all, his secretary informed me she couldn't find the original request and reply, and after I found it for them and sent it I received a two line reply from Mr Bentham informing me that the request had been denied. So angry was I with confirmation of the shock response that I can't reproduce it here for you now, I think I crumpled it up and threw it! I did the same with my next equally terse reply when, after asking him why, he replied that 'The proposal is not worthy of the commitment of our scarce staff.' The latter bit was news to me – we didn't need any members of the cathedral in attendance, and certainly hadn't asked for any.

Wondering what I could do next, if anything, I put my tale of woe into a correspondence sent to the Archbishop of Canterbury at Lambeth Palace, Dr Rowan Williams. Surely if he was the Head of the Church in England he might have a sympathetic ear. The very helpful and sympathetic response came from the ear of his secretary who educated me to the fact that Dr Williams can't intervene or overturn any decision reached by its own cathedral officialdom. So much for being Head of the Church, Rowan! Even the very wonderful Erica Utsi, Director of her Company couldn't sway them, approaching them on my behalf and making it quite clear we didn't need a representative from the cathedral staff present. Roy Bentham's reply held only the slightest glimmer of hope – I should put a request to the cathedral archaeologist, Ron Dixon, asking if he would make a report on Margaret's for me (and for a fee of course). I did just that, but Ron never replied, by which time I was beginning to get the message.

CHAPTER THIRTEEN
THE GRAIL AND THE STONE SCULPTOR

For those who seek an alternative to the age old assurances of a Grail-related Templar treasure somewhere in the region of Rennes-le-Chateau, you are always most welcome to return with me, and to my very alternative means of deduction, to Lincoln Cathedral, England and to the final conclusion to the mind-boggling Rennes-le-Chateau mystery and hidden Templar store. There is a definite dichotomy regarding this ongoing secret doctrine concerning alleged tombs and treasure contents, many dismissing the entire affair out of hand as nothing more than a surrealist prank, the handiwork of the now deceased trio of Messrs. Plantard, De Sede, and De Cherisey. There is a simple, yet effective, compromise between those who choose the hoaxer's theme and those who accept it at face value, and it is the product of that psychological realm, the mechanism of the Collective Unconscious, the dwelling place of surrealistic expression – and every possible hidden imagery you can think of, Surrealism alone – and our French Three were all of its persuasion – allows you to take your mind where it doesn't usually go, a realm where fact and fiction will blur into one. Little surprise that Dan Brown's *The Da Vinci Code* was so popular! French poet and novelist Jean Cocteau, allegedly the last Grand Master of the Priory of Sion, was also a surrealist.

When the 'Collective Unconscious' seeps through a creative individual – irrespective of their awareness of this mechanism – it has the entire content of humankind from which to access in order to ensure that (in our case, this historical 'treasure hunt') unconnected clues are deposited where required via the medium of innocently, unsuspecting individuals. Even those who may initially set out to hoax or consider themselves hoaxers. Author Robert Anton Wilson was always amazed when things he confessed as making up in his excellent 'Cosmic Trigger' series from the middle seventies onward would often become real. You can just imagine Plantard, De Sede and De Cherisey having a right old laugh between themselves, as they constructed their Rennes Parchments, making them up out of thin air and thinking how their clever hoax would fool one and all, without realising that what they were choosing was, in fact, transmitting from the Collective Unconscious via their brains, and what they thought was insignificant and entirely made up, was - in fact - invaluable, using the trio as an unwitting medium!

It makes me wonder, do we totally own our own brain? If the Parchments are a hoax direct from, and involving, these jokers – and I think there is no doubt they are far more recent than originally thought, certainly not ancient even if copies – it really doesn't matter! They have still provided the information that will check out. Surreal painters like Cocteau, and sculptors, often produce works that bypass the rational mind's preference to censor, surrealism and its followers bring vision and symbols of the Unconscious Mind including the Collective Unconscious to light. The joke may end up on the jokers as 'Many a true word is spoken in jest'. Cocteau is a classic example. Maybe he was privy to secretive information and he painted it in his work deliberately. Maybe he painted it innocently and unconsciously. Either way, it remains there for closer scrutiny and decipherment. And this could have been going on for centuries throughout history. The archetype of the ever-elusive Grail moves about as a glob of mercury should you try placing your finger upon it, and why not...don't people who are being pursued continually keep on the move?

The suspicion of historians is that the Grail has relocated six times since arriving in Europe from Jerusalem, now residing somewhere in England, with the reassuring - if puzzling – statement of affirmation that you do not find the Grail, it finds you! Tell it to Henry Lincoln who went to France to find what was already being hinted at in his chosen surname! How else could this be if it wasn't with the assistance of our own boundless Unconscious Mind? How did ancient buildings innocently manage to place their churches on what we have now discovered as ley-lines? How did Tibetan sages over two thousand years ago manage to compile mantras that modern day neurology now knows affect enzymes in the brain to alter consciousness? In 2000, I had a routine tomographicall CAT brain scan at the Boston Pilgrim Hospital in Lincolnshire, having had a problem involving a bleaching effect with a colour in my left eye. Whilst laying still and passing through the inner rumblings of the machine intimately on either side of your head that break the otherwise total silence, I thought I recognised the sound. It came to me there and then, it resembled an intoned mantra to the Tibetan Goddess Tara! How could that be! I even joined in mentally with it! We have all experienced during sleep how there is no time in dreams, where past, present and future somehow merge, rather like clues left by centuries old secret societies and Masons, only now being recognised today in paintings and Gothic architecture. Isn't it a strange experience when you can fall asleep for moments, a 'cat nap', and how when you wake you remember dreaming, and yet in the dream your adventure with numerous sequences and scenes appeared to last hours! This is how they said was the passing of time in Faeryland!

I am not the only person to have been drawn to the city of Lincoln, the might of Tinsel Town and Hollywood arriving here in 2005 to film their own version of codes leading to a Grail, and the year earlier a group of Tibetan monks came on an unconscious pilgrimage from Drepung Monastery in Tibet to the Bishop's Palace, only a few hundred yards away from my marker tomb that pinpoints the Cathedral

Code, to construct a mind-blowing sand diagram mandala. This, upon completion, they marched off to the Waterside River to empty it out to emphasise how everything is impermanent. From mystical Tibet to mundane Lincoln, that's some way to come, unaware of how spiritual their journey actually was...a Tibetan pebble's throw away from most sought after holy relics in Europe and the Middle East. Robin Griffith-Jones, Master of the Temple Church, London was drawn to the cathedral in 2006 to give a lecture on modern day Grail associations. One of my favourite synchronicities is, we all know, that the name of the man who started all the modern day Grail search is Lincoln, and his co-authors who wrote *Holy Blood, Holy Grail*, Michael Baigent and Richard Leigh sued Dan Brown in the London courts for plagiarism of their book. Nothing synchronistic about that, until we learn that the name of their QC who represented them was Raynor James...the same sounding name as the Rayner family whose name is on the Lincoln Cathedral marker too. Perhaps 'Lincoln' is a strange connotation in its own right?

The most famous worldwide example of synchronicity may well be that between the assassinations of President Lincoln and Kennedy, at which point I suggest we stop off for a few moments to look at the major synchronisations. Lincoln was elected to Congress in 1846, Kennedy in 1946. Lincoln was elected President in 1860, Kennedy in 1960. Lincoln's wife lost a child while living in the White House, as did Kennedy's wife. Lincoln was directly concerned with Civil Rights, as was Kennedy. Lincoln had a secretary named Kennedy who told him not to go to the theatre, where he was shot. Kennedy had a secretary named Lincoln who told him not to go to Dallas, where he was shot. Lincoln was shot in the back of the head in the presence of his wife, as was Kennedy. Lincoln was shot in the Ford Theatre. Kennedy was shot in a Lincoln car, made by Ford. Both were shot on a Friday. Lincoln's assassin, John Wilkes Booth, was known by three names comprising fifteen letters, as was Kennedy's assassin Lee Harvey Oswald. Booth shot Lincoln in a theatre and fled to a warehouse. Oswald shot Kennedy from a warehouse and fled to a theatre. Both Booth and Oswald were killed before coming to trial, there being theories that both were part of a bigger conspiracy. Lincoln's successor was Andrew Johnson born in 1808. Kennedy's successor was Lyndon Johnson born in 1908. After that one, I think we need a rest from Presidents!

The first alleged alien abduction case was of Betty and Barney Hill whilst driving through Lincoln, New Hampshire...the biggest lottery win ever in USA history - $365 million in 2006 – was at Lincoln, Nebraska. Even the start of the recent movie *National Treasure 2* starts with President Lincoln and its fanatical treasure hunter is called Wilkinson, the apparent real name of 'Bloodline' treasure hunter Ben Hammott. Is it any wonder that the abbreviation for the County of Lincolnshire is 'Lincs'!

Carl Gustav Jung announced in 1947 that when we begin to see strange aerial phenomenon this would mark the herald of a consciousness change, the end of an era in history and the beginning of a new one, his symbols for this being the rounded 'UFO' and the mandala. Other rounded symbology is the Grail, and more recently, crop circles – another phenomenon that has enlisted the occasional aid of hoaxers. Even though some of these hoaxers have owned up to making hundreds of corn circles ranging from the basic to the intricate, I have no doubt that – as with Plantard, De Sede and De Cherisey – these hoaxers are totally unaware that they have been 'used' and in fact have contributed to facets of the particular mystery. What they intended to pass off as hoax to the many is just as likely to have been crucial to a lesser audience. The knack is in having the intuition to notice these things with the understanding that all things are connected, no matter how apparently tenuous or flimsy. The Collective Unconscious is now pouring through on a global scale, affecting and influencing us all, the information we collect, identify and piece together drawing closer to a conscious awakening in us all. 'Alien abductions' during the sleep state are occurring all over the world in all countries to all manner of people, some who have no interest whatsoever in UFOs or aliens from space. Either hundreds of thousands, and probably millions, of people are going mad in a pandemic mental health crisis, or there is some underlying psychological and/or neurological message wrapped up in this type of scenario presenting as saviours or interlopers from light years away.

Back at the Rennes-le-Chateau church, there is a particular stained glass window that shows Jesus with Martha and Mary. What is even more significant is that between the assembly we see a dead ringer for our Cathedral Code marker tomb as it is today – it even has a small cross in the middle to indicate that the tomb stands where there once was a church – the church of St Margaret that was demolished in 1781, the same year as Marie De Negre died, and - with her - the secret of Rennes-le-Chateau. Whether Marie's death and the church being finally demolished were a straightforward synchronicity, or whether the demise of the church was taken as an advantage in the hope that both custodian of the secret, and its secret location, were both lost forever in a double whammy cannot be known. Either way, the effect was the same. Within Lincoln Cathedral there is the painting we are told is of the Annunciation. We see a pregnant red-haired female who is meant to be the Virgin staring over at what is the Rayner tomb as it stands today, with scrolls upon its top. (These scrolls may well lay below). How did the painter innocently paint such breathtakingly accurate clues, unless it was the Collective Unconscious at work yet again? In Dan Brown's *Da Vinci Code* fiction, the final resting place of Mary Magdalene and her secrets lay under a three foot structured pyramid. The Rayner tomb, all three foot of it, has a pyramidical top! Has the Collective Unconscious connected Brown's fiction with a city of Lincoln reality?

Let us look at the Rayner family crest. The name 'Rayner' was undoubtedly introduced into England from France circa 11th Century. The crest features an ermine fur with 23 visible indents and two etoiles on an azure background. The etoiles, or stars, are each what is known as a Marian star, six-pointed, which can also be identified with the Jewish emblem of the Star of David, the number 23 is significant in our Lincoln Cathedral Code as it is connected with the 23rd day of July when the dog-star Sirius is in conjunction with our own Sun. Even the word 'ermine' can be investigated..

'ermine', a fur once reserved for royalty, comes from the French 'hermine'. 'Her mine?' To mine is to bring about an excavation dug under a position to give secret ingress. Mary Magdalene's mine? Not far away from the cathedral, only a matter of minute's walk at Greetwell Gate, stands a public house dating back to 1781, again the same year as the death of De Negre and the end of all evidence that a church ever stood at the burial grounds of St Margaret. Facing the east of the cathedral it is called *Morning Star*. An inescapable reference to the bright and morning star of Sirius. Should we wonder why the chapel in the cathedral dedicated to Mary Magdalene is called 'the Morning Chapel'? However, just a short distance along from this Sirius-titled pub on a corner, there is a building that is clearly of Masonic origin with the compass masquerading as a letter 'A' in its foundation stone. It has two stars – or etoiles - as on the Rayner crest. Is it hinting at the tomb? It is a fact that you cannot linguistically pronounce 'Rayner' without it sounding like a blunted 'Rayn', or REINE, which in French means 'Queen'...the missing piece in this chess – or 'chase' – game. In 1979, Henry Lincoln named one of his BBC documentaries on Rennes, 'The Shadow of the Templars'. Revealingly, in Jungian territory, a shadow is an archetype that is an inferior of the 'Self' which we hide from others. What an appropriately titled work!

Another talented individual who was drawn to Lincoln Cathedral with appropriate and curiously innocent titles to his work, was Michael Dan Archer, an international stone sculptor who, in 2002, contributed numerous examples of his sculptures in and around the gothic building. One, opposite a wood carving of the Stations of the Cross which contains one of my dog clues, at the Chancery, he titled 'The Portal'. Today, at the SE corner of the cathedral where so many clues amass and congregate, and you can still see his gateway entitled 'Between two worlds'. Peeping through it you can see straight across to the Rayner marker tomb! I contacted Michael in 2008 and he told me how he did receive his inspiration for his work and titles through dreams, and how he had once been interested in the Knights Templar. However, no longer with us is the sarchophagus-shaped slab that was placed outside the Great East Window, starting point for the Cathedral Code with the Last Supper. Facing at an angle to point over at the St Margaret's burial grounds containing the Rayner tomb, its sculptor chose it a most fascinating title. Michael named it 'The Secret'.....

MARY·HATH·CHOSEN·THAT·GOOD·PART·WHICH
SHALL·NOT·BE·TAKEN·AWAY·FROM·HER ✥

Erected to the Glory of God in loving memory of
Mary Forrest of Ardow. Died 23rd October, 1904,
by her affectionate sister, Isabella D. Forrest.

CHAPTER FOURTEEN
SYNGENESIS

High up on a stained glass window at the church of St Mary Magdalene, Beziers, France, the village that in 1209 had its 20,000 population slaughtered by the Catholic Church on Mary's Feast Day of 22nd July for their belief that Jesus and Mary were married, there is a rather unexpected figure at the feet of the Virgin, so small as to be almost imperceptible. It is a dog! To its left we see the crest of Pope Leo XII, which can also be found above the church doorway at the Rennes-le-Chateau church with the added Latin motto *'Lumen in coelo'* meaning 'Light in the sky'. Is this light in the sky the brightest of them all, the dog star Sirius? The motto contains the encrypted place name of 'Lincoln', and here at the Great East Window of the Gothic Cathedral, at the scene of The Last Supper, what do we see upon Christ's plate? A dog! Outside in the cathedral precincts there is a statue of Grail Poet Laureate Lord Tennyson with a black dog looking up, in the church of Rennes-le-Chateau, St Roch stands with a black dog looking up, too. Not only is St Roch also a patron saint of dogs, but his Feast Day is one day after, as if a closing declaration of, the ending of the Egyptian 'dog days' on August 15th. The demon guardian statue in the Rennes church has his right leg over his left. Alongside him, St Roch is bearing his right leg. The demon guardian imp at Lincoln Cathedral has his right leg over his left, and the dog at Beziers has his crossed over his left! What are these reoccurring images indicating to us? Furthermore, we learn that the Greek word for 'dog' is 'Cyon', sounding the same as 'Sion', recalling that the word 'imp', our Lincoln demon, derives from Old English 'impa' meaning 'shoot', 'offspring', 'graft', and in Masonic architecture a graft is 'the place of junction and stock and scion'.. 'scion' a word from Old French 'sion' meaning a young member of a family, descendant, offshoot. In Egyptian, Sothis (Sirius) means 'pregnant' or 'to be pregnant'. Can we tie in a pregnant Mary Magdalene here with our dog symbology, accompanying attendant guardian demons, and Priory of Sion?

The dog was always the guardian of knowledge at the entrance to the Underworld - and it is here we must look for a possible explanation for all our re-occuring symbologies, icons and archetypes – and what is referred to in psychology as the

Collective Unconscious, the universal memories and experience of humankind, represented in the unconscious images of all people..a reservoir of the experiences of our species that directs the Self through archetypes present in mythologies, dreams and intuition...a treasure hunter's most unlikely tools! As a researcher attempting to locate a lost 'treasure', I have always employed the wondrous and magical tools of synchronicity, coincidence and this Collective Unconscious, for this is where our 'lost' memories reside deep in this watery realm, with occasional bubbles rising to the surface of our daily waking consciousness or seeping through. It is also a mechanism whereby hoaxers are only hoaxing themselves when their handiwork becomes meaningful to an unexpected recipient elsewhere. What a convoluted means of communication! By employing this strange medium, in 2005 I was able to translate the famous Rennes-le-Chateau Parchments – which some still argue are fake – and their presenting conclusion, an 'X' marks the spot, in convincing fashion at the St Margaret's burial grounds opposite the SE corner of Lincoln Cathedral, itself replete with the archetype of the dog, guardian of knowledge.

One contender for discovering the most sought after treasure and/or tombs of the Rennes mystery arrived in the form of one French researcher by the name of André Douzet, who presented one and all with a model maquette, or model map, entitled 'Jerusalem' - which was allegedly commissioned by the priest Sauniere two years before his death in 1917. According to Douzet, the maquette reveals two tombs close to Rennes-le-Chateau, an area nearby the village of Perillos, (although critics are quick to point out that when compared with IGN maps it bears no physical resemblance to the topography of the area, some supporters of his claim still argue it does). One of Jesus, the other of Joseph of Arimathea. Other researchers who have good reason to suspect the veracity of Douzet's work have since declared finding that initially there were two twinned model maquettes that were excavation models employed as a teaching aid in the classroom, and owned by Professor Enrico Galbiati. Apparently, these model maps were used before and after to explain the excavation sites carried out in Jerusalem at the Holy Sepulchure, and that Douzet's copy is the pre-excavation copy. So we are left with those who dismiss his claim entirely out of hand, and some who still attempt to point out similarities in the area of Perillos with a map of Jerusalem. I can go one further...and better! Three miles outside of Lincoln there is a small village that is actually called 'Jerusalem', which dates back to at least 1436! There is no other such identical place name in the British Isles, and the few people who live there are at a loss to explain exactly why they have been left with the name. Possibly, it has to do with the Knights Templar's influences at nearby Eagle, itself a curious village south west of Lincoln where the Templars once had a house in 1312. Eagle is a small, quiet village and is arranged in an 'X' shape!

Anyway, what I can tell you is that Douzet's controversial maquette matches with equal ease the crucial terrain that concludes the Lincoln Cathedral Code, the cathedral itself, the castle and the St Margaret's burial grounds where, in relationship to the maquette, a rounded greenish stone purporting to be one of Douzet's tombs is exactly where the Lincoln Cathedral Code concludes! Maybe we should also be reminding ourselves here of our German Grail tale involving Lucifer's emerald Grail! Although one would like to think this is unbelievable, it isn't. It IS believable, one only has to compare the maquette and the map of Lincoln. This can only be made possible by an acceptance of the Collective Unconscious, and how a genuine model map that originated in a Jerusalem classroom, and was taken to lay claim to a replica landscape for the sake of announcing a stashed treasure, can then actually indicate a more credible resting place allied to the actual title of the model!

If we now nip off to the Museum of Antwerp, and to a specific painting that hangs there, we will also see another confirmation for the location of the Lincoln Cathedral Code being correct, as well as the unconscious offering of the Douzet's maquette. Entitled 'The Invocation' by Belgian artist Eugene Samain, we see a guardian sitting at the SE corner of the familiar stonework of Lincoln Cathedral facing what would be the St Margaret's burial grounds, where under plot number 28, as revealed by the Cathedral Code, still hides the lost treasure of the Knights Templar. Elizabeth Van Buren preferred to refer to this painting as 'Grail Temple'. It was also featured on the cover of the book *L'ile des Veilleurs* (The Island of Watchmen) by author Alfred Weysen, who had known and met Philip de Cherisey of the Rennes Parchments infamy. Who does the sentry in the painting guard? A naked female in an open coffin

The Maquette overlays the topography of Lincoln - the Collective Unconscious.

with her head covered by cloth. The symbol on his seat is the Seal of Solomon – she is Jewish. He holds a thistle, which in Latin translates as 'cardu'. It is phonetic for 'Card Two' in the tarot, which is the card representing the High Priestess, in turn, Mary Magdalene! He has four buttons down his tunic sequentially followed by seven small squares containing an 'x'. $4 \times 7 = 28$. A female in a coffin without a lid was actually discovered alongside Lincoln Cathedral originally in the '60s, and rediscovered in 2005 - the week Hollywood was filming for *The Da Vinci Code*, and is now referred to as 'The tomb of the unnamed woman'. She, too, was 'headless' (in the very real sense) with a missing lid. The veiled woman in the painting is pointing at a green pearl. The name 'Green' originates from 'one who dwells at a grassy mound' or 'the green hill'. 'Pearl' is a word from the Greek form of the name Margaret. (St Margaret ended her days decapitated). Thus, the entire painting can be interpreted as telling us 'Plot 28, St Margaret on the hill, opposite SE corner of Lincoln Cathedral, the Jewish High Priestess Mary Magdalene'. The silhouetted background shows a section of Lincoln Castle from a certain angle as if approached down a side street from Castle Square.

Let us take a closer look at Lincoln Castle itself. Like the cathedral, whose Patron Saint was St Hugh and whose emblem was the swan, it also contains swan symbology, albeit hidden. Given that you can see the Lincoln Cathedral Code marker tomb 28 in a direct line from the Castle's Observatory Tower - (could it have been constructed for that purpose in particular, to observe the tomb?) does this make the castle, where some of the finest prison carvings in Europe can be seen to this day carved by imprisoned Templar Knights, a candidate for the mythic Grail Castle, where lived the fabled Fisher King? Rumours have always persisted of a concealed tunnel leading from the castle to the cathedral. I suggest we look at the name that is kingfisher, the bird that is otherwise known as the halcyon, containing the Greek word for dog, 'cyon'. In Greek mythology, Alcyone, daughter of Aeolus, ruler of the winds, married Ceyx, son of Eosphorus, the morning star. This is interesting as legend tells us that it was the wind that blew the Lincoln Imp into the cathedral that contains so many references to the dog star, the bright and morning star Sirius. Alcyone and Ceyx were so happy that they sacrilegiously began calling themselves Zeus and Hera, so angering Zeus himself that he threw a thunderbolt at Ceyx's ship, drowning him. When Ceyx appeared to Alcyone as an apparition telling of his fate, she threw herself into the sea in grief, her story ending when she is transformed into a kingfisher. The word 'halcyon' originates from the Greek 'hals' meaning 'sea' and 'kyon' meaning 'conceiving'....again a reference to a birth. Mary and her child, the Grail?

From the old French version, the name of Grail Castle was Corbenic, and in Malory's version, Carbonek. Within the 1068 castle is the 13th Century Cobb Hall, where the Templars at Bruer where imprisoned after their trial at the cathedral Chapter House, and where they carved their strange handiwork in stone. The German composer Wagner used the swan to symbolise the Grail Knights, the bird considered sacred by them. A 'cob' is the name for the male swan. Young swans are known as cygnets from the Latin word for swan, 'Cygnus'. Phonetically, we revert to 'signet' as in a

Martha, Mary and Jesus with the Lincoln Marker Tomb in the middle – stained glass,
Rennes-le-Chateau church

seal – an obligation to secrecy. At the castle there is also Lucy Tower. In Latin the name Lucy means 'light' and one of its variant forms, Spanish and Latin, is Luz, an early name for the biblical town of Bethel, mentioned in the story of Jacob, and the ladder whereupon Jacob ascended to heaven. An inscription relating to this is also above the church doorway at Rennes-le-Chateau. Is Lincoln Castle, with the Grail evidently hidden but a short distance away opposite the SE corner of the cathedral, a candidate for Grail Castle?

We will learn shortly of an important confirmation from the stars that it is! Could it not be Corbenic, but again with the ploy of phonetics, a favourite of the Templars and Masons, 'Cob neck'...the visual trademark of the swan? Both swans and kingfishers can be seen at the nearby River Witham below both castle and cathedral. There is one Templar prison carving in particular that appears as if it is trying to tell us something. Found just as you enter Cobb Hall, on a wall to the right, the knight shows us an arrangement of four fingers on one hand and five on the other. Behind him is a cross. If we 'cross' 4 x 5, we arrive at 20, the exact number of days before and after the earth-Sirius conjunction...the number of the dog days and the number of the fifth down and fourth across roundel out of 64 at the Great East Window, where we see the dog on Christ's plate at the Last Supper. Is the Cross behind him an Eleanor Cross, associated with Eleanor of Castille at the SE corner of the cathedral who looks directly over at the Cathedral Code marker tomb in Margaret's burial grounds? (A remaining remnant of an Eleanor Cross now stands within the castle grounds).

And so to the maquette, which also curves in places itself. Although there is no scale, taken from the aerial view, it fits rather comfortably as well as any efforts in France, and even with the layout of modern day Lincoln! Apart from the obvious castle and cathedral, there are two other noteworthy features. One is where a stone oblong appears on the maquette – it is reflected by the Lincoln Water Tower constructed in 1905, ten years before the model map was constructed! The tower is adorned in multiple decoration, with the very symbol of France, the fleur-de-lys. The relationship of tower to castle is strikingly the same as the water tower at Rennes-le-Chateau to its castle! As precise is the break in the map nearest the bottom. It is exactly where stands Jew's House and Court, Lincoln being one of the most important Jewish communities in England, established well before officially noted in 1154. Here it is once believed stood a synagogue. Plenty of Jewish connection here then for a Jerusalem, as well as the aptly named village only three miles away! We must also remember that, like the Holy City, Lincoln under Roman occupation was also a walled city, some of its gates still standing today.

Also of great interest to me is the discovery that if we walk down the Nave of Lincoln Cathedral to the corner of the north east Transept, we will come across what is known as the 'Trondheim Pillar'. Not to be outdone, Trondheim Cathedral in Norway, perhaps known better as Nidaros Cathedral, has its own 'Lincoln Pillar'! The reason for this is not coincidental, for it was Lincoln masons who set about building Nidaros in 1070. So why are the cathedrals twinned in this way? Well, Trondheim forms part of the Golden Section sacred geometry of the 'Viking Serpent', founded by Harald Boehlke, son of a Norwegian diplomat, the measurements being numbers that show the church to be candidate for a New Temple of Solomon, a heavenly Jerusalem. When I informed Harald of a Lincoln Pillar twin, he had no idea! If we look closer at the place name 'Nidaros,' the lost mother tongue reveals it to be: 'Niddah-Rose'. In Hebrew, 'Niddah' describes a woman while she is menstruating. A holy blood and rose association? Who can we be talking of here other than Mary Magdalene? Before I leave the subject of Lincoln's own Jerusalem, I cannot rule out that it is the one here in the East Midlands that is given a cloaked reference in the famous 1804 short poem and hymn 'Jerusalem' by the mystic and visionary William Blake, inspired by the apocryphal story that a young Jesus and his uncle Joseph of Arimathea visited Glastonbury to create a temporary Heaven in England, in contrast to the 'dark satanic mills' of the Industrial Revolution of his day. 'And was Jerusalem builded here, Among these dark Satanic mills'. A contested view is that these dark satanic mills are a metaphor for the great churches of the established Church of England. With Lincoln Cathedral and its own devilish associations, only three miles away from our own Jerusalem, and surrounded by a number of other churches, it could be that Blake may have been privy to the secret about the alleged wife of Jesus actually being buried opposite the cathedral.

Adherents of the maquette being in France claim that there are two tombs where names are marked, but my suggestion is that if we go with the greenish-tinged stone to the far right we ought not to be surprised that this location is exactly at the conclusion of the Cathedral Code – as revealed by the Rennes-le-Chateau Parchments and the Samain painting – St Margaret's burial grounds at GREESTONE Place! Has the Collective Unconscious gathered us the clues and led us here? If so, how this mechanism works may well be the greatest mystery of all.

MARY·HATH·CHOSEN·THAT·GOOD·PART·WHICH
SHALL·NOT·BE·TAKEN·AWAY·FROM·HER ✠

Erected to the Glory of God in loving memory of
Mary Forrest of Ardow, Died 23rd October, 1904,
by her affectionate sister, Isabella D. Forrest.

CHAPTER FIFTEEN
TUNNELS AND U-TURNS

My first fascination with tunnel systems as we read earlier on, was inspired by the author Alec McLellan and his Wharfedale-Atlantis adventure, an interest in access point below and through the ground remaining high on my list. I, as we have seen, later found myself below ground level in areas as far flung as Malta, South Shields and Royston, not to mention the conducted tour of Cheddar Gorge and its 40,000-year-old cathedral sized cave of outstanding natural beauty. Given half a chance I'd have been down that sealed rock crop tomb at Rennes-le-Chateau, too! You bet! Synchronicity and the surfacing subtle hints of the Collective Unconscious are the tools that make Dan Green different from all others who set out searching for the hidden. Adventures at Rennes-le-Chateau , France, in 1986, and finding a rock crop tomb with two sealed entrances there, that I later discovered had been painted by Da Vinci at the top of one of his two versions of 'Virgin of the Rocks', brought me - twenty years later - to Lincoln Cathedral and a burial ground opposite its south-east corner where overwhelming evidence suggests that here, below the ground at a precise spot, resides a precious 'treasure' placed and hidden there by the Knights Templar, central to the Rennes global mystery. Initially, the Cathedral agreed to allow me permission for a GPR ground penetrating radar scan to see if indeed my deductions were right, but then rather mysteriously, they reneged!

My Lincoln Cathedral Code had came to a sudden and disappointing end - until Winter 2008 - and a very unexpected fortuitous find! My son had just ascended the summit of Greestone Stairs with a view of the cathedral in sight, when his newly acquired college friend announced, 'Do you know we're standing above an underground chapel?' This fellow knew nothing of my son's connection to me and my own work, but my son's ears pricked up to ask him what he meant. 'Oh', he replied, 'My mother used to work in a house over there and there's a tunnel that leads to the Chapel'. The house 'over there' I found was in the Medieval Bishop's Palace, adjacent to, and only hundreds of yards away from, my nominated Templars cache underground site, the Chapel referred to being the church of St Margaret, demolished in 1781.

This was the very spot I had been denied my GPR scan! I had always suspected there may exist a tunnel from the cathedral to this nearby church. Unfortunately, I couldn't elicit any further information from the mother now living in Cyprus, so I thought I'd ask the palace themselves, expecting that they would probably brush off talk of a tunnel as hearsay. Surprisingly enough, I received a very warm reply from the Chief Executive's Secretary stating (quote): 'We too have all heard about the tunnel...' Could this be the way in to finding the Templars cache?

Legends and rumours of a honeycomb of tunnels at Lincoln Cathedral and in Lincoln are aplenty, as I have discovered, and I have had all sorts of stories forwarded me by helpful sources, one of the most appealing being a tunnel at the church of St Hugh's on Monks Road, close to the cathedral and allegedly leading up there. St Hugh was the Patron Saint of Lincoln Cathedral and was responsible for building the Bishop's Palace. Another dark rumour spoke of a tunnel leading to the cathedral all the way from the site of the old lunatic asylum at St John's, 1892-1990. Many stories about tunnels arise from a combination of observations that have been made over many years referring to limestone quarrying, and mining carried out from the Roman period until the 19th Century with surviving underground mining shafts, ironstone mining within areas of the city, Roman stone-lined sewer chambers running under the upper city, which are seen occasionally during road works, and the many wells in the Uphill area. However, throughout the British Isles there is almost a culture of tunnels that have been unearthed concerning castles, cathedrals (Lincoln have both at no distance away from each other), churches, old inns and breweries. The church of St Hugh's was built on the site of an old brewery! Castles in England who have confirmed tunnels and underground passages are at Ashby De La Zouch, Bungay, Dover, Hastings and Nottingham, and in Wales, at Carrey Cennan and Pembroke. Cathedrals with confirmed tunnels are Canterbury and Norwich. So why not Lincoln!

It amuses me when archaeologists tell me there are no secret tunnels simply because they haven't found any. Precisely, that's why they're called secret! During 2008, I came across a group of intrepid 'urban guerillas' who set about uninvited exploration of interesting derelict sites all over the country. This often means they have to bypass security guards and enter illegally, although, armed with cameras, they leave these places exactly as they find them causing no damage. Because of this, they have to keep their identities unknown and so I will only refer to my contact as 'Tims'. Tims informed me of a great deal of information concerning both tunnels he knew of and suspected ones in Lincoln, some apparently still accessible, others sealed, as he and his twilight army also undertook underground explorations, many of the original leads for these stories corroborated by workmen witnesses. The website for their recorded activities is called '28 Days Later', for me yet another meaningful link and re-occurence with the number 28. One of the more intriguing leads that came my way is as follows:

In uphill Lincoln there was once a property owned by a family called the Emilianis who had the Ricardo Emiliani garage that was Lancia, and then became Honda. Apparently, there was a basement in the dealership for storage purposes as big as the above room space above it, and when our correspondent was 13, whilst looking at a car being restored down there, he came across a big wooden door. Enquiring what it was, he was told it was the entrance to a very long tunnel network that led over to the cathedral and the castle. Years later his persistence and persuasion paid off, and he was allowed through into the tunnels. He claims that an architect's report in existence at the time showed the tunnels to be long, and that when traversing them he counted 20-30 junctions in the quarter distance only that that they went. Direction wise, it looked as if they were heading toward the cathedral in one direction and down Greetwell Road, towards the County Hospital, in the other. The Emiliani entrance is now defunct, the tunnels filled with tonnes of concrete to create the foundations for flats that now stand on the spot, although the teller of this story still maintains that there may be unfilled offshoots.

One other interesting contribution to exposing Lincoln's tunnel network returns us back to approximately 1988 when another correspondent alleges that someone at the cathedral contacted the Lincoln scuba club to investigate a suspected leak from what was understood to be underground water tanks built as a reserve for fire-fighting activity. Holding the ladder for his father and others in their scuba gear to enter the tank through a manhole about 18 square inches, an old chap who had been watching the activity sauntered over to ask if they were 'going into the tunnels?' This correspondent alleges that Lincoln's local TV programme, 'Calendar News', managed to capture the moment for posterity. The Lincolnshire Paranormal Research Team some years back spent a dark midnight filming in the spooky transportation cells under Lincoln Castle. My friend Garry Ross, who led the team, told me there are what appears to be evidence of certain walls being sealed, the difference in the brickwork being apparent. When I heard this I asked the castle if I could investigate, but access was denied as by then a protected colony of bats were roosting down there and couldn't be disturbed! At Temple Bruer, twelve miles away from the cathedral and a part of the Cathedral Code, there have been two incomplete excavations that have already confirmed tunnels. The owner of Bruer, Mr Broughton, once told us that his workmen often hit tunnels when digging in the fields around about. In November 2008 I accompanied a Shepperton Studios team from Classic Media who were investigating Bruer for their DVD Templars' series 'The Quest', and we witnessed Tony Peart of his excellent Templar Mechanics website locate the site of the tunnels via dowsing. In December of that year, Tony alerted me to some unexpected air vents he had discovered in the undergrowth at a place called Griffin Wood, not too far from Bruer. There were a number of them all at distances to each other. Sworn to secrecy, he took me with him to investigate and we took some photographs only, narrowly deciding not to dig. The actual church at Temple Bruer a short distance away from the tower ruins has in its graveyard a plot with a carved griffin. The symbol of the griffin, in Greek mythology, is, of course, considered a guardian of hidden treasure.

My interest remains in this hidden tunnel at the Bishop's Palace, a residency that was for almost 500 years the Seat of the Holy See in England. From the viewpoint of a church hoping to keep the secret concealed, what better a place to have a secret tunnel leading to the most sought after historic treasure of all? And could it connect to the cathedral? There is a carved illustration of a ship on one of the walls of the 15th Century entrance tower, which could be a Templar reference, along with some Masonic symbols. Elsewhere you can find a Latin motto *'Benedicat tibi dominus ex Sion'* alongside the Star of David dating back to Sauniere's key year of 1885. Translated, we find it comes from a quotation from Psalms 128-5 and is a 'A song of Degrees', although experts are not certain what this Hebrew superscription means. Degrees, of course, is associated with Freemasonry. The translation reads, in full, *'Benedicat tibi dominus ex Sion; et videas bona Jerusalem omnibus diebus vitae tuae'*. 'May the Lord bless thee out of Sion, and mayest thou see the good things out of Jerusalem all the days of thy life.' Has this been chosen deliberately to make a reference to Lincoln's own Jerusalem?' A lady from Boston in Lincolnshire contacted me to say that back in the early '50s, when she was a little girl on a school trip to the cathedral, they were shown a series of tunnels under the floor and told that they would be permanently sealed off as they were unsafe. Humans do have an irritating habit of sealing off tunnels! And now, for another most helpful synchronicity. During a conversation about tunnels in the city, a source that I would trust with my life told me this story.

At a 1780 property at Steep Hill, which leads to the cathedral and castle, during 1963, she was privy to a conversation held by staff at a City and County Home for Girls. The home was for girls awaiting court appearances and if they were naughty they were sent down into the cellar for a solitary confinement punishment. On this occasion, the girl who had been sent down there had gone missing – she had found a tunnel in the cellar! The staff had to go find her and it transpires that this tunnel went along from the home, the direction it followed meant it also passed under the nearby Church of St Michaels on the Mount, and on, to the cathedral. The person relating me this story even saw the tunnel hole in the cellar for herself. Steep Hill is not so named for nothing, it has a 1 in 7 gradient – it is like ascending Glastonbury Tor, itself suspected to have a tunnel system - and has a few other interesting buildings including the 12th Century Jew's House (England's oldest domestic residence) and, only a few hundred yards along, The Norman House (1170) which at one stage was owned and leased by the Knights Templar themselves. Lincoln was the second most important Jewish community in England during the twelfth century, thus making it quite believable that a treasure relating to them could find its eventual way to the area. Some architecture in Lincoln Cathedral is even influenced by Jewish legends. During the '80s this once Home for Girls, a listed building, was subdivided and converted to residential use. Could that cellar, if still accessible, prove the existence of this tunnel, if only now to show a sealed wall?

And now, time for two loose threads to pull together in a rather interesting fashion. The church in question, under which the Steep Hill tunnel passed, the medieval St Michaels on the Mount situated within the cathedral quarters, built in 1560 and declared redundant by the Church of England in 1990, was sold in September 2007 to an unnamed mystery buyer who paid 200k over the asking price of 350k to secure it! Estate Agents Walters, Lincoln who made the transaction even themselves referred to the church as 'a very unusual property'. Does it have a significance because it contains or connects to an important tunnel? Who might be the mystery buyer? On 23rd December I approached the Dean's Secretary back at the Bishop's Palace one more time. I had heard from yet another source that apparently there is a plaque somewhere within the Judges' Lodgings associated with the Palace, referring to tunnel entrances. Although she hadn't heard of this her reply reads: 'The Judges' Lodgings are now closed having being sold off for some inappropriate reason, so no access there at present.' Some 'inappropriate reason'? How peculiar a phrase. Certainly not appropriate for my advancement, but I wonder if it may well be for somebody else with a vested interest in tunnels and the hidden Templar treasure only a short distance away?

The plot thickened a little further when on March 2nd 2009 I decided to return to the quizzical remark of December and asked the Dean's Secretary, Joy Schneider, if she would care to enlarge on the closing of the Judges' Lodgings and its 'inappropriate' reason for sale. The email response within a day portrayed a different tone from the same lady who was used to referring to me on first name terms. Opening with 'Dear Sir', it went on succinctly, 'I do not recall saying anything of this nature and I fear you may have noted my comments incorrectly'. This smacks of the cathedral's tried and tested ability to U-turn, and I found it all rather odd. Just as well I still have the original email and declaration in my safe keeping.

My son's peculiar knack of being in the right place at the right time proved useful again, for in June 2010 Ben happened by chance to engage in conversation with a fellow who tends to the Bishop's Palace, and when he mentioned the subject of tunnels to him, the man casually informed him that a cave had been discovered within the vineyard, which is at the back of the palace within its grounds, after a hole had appeared caused by subsidence! I quickly contacted Charles Rodgers of the English Heritage organisation for confirmation of this find. Without offering a date for the incident, he replied by email: 'I'm aware of a 'void' that appears to be under the vineyard which became apparent when a small hole opened up close to one of the vines. I have no idea how extensive the void is, or whether it could be described as a cave. The vineyard area remains the responsibility of the diocese, and I'm not aware that any investigation of the area has been undertaken.' With this, I decided it was time for me to investigate, laboriously combing the avenues of vines, and then I found it! A small hole still existed at the foot of a vine! When I pushed a straw down it fell about an inch or so and below that it was sealed over with soil. There are a number of avenues of vines, starting with two that are shorter than all the others. Beginning with the longer ones, from left to right, the hole was located along the 2nd full avenue, 8th vine along...2 and 8...28. Here we go again, that reappearing and synchronous number – and another sealed opportunity.

MARY·HATH·CHOSEN·THAT·GOOD·PART·WHICH
SHALL·NOT·BE·TAKEN·AWAY·FROM·HER✧

Erected to the Glory of God in loving memory of
Mary Forrest of Ardew, Died 23rd October, 1904,
by her affectionate sister Isabella D. Forrest.

CHAPTER SIXTEEN
STARRY GUARDIAN OF THE CHATEAU AT RENNES

I t was time for me to recap. As a long-term researcher into the enduring global mystery that began at Rennes-le-Chateau, in an attempt to try solve at least a part of whatever is the conclusion of the enigma, I had tried to explore every possible aspect, my starting point being somewhat original, having drawn attention to parallels between the famous village and the Gothic Cathedral of Lincoln in England on the ground, soon to finally lead me upward into the starry heavens! I had experienced what, on reflection, appears to have been something of a puzzling, destined visit to RLC in 1986, involving some interesting adventures there, including the discovery of a rock crop tomb sealed at two points of entry not too far away from Les Labadous, home of the authoress Elizabeth Van Buren who also had stumbled across this tomb, visiting it to sprinkle holy water and call it her 'special place'. Contemporary Godfather of Sacred Geometry, David Wood also knew of this tomb, and apart from our young French guide Daniel, who still lives in the Rennes environs, I wondered who else knew at the time, or even now, of this location which has a stone marker nearby and a babbling stream that you swear you can almost hear whisper. Leonardo Da Vinci in his version of Virgin of the Rocks (Mary without halo) paints it as an incidental inclusion at the top of his work.

My visit to Rennes left me musing my original major comparisons – how here was a church dedicated to Mary Magdalene at the top of a high hill, and containing a demon guardian statue. Back in Lincoln, at the Gothic Cathedral, high up a hill until 60AD there stood a church dedicated to Mary Magdalene, shamefully knocked down to make way for the minster in 1097, which would in the 13th Century introduce its own demon guardian, the notorious 'Lincoln Imp'. Three quite unique similarities there, I thought. Then, in 2005 it was discovered that at the scene of the Last Supper at the Great East Window of the cathedral, having gone unnoticed since the windows were placed, there sits a dog on Christ's platter, rather than a loaf of bread or glass of wine! Deciding to collect up any other anomalies within the cathedral, I had soon found out our canine friend reappears a total of three times, and when my collection was complete the 'Lincoln Cathedral Code' was born, synchronising perfectly with the many clues associated with the Rennes mystery in France.

The Quest

Front page of the mysterious Wyville document, Grantham Library.

We had a pregnant shepherdess, clues relating to painters Poussin and Teniers, the enigmatic '681', the 'horse and cross of God', our demon guardian friend, and the phenomenon of 'blue apples' whereby the sun striking through a pane of glass on a specific time-date causes the dancing, dappling effect upon a key area. Assembling all these clues into a sequential paper chase led to a precise spot at the burial grounds of the shepherdess St Margaret, opposite the SE corner of the cathedral, where once stood Margaret's Church demolished in 1781 to parallel the same year of the death of Marie de Negre who almost certainly knew the Rennes secret. Attempts to GPR scan under this location where a tomb belonging to the Rayner family stands were initially granted by cathedral authorities, only for them to later renege and go silent without any believable explanation.

Then, I discovered another parallel aspect between RLC and Lincoln Cathedral, almost as puzzling as the entire mystery itself! Readers of the best selling *Holy Blood, Holy Grail* will be well aware of what is held to be a spurious document 'The Dossier Secrets', deposited in the Bibliotheque Nationale de France in 1967 - purporting to be part of the history of the Priory of Sion - and it turns out that the Lincoln Cathedral Code has its own! I first stumbled across this work by chance, serendipity working its magic yet again to have something find me. In 2005 my friend Simon Brighton, author of *In search of the Knights Templar*, excitedly told me that he had heard that the cousin of his friend Terry Welbourn (who is now co-author with Simon of *Echoes of the Goddess: A Quest for the sacred Feminine in the British Landscape*), author and ex-BBC correspondent Peter Clawson, had years ago been caught up in an incidental conversation with a local, advising him to find his way to a strange document deposited in Grantham Library, some twenty miles south of Lincoln, that was purportedly written by France's most famous novelist Victor Hugo, an alleged past Grand Master of the Priory of Sion, entitled 'The Quest'. Handwritten and illustrated, it claims to be the handiwork of France's most famous novelist, although having compared the calligraphy, it clearly isn't! Hugo was exiled from France in 1855 – the very year that the restored window at the Great East Window at the cathedral was installed - and lived in Guernsey until 1870. There is no official record that he ever frequented England. Over thirty pages long, the document is dated 1917, the year that Sauniere died, and yet nobody at the library can recall how long it has been deposited there, or by whom. It has certainly been there a long time, outliving the memory and many years of long term staff. This encounter of a Quest also surfaced in a magazine the *Lincolnshire Highlights* in 1983, the first five pages presenting itself as a search for a 'lost cathedral and city of Wyville', as opposed to the small actual hamlet of Wyville where the quest starts. Wyville is situated SW of Grantham on the Lincolnshire/Leicestershire border not too far from a Knights Templar Preceptory that once existed at South Witham and where in 2008 I found a hidden 14th Century coffin slab relating to the panel painting Head at Templecombe. How peculiar, a quest starting at an actual village called Wyville setting off to discover Wyville!

The document has hand drawn illustrations down its sides, and the very first is that of a dagger, which we will investigate further later. The fantastic, if spurious, account ends at the top of a hill with a spring head, five houses and the word 'Thalassa' which is rather intriguing as the Lincoln Cathedral Code quest also ends at the top of a hill that once had five houses and a (lost) spring head. The word 'thalassa' is actually one of the meanings assigned to the name Mary in Martianay's edition of St Jerome's works 1699. 'Pikra thalassa' means 'bitter sea' based on the assumption that the name 'Miryam' is composed of the Hebrew words 'mar' (bitter) and 'yam' (sea) The translated inscription upon the headstone of Rene d'Anjou's 'La Fountaine', that some researchers involve in the RLC mystery, mentions bitter water. Amidst the cryptic 30 pages are numerous passing references including 'a stone coffin at present lying in the small churchyard, its date not later than the 12th Century', 'the hidden story written in the stones', 'and what kings sat throned upon that hill'. Two poems are also in the library file, one entitled 'The Quest' also, from 1917 initialled H.P., and another 'To Wyville', this search starting as far away as in Scotland, no less! 'The Quest', allegedly written by Hugo, appears to be a search for a lost cathedral, and I wonder is this the 'lost' cathedral of the Magdalene given that Lincoln Cathedral may have been secretly known to be dedicated to her and not the Virgin Mary. Is the stone coffin and the churchyard references hinting at the actual St Margaret's burial grounds where until, 1781 it stood, where 'For Dagobert II King and for Sion is this treasure and it is death' as reads one of the RLC parchments? Is the story written in the stones referring to the many anomalies of the architecture of Lincoln Cathedral that parallel with RLC, and does 'what kings sat upon that hill' mean lost Rose-Line descendants? Apart from 'The Professor, who first heard of Wyville, a man who digs for earth's treasures', the most interesting figure mentioned throughout the account is referred simply as 'The Padre' ..very Sauniere-like! I suspect that this lost 'Wyville' is a Masonic play-on word for 'Wife Hill', the hill upon which something belonging to Jesus' wife Mary Magdalene belongs. The word 'Wye' almost certainly originates from the Old English 'weoh' meaning 'idol shrine'. The search for Wyville also includes seeking out the 'lost cathedral'. Not as if I needed any further confirmation about this document leading to St Margaret's on the hill, I still got it. This 'lost cathedral' is none other than Lincoln Cathedral itself, for on numerous occasions throughout the year on a foggy, misty morning, it is enshrouded and covered over and vanishes from sight from a distance…it simply is not there, it is lost!

Strange stuff indeed. Interested readers can see the file for themselves at the Grantham Library even though the puzzled library themselves cannot offer any information as to who donated the items or exactly when. Two concluding strange parallels with RLC and the 'Secret Dossier', are the facts that Grantham Library resides inside the Isaac Newton Shopping Centre with his statue facing it outside, Isaac himself an alleged Grand Master of the Priory of Sion from 1691, and that the Wyville family crest is a hidden representation of the Masonic compass within a letter 'M', and bears an almost replica likeness to the device below the famous 'Penitence, Penitence' motto of Mary Magdalene at the foot of her statue in the Rennes churchyard.

Having had enough of stuff on, or under, the ground that seem to indicate resonance between Rennes and Lincoln, I felt it was high time to investigate any possible links involving the starry heavens. As this was way above my head (pun intended) and beyond my abilities, I sought the aid of a far more capable individual by way of a mathematician by the name of Greg Rigby. He had already contributed to the Rennes saga by way of having discovered pentagonal geometry in Poussin's 'Shepherds of Arcadia' masterpiece – key to the RLC mystery, and in 1996 having written a book entitled On *earth as in heaven - Revelation of French cathedrals*, in which Greg announced that the ancient Celts established holy sites in Northern France reflecting on the ground the constellation Ursa Major with its handle pointing to Rennes-le-Chateau as Polaris, the Pole Star. As our starting point, Greg came over from Florida to precisely orientate and align Lincoln Cathedral for me and with the aid of his computer software, astronomical star maps, co-ordinates and alignments, set about to discover what secrets the cathedral may have been hiding, and if we could correlate it with what was known over at Rennes.

All Gothic cathedrals have their Rose Windows at the west – not at Lincoln though! Here we find it placed at the north, disguised as a Northern 'Star Clock', whereby if the glass were removed and one were to stand in a certain position within the cathedral at night one would see the revolving northern constellations including Ursa Major. Not surprisingly, to me at least, there was something of a significant discovery. The star that is reflected on the ground by Lincoln Cathedral is Arcturus, found in the constellation of Bootes and the third most brightest in the night sky. Arcturus is the 'Guardian of the Bear' that is Ursa.

January 17th is a most celebrated date in the RLC Mystery. Not only is it a date when it is alleged certain key figures including Sauniere died, it is also the date when, at mid-day, the phenomenon of the 'blue apples' occur in the small church, and confirm a part of a coded cipher, the sun striking through a small pane to create the impression of blue apples joining red ones – red and blue circles – that slowly moves along to settle upon the altar and later a statue of Saint Anthony the Hermit. Lincoln Cathedral is a veritable orchard of blue apples all year round, courtesy of its decorative southern windows, this phenomenon, by contrast with Rennes, falling upon a crucial location relevant to the Cathedral Code at mid-day on 22nd July, Feast of the Magdalene, dancing alongside the tomb of Queen Eleanor of Castille who stands high up the SE corner of the cathedral in direct line, pregnant, and staring over at the Lincoln Cathedral Code location at the burial grounds of the shepherdess Margaret. What is most important, however, is that at mid-day at the cathedral on 17th, not only is the constellation of Ursa Major overhead, but the cathedral altar faces directly at Arcturus and resonates with St Anthony at the chateau when we learn that Kabbalists associate the star with the 9th Tarot Trump, the Hermit. The cathedral initially drew my attention with its dog symbology, to ponder if it may be a concealed temple to the dog star Sirius, but Greg and I struggled to find any confirmation and it may possibly just be drawing reference to the blazing star known to be Sirius that is found in Masonic Lodges, given that the structure was laid out to Templar influence, as was the very structure of Masonry.

According to ancient China, the stars of the Great Bear associated with the celestial Palace of the Lord on High, Star God of Longevity, the Heavenly Mountain, Paradise of the Immortals, and Sirius the Heavenly Wolf guarded this celestial palace. Utterance 302 of the Pyramid texts found on the northern face of Unas' pyramid also provides a link that may exist between the heliacal rising of Sirius and Ursa Major, and it is something that we should take a little time to study, as there appears to be evidence that two step pyramids constructed at Saqqara, Egypt, were built as if to face one another, being designed deliberately to coincide and align with stellar symbolism, and involving Sirius and Ursa Major. With strategically placed inclined northern entrances, it appears that the notion was to make a passageway accessible for the dead king to rebirth in the preferred stellar region of Ursa Major, the 'Great She Bear'.

There are three different ways of viewing this constellation, the ancient way providing the bear with a tail so unusually long that it is out of character with the animal, and an older way that has no resemblance of a bear at all. With this is mind, and bearing in mind (pun intended!) that all constellations were named from this side of life, maybe the Collective Unconscious will suggest that the 'bear' we are discussing, is not the animal, but the 'bear' of the act of bearing, to bring forth, to give birth to, which of course involves our recurring theme throughout this quest of pregnancy. I, for example, have no difficulty in viewing the bowl of the dipper as possibly being an amniotic sac and that the handle is an umbilical cord. (Everything to do with a dipper is associated with immersion and water, already suggesting baptism!) The Pyramid texts are not alone in suggesting that the most fortuitous time for this rebirth involved the dawn heliacal rise of the dog star, later funerary texts attesting similar. The full text of Utterance 302 of the Pyramid Texts, tells us; ' The sky is clear, Sothis lives, I am a living one, the son of Sothis,and the two Enneada have cleansed themselves for me in Ursa Major, the imperishable. My house in the sky will not perish, my throne on earth will not be destroyed, for men hide, the gods fly away. Sothis has caused me to fly up to the sky in the company of my Brethren..' Nothing ambiguous about that! In 1800BC the rising star Sirius coincided with the Ursa Major star Al Kaid's lower culmination, affirming a connection between these two stars, at least. Lincoln Cathedral has its own Sirius dog symbology as we have seen, and is presided over by the star Arcturus, Guardian of the Bear Ursa Major. If Ursa Major is an area of the heavens to do with birth (which obviously entails some involvement with pregnancy) potentially a cosmic birth beyond our ken, can we then say that the cathedral clearly has a connection with birth and bearing? With Arcturus now announced as the minster's overseeing star, and its role as guardian of the Ursa bear of which Rennes-le-Chateau is the pole star of this constellation and birth, would it not be surprising then to find the most current symbol of pregnancy and birth - the pursuit of Mary Magdalene, the 'treasure' that Rennes announced to the world via the priest Sauniere, guarded nearby?

The final word we reserve for the Collective Unconscious, that mechanism that can bring anything about it so needs, be it physical materialisation or mere hypothesis and inspiration through the human agency of brain and body. On September 24th 2008, a Cambridgeshire-based company called Ringspark.com, stunned the media by announcing they were seeking planning permission and unveiling plans to construct a stone pyramid larger than the Great Pyramid of Giza! Rising to a height of 502 feet with a base length of 800 feet, the footprint cover area of 640,000 square feet would require 2.6 million stone blocks at an average weight of 2.5 tons each, brought to the site by road and canal. Worldwide funding could ensure the project being finalised in 18 years. Of all the places in the entire world, where do you think the notion to place the world's biggest pyramid had been concluded? The choice was the open spaces of the Lincolnshire countryside, thirty miles away from Lincoln Cathedral. Whether it ever happens may at this stage be unlikely, but at least it's the thought that counts.

MARY·HATH·CHOSEN·THAT·GOOD·PART·WHICH·
SHALL·NOT·BE·TAKEN·AWAY·FROM·HER❖

Erected to the Glory of God in loving memory of
Mary Forrest of Ardow. Died 23rd October, 1904,
by her affectionate sister Isabella D Forrest,
Wolses of Ardow

CHAPTER SEVENTEEN
MIND, MOTION AND THE MAGDALENE

In 2005, local newspaper the *Lincolnshire Echo* ran the story 'The riddle of Jesus, the Last Supper and Lincoln's own Da Vinci Code' referring to the discovery of a dog on the platter at the scene of the Last Supper upon the Great East Window within Lincoln Cathedral. The notion of Lincoln Cathedral having its own 'Da Vinci Code' appealed to me within an instant, I set about investigating it and the rest is now modern history. From the very onset, synchronicity played its part – the fellow who discovered the dog on the plate during repairs to the window had the word 'cup' in his surname, the Grail once held to be a golden cup or chalice; Tom Kupper, being leader of the cathedral glazing department. As I was making exciting progress in pursuing this chance find of a factual Cathedral Code, the most unbelievable announcement was made – in July 2006 Hollywood was going to come to film scenes for Dan Brown's fictional *The Da Vinci code* within the cathedral! Here was I seeking to authenticate a factual code there, when the film version of the best-ever selling work of fiction was about to tread on my toes and share the same stone floor. I thought this visiting significant synchronicity would never be repeated, but during March 2010 lightning struck again.

On March 12th, the 36.5 centimetre tall, 5kg solid gold soccer World Cup, the most iconic sports trophy of all time, was going to pay a solitary visit in the UK during its global tour ahead of that year's summer tournament in South Africa. Where to? The soccer giants of Manchester United, the world's second richest club? London's top two, champions Chelsea or Arsenal? Previous European cup winners Liverpool, perhaps? No - against all conceivable odds, and described in the press as 'truly fantastic' and 'totally unique', it was brought to lowly second division football club Lincoln City of the fourth tier of the English football league system, at their Sincil Bank ground, lowered down by helicopter before the game with visiting Hereford United, as a token acknowledgement to the club's 125th anniversary. The news was a sensation and an unlikely event to soccer fans in the city, with waves of envy rippling through all other clubs and soccer followers in the country who would love a one-off chance to glance this cup of cups. If we remove the exoteric explanation for this still-unlikely happening, we can take a look at the esoteric, for as many of us have learned, or at least suspect, all is not exactly as it seems in this world; deep multi-layered explanations abound for many far subtler reasons.

With synchronicity now being a way of life for me, I immediately recognised the mechanism of the Collective Unconscious at work again, and was - for a second time - responsible for drawing a specific arrival to Lincoln. The symbology of the 'Blade and the chalice' is a confirmatory requirement of the Grail seeker's search, with even Dan Brown mentioning it in his *The Da Vinci Code*. And here it was, finally announcing itself in the very city where I had already placed evidence of the final resting place of the Magdalene. The helicopter (blade) bringing the world cup trophy (a golden chalice) – the blade and the chalice. The original octagonal World Cup with the title of 'Victory' and retired in 1974, was made of gold plated sterling silver and lapis lazuli, depicting the female figure of the Greek goddess Nike. Its replacement now depicts a male and female holding up the earth. After its incredible arrival in Lincoln, the trophy coincidentally travelled to Paris where Dan Brown placed the Magdalene under the inverted pyramid at the Louvre.

To explain the consequent synchronicities of this trophy arriving at Sincil Bank, we must take a look at the visiting team, Hereford United. Hereford Cathedral is the home of the 158cm x 133cm golden 13thC Mappa Mundi or 'Map of the world'. It is attributed to Richard de Bello, Prebend of Lafford in Lincoln Cathedral, but what also connects Lincoln Cathedral with Hereford is a medieval writer with an appropriate surname, Walter Map (1140-1210), chancellor of the diocese of Lincoln, later becoming Precentor, and then later Canon of Hereford. Map was long considered to be the author of a lost prose version of the Lancelot story entitled *Quest of the Holy Grail*, on which later accounts of the Arthurian legacy were based. In the centre of the Mappa Mundi is placed Jerusalem. Three miles to the west of Lincoln Cathedral we have the uniquely named small village of Jerusalem. Curiously, the labels for Africa, host to the year's World Cup, and Europe are in reverse. The connections deepen when we learnt that the favoured nickname of Hereford United is 'The Lillywhites', the white lily being an emblem of Mary Magdalene. Lincoln City's football ground, Sincil Bank, was built in 1895, which was the very year that Berenger Sauniere began his construction of the Villa Bethany. The origin of the name 'Sincil' is a puzzle, and is rather untraceable as British, but if we resort to the matrix of the mother tongue, the expression of the language of Collective Unconscious, it reveals the phonetic 'Sign Seal'. So now we have a synchronised collection of the blade and chalice of the Grail, a sign, and the seal, a means of authentication or attestation. The arrival of the World Cup trophy, the blade and the chalice, brought about by human agency is the unconscious sign strengthening the belief that the Grail is in Lincoln.

My own investigations, aided and abetted by arrangements from this Collective Unconscious and its tool of synchronicity, have placed a Templar treasure concerning the secret of a pregnant Magdalene opposite the east corner of the cathedral, at the burial grounds of St Margaret. At this angle of the Gothic structure are two prominent carved figures presumed to be of King Edward and Queen Eleanor, heavily restored in the 19th Century, and thought to have not originally intended to depict the couple. After her death and embalming - which involved evisceration – her viscera only was buried in her tomb in Lincoln, with the rest of her remains being buried at Westminster Abbey. Interesting synchronicities here are that the statue on the outside clearly shows a pregnant female. The statue of the gravid Eleanor looks directly over at the location of the marker tomb where my final location resides, and behind her, inside the cathedral, is her own viscera in a tomb placed under the Great East Window. The 1891 structure is an exact copy of the original that was defaced and smashed by Cromwell's men at the time of the Civil War. That it is her viscera alone that remains within her tomb at the cathedral is vitally important, as we will soon see. I suspect also that this is the tomb brought to the attention of Berenger Sauniere who mentioned in his casual diary entry for September 21st 1891 - 'Letter from Granes, Discovery of a tomb. Rain in the evening.' His Masonic punning on the word 'rain' has nothing to do with a commentary on weather conditions. It is more a reference to the figure whose tomb it is, in this instance that of Eleanor who had a 'reign' or time of reigning. 'Evening' has the meaning of 'the decline or end of life', and it is her tomb that is clearly a declaration of that finality. It may even be a reference to the Thomas Rayner, marker tomb. Eleanor, incidentally, is reputed to have saved the life of Edward when he was stabbed by a poisoned dagger from a Moors assassin – again the appearance of a dagger in our storyline. As there is no dispute that the original carvings had uncertain identities, is it possible that these statues were once showing the King of Heaven, Jesus, and his pregnant wife Mary Magdalene?

The Collective Unconscious, a tool that has aided and abetted me throughout my investigations, has no human limitation like the concepts of time and space, and this is how it may offer omens in the timeless realm of dreamland. We are now going to return to 'The Shepherd's Monument' at Shugborough. To study the pregnant shepherdess figure in Poussin's 'Shepherds of Arcadia' – who translates as our Queen Eleanor at Lincoln Cathedral - one could be forgiven for thinking that the female is a ghostly figure, as the gathering shepherds show no indication of being aware of her presence, more as if she is invisibly trying to comfort them at her graveside. The kneeling shepherd is painted to look very like the figure of Thomas, who has his finger pointing upwards, as seen in Da Vinci's 'Last Supper'. Note that the garb worn by the ghostly shepherdess is the same colour as the Mary Magdalene figure in Da Vinci's canvass. Next, we visit the enigmatic 'Shepherd's Monument, a 20-foot high, marble tablet mirror-image relief copy of Poussin's original, found at Shugborough Hall, ancestral home of the Earls of Lichfield, in Staffordshire, England, and shown in a contrasting portrait format rather than Poussin's landscape, which some argue highlights the mountainous region of Rennes-le-Chateau in the background. There is an inscription at the foot of the monument that has never been conclusively de-coded, despite a number of claims, and with speculative examples. Leaving some of these possible solutions alone, our need is to concentrate on the tombstone in the portrait as it is now raised higher from the ground than the Poussin scene, with an additional part typical of a popular Victorian embellishment. Surrounded by trees and what appear to be clouds, the tablet is, of course, here in England, and so too may be what it is attempting to indicate, a tomb high up somewhere.

Now, let us flip a photo of the monument so that it is no longer a mirror-image of the painting, but a mirror-image of itself. The kneeling 'Thomas' shepherd stands out from the sculpture further than the other two and is directly pointed at by his adjacent shepherd. Thomas points to the famous, now reversed, *ET IN ARCADIA EGO* inscription, his thumb pointing to the letter 'R' and his finger which is now 'missing' would have pointed to the letter 'N'. Between the two is a letter 'A' and a space – missing letter. In our reversal, this 'Thomas' figure is pointing to 'RA_N'. Could the missing letter have been a chalice shaped 'Y'? Either way, 'R A_N' with phonetic emphasis on the 'A' produces a sounding 'RAYN'. Is this telling us we are at the tomb of Thomas Rayner, the very marker tomb indeed located high up the steep Lindum Hill and surrounded by trees, under where hides an undiscovered crypt associated with the secrets of the Magdalene?

Although Shugborough Hall date their monument as having been built between 1748 and 1763, and the Rayner tomb dates only to 1820, the Collective Unconscious working through Flemish sculptor Peter Scheemakers has still enabled us, whatever his own intentions or instructions may have been, to be led back to the unseen space it occupies. That is the crypt below of the demolished St Margaret's Church, which dates back to the 11th Century. It is interesting that Scheemakers has the initials 'P.S', as in the Priory of Sion. Another vital clue to the solution stands alongside the pregnant 'Mary' statue that looks over at the Rayner marker, the equal spacing of the 681 of the East Dial of the cathedral (681 being part of the coded Rennes Parchments) 30-foot up the buttress of the SE corner of the Transept. The Dial is an important part of the enigma as the original name of the Tour Magdala, the tower dedicated to Mary in Rennes-le-Chateau was 'Tour de l'Horlogium' – 'The Tower of the Clock'. Back at Shugborough, near the Shepherd's Monument we will also see a so-called horlogium, water clock and wind tower. In May 2009 staff at Shugborough Hall announced that they had found an ancient paper cross in their roof space believed to have remained hidden there since being torn from a 1794 newspaper. The cross is, more specifically, in the shape of the Cross of Lorraine, the Templars emblem, which is also the shape of Lincoln Cathedral when viewed from the air. Is this yet another secret kept for over two hundred years, that Shugborough and its monument link with Lincoln Cathedral? Charges brought against the Knights Templar at the time was that they worshipped a mysterious cat or head. Could this cat or head have been concealed within the word 'CAT-HED-RAL', Lincoln Cathedral?

CHAPTER EIGHTEEN
GENOCIDE OF THE HOLY BLOODLINE

Having been a historical detective for twenty years on a case that had provided a final resting place afforded by many, many clues, I could have been forgiven for thinking that it was time for closure. I had been pushed through many a hoop, followed many a trail and many a paper chase that presented itself to me. I would be glad to take a well-earned rest. But there was one last and unexpected hoop I could feel myself facing up to that would complete the final circle of the mystery. One of the tools of a sleuth is that of the hunch, that intuitive feeling that appears from nowhere but follows you about relentlessly demanding your attention. The word 'hunch' clearly resonates with the 'unc' of the Unconscious, and if I were receiving this signal from that faultless repository then I was going to have to act on its insistence. The nagging doubt and direction it was pushing me in led me back to Da Vinci and his 'Last Supper.'

Just about everything imaginable has been either said or suggested about the biblical figure presented to us as Mary Magdalene. That much we can agree. The most favoured and recent of the many hypothesis is that she was the partner of the historical and biblical figurehead Jesus, carrying his child and along with that the continuation of a Holy Bloodline. This Mary figure, who - after the biblical account where she was the first to visit the tomb of the rising Christ - simply vanishes from record. Yet she warrants becoming an object of character assassination by the Catholic Church and added to their tarnishing of all things female by virtue of Original Sin propaganda and inventing us the lie that she was a prostitute. This enigmatic Mary must have been a potent female, in particular an actual spiritual teacher who had a following, and whose importance may well have been thought better removed in order to satisfy a preferred emphasis on a male Jesus figure to cater for the deep-seated homosexual tendencies that have now been brought to light by the exposure of systematic and covered up Catholic Church child abuse in both USA and Ireland and suspected in many other countries, if not all where Catholicism is rooted. That the figure of Mary Magdalene may well have been far more important in history than we could have imagined, eclipsing that of the male Jesus storyline as it is told, may well be one of the better secrets held in relation to her, and the mystery attached to Rennes-le-

**'The Death of Mary Magdalene', Luisa Roldan –
Mary is incised in her left side by a dagger.**

Chateau. Is her connection with blood – menstruation – the one thing a male church hierarchy loathed, to menstruate being 'men's true hate'? Was this enigmatic Mary considered such a threat that she was physically removed from accurate recordings of history that would displease the Church, preferring an emphasis on an elevated and deified male Jesus figure? This story line may be some two thousand years ago, but in that time human nature has changed little, and powerful women who worry the residing male authority of the day are usually removed, from as far back as Jeanne D'Arc to more modern examples of Marilyn Monroe, Princess Diana Spencer and Benazir Bhutto. Diana's assassination, as many now believe it to be, having followed the vast evidence, in particular, shows her as a modern day Magdalene figure, and amongst that evidence we cannot rule out that she was also pregnant at the time of her arranged death. I was now having to face the real possibility that it was now a crime to solve. With more than a character assassination to consider, could a pregnant Mary Magdalene have been demised?

Throughout my work I have learned that sometimes such secrets are knowingly safeguarded by secretive societies and Masons, and other times not. The fact is that the Truth will always out, as the Collective Unconscious will ensure key words, phrases and pictorial clues are perpetuated through the unwitting medium of the human agency, waiting to be spotted and gathered up like a join-the-dots puzzle to preserve a true picture. Painters may, unaware, paint clues on their canvass and sculptors may carve anomalies on their architecture without the knowledge that they play their part in defending Truth. Another painting that figures in our Lincoln Cathedral Code and of the Magdalene, although not presented as such, is the one within the cathedral called 'The Annunciation' showing a pregnant red-haired female in red garb, encapsulating the imagery of the sacred feminine, and is allegedly the Virgin Mary being told of the birth of Jesus. It was painted in 1800 by Matthew William Peters who had been a student at the Royal Academy of Art and famed for his portrayal of salacious women – as the Magdalene had wrongfully been portrayed – who quit to join the Church and became the Canon at Lincoln Cathedral. The female in the painting looks over at a monolith that resembles the marker tomb that concludes my work. The canvas was originally placed in the prestigious position of being behind the High Altar, however in 1855 when the image of the dog on the plate was installed, it was moved and stashed away, many clergy at the time finding the art 'distasteful and hideous'. Showing the painting to Margaret Starbird, she confirmed that here was a clear illustration of the sacred feminine.

There is at least one another example of Mary Magdalene being passed off as the Virgin that I have found. A closer look at Caravaggio's controversial canvas 'The death of the Virgin' from 1606, painted at a time when the assumption of the Virgin was not accepted, shows her looking far younger than the 50 or so she was supposed to be. I believe this is because, like the painting of the sacred feminine in the cathedral, she IS Mary Magdalene, who is supposed to be the grieving female in front of the 'Virgin' with her face covered in her hands, but the painting conceals a deliberate transposition of both women. Another indication is that Caravaggio deliberately modelled a prostitute, the title given to the Magdalene by the Church, as the Virgin. The most famous of all paintings hinting at imminent foul play concerning Mary returns us to Da Vinci's famous 'Last Supper'; the scene of a double cross that has been open to so many interpretations involving hidden imagery, mirror-images, and complex sacred geometry to name but a few. Whereby this may be so, in my own instance I choose to employ 'Occam's Razor' to elect that the most simple and obvious implication is the one intended by its artist. Accepting what many now do, we see Mary Magdalene to the left of Jesus. The traditional betrayer of Christ, Judas Iscariot, features behind Peter whom the Gnostic Gospels tells us hated Mary - Peter is making a menacing gesture along the throat level of Mary. This symbology has survived with us today and is commonplace in motion movie-making to designate a 'cut', a cessation or the end of a scene and in musical recording to announce the end, or abrupt ending of a take. This, now infamous, disembodied hand wielding a knife in the painting, is attributed, by many, to Peter. Doesn't this simply suggest, as Leonardo does, that Peter, upon whom the Catholic Church was founded, has ill-intent towards the

The crypt of Mary Magdalene, Le Carol - Mary shows the dagger incising her left side

Magdalene and that the offending weapon to inflict a sudden cessation is that of a knife or dagger? Is this weapon one and the same as the illustration on the Wyville document, which also mentions 'knives with blades but not handles', and the dagger carved on the cave wall at Royston? And if the Quest leads us to find Mary, why with a dagger association?

I turned my attention back to Leonardo recalling how, in 2002, an interesting development came to light in the art world and continues the theme of Leonardo attempting to convey a message. A previously unseen Da Vinci turned up in a private Swiss collection: a portrait of Mary Magdalene on a wooden panel (the Templar related artwork known as the Templecombe Head was also painted on such a panel) authenticated as being completed by him with help from one of his pupils around about 1515, shortly before his death. The painting shows Mary dressed in a red cape and holding a veil over her lower stomach. The veil is to simply tell us there is something 'veiled' within this painting, and if - under enlargement - we take a closer look through this film at the level immediately above the crumpled red garb she holds with her left hand, we will see what can be interpreted as a stretch of scar tissue over her left lower abdomen, the dark folds contained within the piece of cloth she grasps even resembling a dagger-like shape. In the traditional storyline we have Jesus betrayed by a figure named 'Iscariot' whose name actually comes from the Jewish assassins called Sicarii, known as 'the dagger men'. Was Mary Magdalene caught up in a betrayal or double cross involving a dagger? When I first discovered the dog on the plate at Lincoln Cathedral's own 'Last Supper' I decided to take a thorough look see if there were any other anomalies about, and of course I found what awaited me. In the same spirit of inquiry, I now decided it was time to take a closer look at paintings or sculptures of Mary Magdalene, Da Vinci having spurred me on to now know what to look out for, details that we would never have spotted because we weren't looking for them ...scotoma strikes again. Look how long it took before it was quite evident that the figure next to Jesus in 'The Last Supper' was a woman!

Stunning confirmation of my suspicion of foul play arrived sooner than later in the form of 'The death of Mary Magdalene' a sculpture by Spain's first female sculptor Luisa Roldan (1652-1706). There is some evidence that before, during, and after the time of the Cathars who were exterminated for their belief in Jesus Christ being married to a pregnant Mary Magdalene, the impending Grail legend had either originated (as Wolfram Eschenbach thought) in Spain, or had found its way there, none more so than in Catalonia, capital city of Barcelona, south of the Pyrenees, where monks of Montserrat believed it to be buried there. It is therefore no surprise that the person responsible for a graphic presentation of the demise of Mary Magdalene and confirmation of my suspicion of foul play arrived sooner than later in the form of 'The death of Mary Magdalene', a terracotta from around 1692 or before, by Roldan. In the sculpture we see a dying Magdalene surrounded by two large angels and a pair of cherubs. As in Da Vinci's veiled Magdalene, we can clearly see a tear in her clothing in the very same area - the left abdomen - the cherub

Mary Magdalene looks over at her Marker tomb.

nearest looking straight at it. There is an expression of shock on the face of both angels, one cradling Mary and the other holding, on an non-obligingly deliberate angle, what we can interpret to be a dagger, the incising weapon. By route of the Collective Unconscious, Luisa was in her lifetime afforded the nickname 'Sheave', for the identically sounding 'shiv', related from the Scottish 'schive' meaning to slice, originates from the Romany word 'shiv', a slang term for a knife-like weapon, as seen held by the disembodied hand in Da Vinci's 'the Last Supper'. During my investigations since 2005, I had used the name 'Dan Green' for a number of reasons. One was to continue the work of Dan Brown. Secondly, it was in respect of the 'green language' a term coined by alchemist Fulcanelli who discovered the Gothic Cathedrals had their own hidden codes or language. I later also realised, perhaps, that I had chosen the name unconsciously as it is an anagram of 'endanger' and for many involving themselves in the mystery of Rennes-le-Chateau, to do so was to put themselves in that position. However, I tell you this because when I approached the current custodians of Luisa Roldan's revealing terracotta, The Hispanic Society of America in New York, the person who watches over its safekeeping is called Dan Silva!

The secret that could no longer be kept seems to have been retained throughout the family, for Pedro Roldan, Luisa's father, studied with Alonso de Mena, in turn the father of Pedro de Mena who in 1664 sculpted the polychrome wood 'Mary Magdalene in penance'. In this beautiful life-like work we see the Magdalene with her left foot thrust out to draw attention to her left side, the word 'thrust' meaning 'to stab, to pierce in a sudden or violent movement forward', her lips are open not to show she is breathing through her mouth, but taking her last breath. Upon her abdomen, we see a dagger knot tied on her sash and it is the very same knot we see worn by Jesus high up above Mary Magdalene holding child at the Judgement Porch at Lincoln Cathedral. Another painting, that of Italian Francesco Hayez, an oil on wood 'The Penitent Magdalene' (1833), also shows the same incision at the same point, the left abdomen, although skeptics will allege it is simply folded flesh. It cannot be disputed that it is looking as if Mary has just removed this object. It is unimportant whether Hayez painted this knowingly in a masquerading fashion, or if the Collective Unconscious provided it for him. Three decades before Sauniere, there was a precedence to his behaviour in the way of erecting puzzling architecture relating to the Magdalene. Father Louis de Coma was left estate as inheritance from his father's death in 1855, 'Le Carol' in Baulou, an Ariege village, west of Foix. Coma was responsible for the haunting 'Crypt of Mary Magdalene' and here we see a statue of Mary yet again appearing to be withdrawing an incising cross from her left abdomen. I should point out that the cross, or obelus, as we know it, is a cross, and it is not known when the first cross image was made. I will call upon the Collective Unconscious for a moment to remind you how, in typography, the dagger, first used in Roman Catholic liturgical books, also represents the Christian cross, the mark in certain predominant Christian regions employed upon Christian grave headstones. In this sense, was the favoured symbol of the Christian Church unconsciously based on a dagger – the implement of its most shameful crime?

The enduring myth is that a pregnant Magdalene gave birth to a female called Sarah. I believe there is a very real danger that a pregnant Mary did not have time to give birth to a child as she was fatally removed from the scene, and the secret we have been left with is that her fatal wound was to her lower abdominal viscera - the name of her mythical daughter being contained in the word 'viscera' - 'vis-cera/sarah'. This is why it is so important, confirmatory and revealing to know that our very own pregnant shepherdess, Queen Eleanor, who faces the Lincoln Cathedral Code marker tomb from the SE corner, has her viscera alone deposited in her tomb within the cathedral. That my work ends opposite Lincoln Cathedral is made all the more poignant when we note that this great Gothic edifice, when seen from the air, is constructed in the shape of a Cross of Lorraine, a Templars emblem, which is also known as the 'double dagger' and 'double cross', and is also a symbol for poison, alchemists once using the icon on bottles containing poisonous substances. Roget's *Thesaurus* providing synonyms for the word poison, include both the words 'kill' and 'murder'.

Maybe my usage of Occams Razor, another sharp metal instrument, is both an ironic and an unfortunate idiom. There is, however, an even more startling and unexpected addition to this secret, the secret that Mary Magdalene was murdered and that, consequently there is no bloodline, the latter appearing to be a contrivance for eventually hoped for attempted Pan-European political purposes, personal esteem and gain. The question to ask - who did kill Mary and why? For that definitive conclusion we only have to wait until the concluding chapter, for that is what it is. First, in belated respect, let us mourn for both Magdalene and her unborn child.

CHAPTER NINETEEN
THE DEATH OF MARY MAGDALENE - THE BIRTH OF JESUS CHRIST

When I was in my twenties, I came across a TV documentary seeking historical evidence for the biblical Jesus, and found myself a bit bemused and out of my depth when the research declared that there was, in fact, very little indication chronicling the life of this key historical figure. Not only did the programme leave me confused, it also left me quite shocked and angry, reminding me that at an even younger age I had wholly accepted that what is known of Jesus' life from a little after his birth until the age of 30, is exactly nothing. There isn't even anything documented to say what he looked like. How can this be so for a person who has had a religion based upon him with millions of followers across the planet? A quick study of serious research available on numerous Internet sites now suggest that this historical Jesus was never a person but a symbol of the divine soul, and that scholars have known this over the last 200 years, and worse still, the disciples, as they have been presented to us, also appear fictitious. There is no record of any Christ-like figure in Roman records, similarly in the Hebrew Talmud. The disconcerting additional fact is that we know virtually nothing about the personnel who wrote the Gospels. The validity of the existence of the disciples - eye-witnesses to Jesus himself - is even in serious doubt, with no corroborative evidence for their existence, with seven out of the twelve having nothing said about them in the Gospels, and seemingly only to exist as names. Bible accounts only mention the death of two apostles, James, and important for us, Judas.

Kenneth Humphreys, British author of *Jesus never existed,* whom I met on the set of a Sky TV show in 2009, states in a private email , 'However plausible a historical Jesus might appear to the rational mind nothing at all substantiates that a figure approximating to the gospel Jesus ever walked the earth.' This area of dispute has been investigated by far more capable and avid researchers than myself for centuries, unable to make widespread their findings for obvious reasons. To make matters worse, our current generation and their siblings, outside of subscription to the received Christian religion, don't seem to care, for at Christmas time – which can only be

**Nov 2011 - The Collective Unconscious brings an exact replica of
Chartres Labyrinth to Lincoln Cathedral**

validated with the birth of Jesus, surely – we now see a stronger and overpowering representation of a fictitious Santa Claus presence, he himself the image iconography of a 1920's American *Coca Cola* advertising campaign. Even more confusing, the name 'Santa' is a pale anagram of 'Satan', and we could argue that another of the adversary's title 'Old Nick' actually comes from Saint Nicholas who - we are told - was the template for the original gift bearing Santa myth. It's all getting rather messy! So, we must ask, if our traditional image of the Jesus Christ figure is far less accurate than we are told, then why?

Given that I have inevitably vested interest in the enigmatic female called Mary Magdalene who, in more recent hypothesis, was allegedly married to Jesus and said to have spawned a Holy Bloodline, I began to worry a little. No Jesus, as we know him, surely meant no married or pregnant Mary? This posed a serious hindrance to my work and conclusions, unless... there is another interpretation of events that until now nobody has ever thought of, let alone announced. Let me begin to unfold

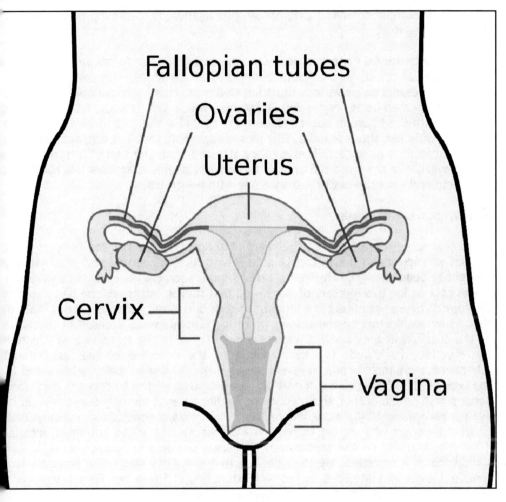

The Fallopian Tubes - a representation of Jesus hanging on the cross.

his series of events from a never viewed before perspective. For to have a pregnant Mary - for a short while at least – we have to ponder who may have been the father of her child. The fact is that at the time of these events there where many people with the name of Jesus, it was quite a common name. Let us assume the possibility and favoured contemporary conspiracy theory that a male called Jesus – and who would soon be hoisted into a deified superstar figure in order to provide an organised religion with unrivalled power – did marry and impregnated a female called Mary Magdalene. This Mary figure who, after the tomb incident where she was first to visit the tomb of the rising Christ, simply vanishes from record, it is agreed, was character assassinated by the Catholic Church and added to their tarnishing of all things females, and their the Original Sin propaganda by informing us the lie that she was a prostitute.

The late controversial historian, John Boswell, argued a case for an approved outlet for homosexual priests in the Adelphopoiesis Rite, a marriage-like same sex union practised at one time by various Christian churches, citing the example of the icon of 4th Century martyrs St Sergius and St Bacchus, which depicts both of them standing together with the figure of Jesus behind them assuming the role of best man. Given the worldwide sex abuse scandal, it is more than ironic that the origin of the place name 'Vatican' is of uncertain etymology attested from the Latin 'Vaticanus', the second syllable of the word the area of the priestly abuse. It appears this Magdalene was completely written out of history along with her status.

Why? What was this status?

Given that somewhere between the years 1110 and 1120 the Knights Templar found a great secret hidden under the Temple Mound in Sion, Jerusalem, and that it is thought to conceal a great historical and religious secret, I now began to wonder it it was concerning this mystery of Mary. And that maybe, after all, she was closer to the 'Jesus' figure we have been taught about in Christianity than any living male by that name. Could this be the reason why the Templars were accused of trampling on the crucifix, as they knew it was not a male figure in the story, and why in 2004 the Bletchley Park code breakers announced the decoding of the Shugborough 'Shepherds monument' code to reveal 'Jesus H Defy' – the 'H' believed to stand for the Greek letter 'Chi' meaning 'Christ' – suggesting that we are to defy the traditional Jesus story? British author and biochemist Anthony Harris daringly suggested in his 1988 book *Sacred Virgin Holy Whore* that Christ was a genetically and physically imperfect woman who set out to fulfill the prophecies of the Old Testament messiah while also carrying on the tradition of the Great Goddess religions, and with Mary Magdalene as a priestess. My thoughts are that this Mary was not a priestess to a female Jesus candidate, but in fact WAS that figure! I feel the French myth of a male 'Jesus' being married to Mary Magdalene is allegorical. 'Marry' is from the Old French 'Marier', phonetic 'Maria' as in Maria Magdalene....both figures being the same person. We have learned that Mary Magdalene was demised by a dagger to her left side. If she was, indeed, a mirroring female image of a mythic male Jesus, we should note that Jesus, whilst on the cross, was pierced in his right side!

The earlier chapters show that my tools of uncovering information are a reliance on the workings of the Collective Unconscious, that mechanism whereby all of the earth's history resides deeply within us and you simply cannot keep the truth from surfacing if only you know where to look for it and how to connect the dots. Now arguably the strongest association with the Jesus figure is the cross and his crucifixion. If we take a deep, psychological survey of the Stations of the Cross, the depiction of the final hours of the passion of Jesus as he carries his cross to Calvary, we will discover a veiled unfolding of the most important of female functioning. In other words, the gynaecological process of early conception and the journey of how an egg leaves an ovary to travel through the fallopian tube preparing for a possible pregnancy, a legacy and memory that is a transposition of a mythical male Jesus with a historical pregnant Magdalene figure. There are 14 Stations of the Cross, the 14th day in pregnancy being the day of ovulation when the rupturing follicle releases the egg, the most fertile day for fertilisation. In fact in obstetrics, the term 'station' is the measure of how far the baby has travelled down the birth canal, the term 'fully engaged' (and here we think of Jesus and Mary in terms of marriage) meaning it is ready to be born. Are we more correctly looking at the (Ge)Stations of the Cross, 'cross' in this instance referring to the 'X' chromosome of the female? These Stations are sprinkled with terms alluding to pregnancy. There are three mentions of Jesus 'falling' on his journey (Stations 3, 7 and 11) and, of course, a woman 'falls' pregnant. It is on day 7 that the egg begins to develop, reaching maturity on day 11. At Station 4, he 'meets with his mother' suggesting the spark of life is at that point within the female parent, for on day 4 the egg starts to develop in the follicle, and at Station 5 Simon of Cyrene carries the Cross for Jesus, 'carrying' being the term for a pregnant mother. At Station 6, Veronica wipes the face of Jesus, and it is from this encounter arrives the legend that when she paused to wipe the sweat off his face with her veil, his image was imprinted on the cloth. However, this imprint of Jesus on her cloth is actually replicating how external genital changes in an embryo develops six weeks after the fertilisation, in this case a sex determination of a boy (as the cross carrying Jesus in the story is male) for although genetic sex is determined at fertilisation, embryonic gender remains undistinguished for the first six weeks of development. At Station 8, Jesus 'meets with the daughters of Jerusalem' and the biblical reference to this encounter, Luke 21-23, has Jesus making yet another reference to motherhood, or the lack of it; 'But woe to them that are with child..' At Station 10 Jesus is 'stripped of his garments' which parallels with an egg, which if unfertile will cause the uterus lining to shed or strip away so that the body can prepare for the next egg and potential pregnancy. Station 12 shows the splayed out arms of Jesus Christ hanging on the Cross, his extended arms a full representation of the fallopian tubes and womb that bleeds, as Christ in this respect is in all women. Station 13 sees his body removed from the cross, for it is at this point of death there is potential of a new birth (as noted in the tarot card 13, 'Death'). In modern Israeli Hebrew, the name 'Yeshu' is given for Jesus, and sounds similar to the word 'issue' – the woman's discharge of blood during a period. Station 14 shows Jesus is laid in the tomb, the fourteenth day of pregnancy when ovulation is most fertile, and it is at this point in the biblical text that Mary Magdalene comes to seek him. From biblical text we are told she thinks the tomb has been looted and he is no longer there. Let me draw attention to the working of the Collective Unconscious here. A 'looted tomb', a tomb looted of a corpse, becomes the 'corpus luteum' ('loot tomb') or what is left of the follicle after a woman ovulates. The 'Spear of Destiny', or Lance of the Roman soldier Longinus, which we are told pierced Christ's side, is indeed one of destiny, for here the egg has been ruptured and bleeds and the menstrual cycle starts again as pregnancy has been missed. Within the name of Longinus is the clue – for Lon gyn us enclosed the word 'gyn', in composition, 'female'.

There are also unconscious female reproductive references to the supposed location in this story, as Jesus has made his way to Calvary. It is not possible to pronounce the word 'Calvary' without noting that as we pronounce the syllable 'Cal' there appears the enunciation of an 'o' as we reach the second syllable, providing us with a 'Cal-ovary', a reference to an ovary. The Garden of Gethsemane, where, curiously Jesus bleeds as he bends down (Luke 22: 54-62) – as a menstruating woman might – contains the phonetic 'gets semen'. Even the last reputed words of Jesus on the Cross, It is finished' can be deemed the end of the ovulation cycle. Still today there is debate over the inscription 'INRI' put on the cross, allegedly an acronym for 'Iesus, Nazarenus, Rex Iudaeorum' to translate as "Jesus of Nazareth, King of the Jews', for there is another version, a medieval motto from the Rosicrucians who employed the rose symbology of Mary Magdalene, 'Igne Natura Renovator Integra' meaning 'By the fire Nature is restored in purity', the fire of synonymous heat, the term used as ' in estrus' or 'in heat' while in that part of the estrus or menstrual cycle, estrus referring to the phase when the female is sexually receptive.

It now will become easier to understand why at Easter time, we cannot help but celebrate with eggs, now commercially shameful and of the chocolate variety, but unconsciously reflecting on the egg which is the ovum egg cell, the female gamete sex cell. A traditional story associated with the Magdalene after Jesus' death and resurrection tells how Mary gained an invite to a banquet held by Emperor Tiberius whereupon she greeted him holding a plain egg in her hand symbolizing the rising Christ. Upon Caesar laughing at the suggestion that Christ rising from the dead was as likely as the egg she was holding turning red, the egg suddenly did just that. From the Greek, another version tells of Mary putting a basket full of eggs at the foot of the crucifixion, symbolic of ovary eggs, painted red by the blood of Jesus. In both accounts we are being reminded that when the (white) egg fails to fertilise, it leads to the red of the oncoming returning cycle of menstruation. Biblical text John 17: 1 has Jesus saying, just prior to his betrayal and crucifixion, 'Father, the time has come...' and timing is what differentiates a fertilised egg from an embryo.

The subject of the 'Eleanor Crosses' may well conceal a deeper insight into our Mystery culminating in Lincoln, given the earlier discovery of the connection of Queen Eleanor with the Magdalene. These crosses were monuments marking the procession route of Eleanor's body on the way from Lincoln to Westminster Abbey. There were twelve crosses erected plus three tombs, Lincoln Cathedral, Westminster Abbey and Blackfriars, making 15 stations of the stopping /resting places of her body, or parts of it. This is the same number of stations of the Cross that found their way into Lincoln Cathedral sculpted in wood by William Fairbanks in 2006, for although not a traditional part of the Stations, the resurrection of Jesus is sometimes included as a 15th. Mary's symbol is found at Station 12, at Stamford, a replacement modern monument carved with roses, and at Station 13, Grantham, where the mysterious 'Wyville' document was placed in the public library there, all that survives is a marble rose at the town museum. At Station 14, at St Katherine's priory at Cross O'Cliff Hill in Lincoln on land once owned by the Templars, there is now a college with an exact copy of the Chartres Cathedral labyrinth, which confirms the importance of Lincoln having its own village named Jerusalem. On November 2011, an exact copy of the Chartres Labyrinth was chalked, for 48 hours only, on the stone floor between the opposing 'Light' and 'Dark' Rose Windows of Lincoln Cathedral! The Chartres Labyrinth can be divided into four quarters, each quarter containing seven 180 degree or U-turns. The 7 x 4 offers up 28 changes in direction, the number 28 being key in how the Lincoln Cathedral Code resolved itself at its concluding marker tomb. Labyrinths were walked by monks as a form of penance, arriving at the centre called 'New Jerusalem'. Has the Eleanor Cross legend, working backwards from London to Lincoln, enacted its own version of the Royal Route that led to St Denis in France, for these crosses bear a striking resemblance to the 'Montjoies' constructed at the end of the X11C and demolished in 1793?

Starting with Dagobert I, this location of the Merovingian necropolis has enjoyed a close association with the French Royal house with almost every French King buried in the Basilica. Here, there is a coinciding with the Zero Meridian and a trail of blood oozing from the severed head of the Saint, reminding us of the severed head of St Margaret, the Lincoln Cathedral Code's shepherdess. St Denis has another unexpected Magdalene connection in that he is invoked against demonic possession, and this inference repeats again in a most unlikely fashion within Lincoln Cathedral. Carved into the back of a seat on the south side of St Hugh's Choir, the second block of seats on the left as you enter and the middle row of that block, there is a carving of a frog appearing to be incising itself with a dagger. The explanation of this image, say the cathedral, is to represent the seven devils being exorcised out of Mary Magdalene...a very strange, almost surreal, explanation indeed! (Note: frogs can be symbolic of childbirth).

Ironically, Rue St Denis, which is one of Paris' oldest streets, is now a notorious haunt for prostitution. Margaret, too, has a hidden connection with the Magdalene. As Margaret of Antioch, she is entwined with the legends concerning St Pelagia who was known as 'The Harlot Penitent', an undeniable resonance with Mary Magdalene. Long before they went to Jerusalem, the Knights Templar had castles in Antioch and therefore must have been aware of, or acquainted themselves with, the Margaret-Pelagia figure. Could it be that the St Margaret's Church that once stood opposite Lincoln Cathedral and protected the concealed conclusion of our Quest, was a secretive Templar church, therefore confirming the legend that the Grail is concealed under a hidden Templar church somewhere in England?

And so, what may we have learned so far? That the figure Mary Magdalene was far more important in history than we have imagined? And that the greatly exaggerated historical figure of a man called Jesus, no divinity or son of God, may have been based on Mary, an actual teacher with a following, to the point that aspects of what we have been given to believe about Jesus have been styled on the workings of the female body – the one thing a male church hierarchy so loathed? Was this enigmatic Mary considered such a threat to a preferred emphasis on an elevated and deified male Jesus figure by the Church, that she was physically removed from accurate recordings of history that would displease the Church, instead placing an emphasis on an elevated and deified male Jesus figure? We return to Da Vinci's 'The Last Supper' and to the traditional betrayer of Jesus, Judas Iscariot, featuring behind Peter who, with one hand, is holding a knife and with the other is making a menacing gesture along the throat level of Mary. Now, to take things a step further. If most of the characters as they appear in the New Testament are recorded for us in a less than accurate fashion to legitimise the claims of earlier churches, then maybe the story of a Christ figure's betrayer is also out of a misnomer. The name of Judas Iscariot, be he real, exaggerated or otherwise in the given storyline, seems as if it originated from a very real bunch of Jewish assassins called the Sicarii. The trademark weapon of these rebels was a small dagger, the sicae. Hidden under a cloak, it is the origin of the phrase 'cloak and dagger', meaning to concern or involve spies, secret agents, intrigue and mystery. In our transposed storyline, which doubts that a male Jesus was betrayed by a Judas, could the reality be that Mary was betrayed and assassinated by the Sicarii? Was this the secret discovered by the Templars at the Temple Mound, that it was Mary who was the most important biblical figure and that she had been murdered?

If the Church were content in its enforcement of a deified male Jesus as presented in the Gospels, then whispers that such a figure had impregnated Mary Magdalene would have been most unwanted. Unless this more recent counter culture of a potential holy bloodline is simply a clever hoax actually started by, and to justify, the Church claims and power, to perpetuate that there was a historical male figure who was indeed a Son of God. An unenvied and no-win position to be in, any historical form of a Jesus would be both enemy of the Roman administrators and the Jewish religious authorities alike. Whereas the former feared a loss of control by Jewish religious leaders might pave the way to a Jewish open rebellion, the latter also feared that Jesus would be able to control the people by usurping their power. In short, a Jesus figure threatened both the prefect Pilate's position charged by Rome to keep peace in Judea, and the role of the Jewish high priests.

The Sicarii, too, appear to have been caught up in an enmity of both Romans and Jews and to further their extremist ends would assassinate Roman officials and Jews who collaborated with them, and so they were not opposed to the pursuit of either faction. Modern interpretations of the 1st Century Jewish Roman historian Flavius Josephus accord that the Sicarii were an extremist splinter group of the Zealots who were equally antagonists to both Roman and Jewish groups that raided Jewish habitations and killed those they considered apostate, eventually driven out of Jerusalem by fellow Jews. If, as I suspect, there was no Judas Iscariot as written, who betrayed a male Jesus as written, there is a distinct possibility that the Sicarii may have followed a Mary Magdalene teacher in the hope that she was a political messiah who might just lead a revolt against Rome, and with her betrayal by assassination further hoped that the outcry would provoke a riot directed at the Romans. As it is customarily written, Jesus had disappointed the Zealots by hoping to change the heart of Man rather than the political structure of the day – perhaps this disillusionment with a hoped-for figure made enemies with a Sicarii who had expected a backing of their politics? Retribution from these robbers and terrorists took the form of violence, assassinations and murder. It is known that the Sicarii often negotiated deals with the Romans by way of kidnap and bribery to bring about released prisoners. Did a disgruntled Sicarii do a deal with the equally unsatisfied figure presented as Simon Peter, allegedly a disciple close to Jesus who so disliked the Magdalene figure? Could he have even been a personality who simply disliked a female Jesus? Are we looking here, at evidence of a sacrifice, or, a 'Sicarii-vice"?

It may be that a Catholic Church contrivance promoted a 'holy bloodline', a ruse originating from a union between an ordinary man called Jesus, and Mary to promote a deified and preferred male figure, or it may simply be that the ruse was to be seen to conspire to eradicate a holy bloodline from existence, again to consolidate that a male Jesus was divine and could not impregnate a mere mortal. Either way, I fear that the dreadful and disgraceful secret once known by the Church is that a pregnant Mary was murdered and therefore could no longer pose a threat either as the original idea upon whom a male Jesus God was concocted, or could ever be proven to have lived long enough to have continued any 'bloodline'. Ironically, the admonition 'Penitence, penitence' that accompanies the statue of Mary Magdalene at Rennes-le-Chateau may have come full circle on 15th April 2010 when, in the wake of the worldwide sex abuse scandal, Pope Benedict Ratzinger asked that all Catholics do penance and pray for their sins. Is it possible that the Magdalene statue is to remind us that it is the Church, and not Mary, that must do penance for implication in her demise?

Ken Humphreys continues in his email, 'The sacred feminine presented a particular challenge to the brash patriarchal cult of Christ, and its votaries spared no effort in bringing the goddess to her knees and silencing her voice. In the diverse, passive women of the gospel yarn and, in particular, in the shadowy figure of Mary Magdalene, is to be heard the faint echo of a life-affirming spirit and a far nobler principle.' Did Mary Magdalene die by dagger at the hands of the Sicarii? Lincoln Cathedral whereupon my work concludes, viewed from the air, is in the shape of the Cross of Lorraine or 'double cross' and was the heraldic device of the Knights Templar, keeper of the secret. Perhaps the secret they found under the Temple Mound was of a double cross, the phrase meaning 'to betray.' The female sex chromosome, note, is XX – a double cross. XY, the male chromosome, symbolically shows a male 'Y' - with outstretched arms hanging on a cross - X . If we return for a moment to Pedro de Mena's 'Mary Magdalene in Penance', we see Mary staring at the crucifix and touching her breast as if to say she is looking at herself on the cross, 'This is me', the hidden message of the sculpture informing us that she, not a male, is this Jesus figure. I must also ponder on the meaning of her being pregnant, for, outside of 'carrying child', 'pregnant' also means 'of great or potentially great importance, full of meaning, significant and threatening' – all easily applicable to what we suspect of the Magdalene.

What are we to make of this iconic female written out of the Bible and history, portrayed undesirably as a prostitute ever afterwards, and the true nature of her identity? Other authors have postulated that Mary Magdalene was a priestess of a female cult possibly of Isis or Diana. I feel that we can find a clue from her inseparable legendary association and primary emblem of the alabaster jar, or box, as it appears in the King James version of the Bible. Although the meaning of the name of the ancient Egyptian Goddess Bastet, also known as Bast, remains uncertain, Egyptian archaeologist and Professor in Egyptology, Stephen Quirke explains it as meaning 'She of the ointment jar' (her name being written with the hieroglyph for ointment jar) and images of Bast were created from the local alabaster stone. Bearing in mind an alleged marriage and child between the biblical Jesus and Mary, it is noteworthy that the word 'bastard', meaning to be born out of wedlock originates from Bast. Another English Egyptologist, the renowned A. E. Budge, postulates that the name 'Pasch', records in ancient documents as being the older version of her name, and from this received the word 'passion' – Jesus' redemptive suffering and death by crucifixion is collectively referred to as 'The Passion'. Priestesses of Bast dressed in her colour, which was red, the same associated with the Magdalene. Some years ago, when I began to study images of Mary's alabaster jar I knew at the back of my mind that it was reminding me of something, but I struggled to recall where I had seen it before. have since rediscovered that misplaced memory, prompted by emphasis placed on an alabaster box rather than jar. We can find the outline of the object contained within the larynx, colloquially known as the 'voice box', and which generates sound and the spoken word. It is used each time we breathe, talk and swallow, the outer wall of cartilage forming the area of the front of the neck referred to as the 'Adam's apple', named after the forbidden fruit in the Garden of Eden, and the vocal cords being two bands of muscle that form a 'V', symbol of the Grail chalice - inside the larynx. This makes Mary Magdalene, truly, the Voice and Spoken Word of God, and this responsibility, held by a female, was erased from living memory by a jealous male orientated Church with a fear and loathing of female, bent, solely on adoration of the male.

EPILOGUE

I n Chapter 11, I explained how the triangular-shaped device at the top left of Rennes Parchment 2 appeared on the West face of the Templar Preceptory at Temple Bruer, and that it was to draw our attention to the dog-star Sirius. I also promised a deeper meaning, and here it is. The Solfeggio frequencies, chants and special tones, lost centuries ago by the Church, were employed in Gregorian chants when sung harmoniously in unison throughout religious Masses, such as the great hymn applied to John the Baptist, bestowing powerful spiritual blessings upon all in attendance, and essentially rediscovered by the late Dr Joseph Puleo during the middle seventies. His own Collective Unconscious led him to probe Chapters in Genesis, uncovering a pattern of six repeating codes, revealing six electromagnetic sound frequencies in correspondence to the missing six tones absent from the ancient Solfeggio scale. In short, he had rediscovered how to utilise sound as a healing tool. The most fantastic element of this breakthrough is when we learn that the third note, known as frequency 528HZ, is the very same frequency that biochemists are now using to repair broken human DNA, the nucleic acid that contains the genetic instruction used in the development and functioning of all known organisms, the genetic blueprint upon which life is based, the very 'Book of Life and Death'. The device from the Parchment and at Bruer, seen vertically shows an 'M' and an 'I', - MI - and this is the very note that relates to frequency 528 on the scale, deriving from the Latin phrase 'MI-ra gestorum ' meaning 'miracle'. Our Mother tongue also shows it to read 'Mirror birth', MI-ra = 'mirror' and 'gestorum' from progesterone that maintains pregnancy, relating to the replacement of the Magdalene with the mythical male figure of the great healer Jesus, and the allusion that she was about to give birth.

A clue pertaining to the lost frequency, the 'words in the tones' (anagram from the Arthurian 'Sword in the Stone'), was placed for us at the Bishops Palace, and can be found on the crozier fitting of the Bishop Grosseteste. It reads, 'By the form of a staff learn the pattern of a Bishop'. When I first discovered this, I thought it would be a chess reference and how the Bishop can only move in a diagonal fashion, but then I found how it was all to do with musical terms. Every piece of music has an overall plan or structure called the 'form' of the music. The staff, or stave, in musical notation originates from musically annotated text through the Gregorian Chants, home of the Solfeggio scale. Most helpful was the unexpected discovery that the word 'constellation' is synonymous with the word pattern. The Bishop is the spiritual overseer in the early Christian church, the highest body. The 'highest body', the one that everything circulated around was the Pole position hidden, the thing that was seen was the constellation circulating around it – Ursa Major! Incidentally, the upper part of the Bishop chess piece, carved into the shape of a mitre, was formerly called the 'archer', the surname of our stonemason friend Michael Dan, who unconsciously directed the way to 'The Secret'.

It is accepted that Berenger Sauniere befriended the internationally famous French operatic singer Emma Calve, in her private life a Cathar and High Priestess of the Parisian esoteric underground around about the time of 1900. Villagers at the Chateau reported hearing her high-pitched singing coming from his Villa Bethania, for reasons unknown. Was Sauniere employing Calve to try to hit certain notes that he felt to be magical? Did my wife Avril do so naturally in her vocal outburst within the church at Bugurach? 'Repairing' the tampered-with Jesus-Mary story has been a quintessential part of repairing the DNA of the Mother planet, the disrepair threatening life and health. It is at the place on earth that accommodates the Gothic Lincoln Cathedral that this restoration and healing process has occurred, despite the original damage caused in the Middle East, the Collective Unconscious having eventually led us here. For whilst intricate DNA repair mechanisms in a cell's nucleus are known to work constantly, effortlessly trying to fix what has broken, we do not know whether the repair work is carried out at the point where the damage had announced itself or at other specific regions of the nucleus. This is why it has been so important to locate the area of the planet's surface that will respond effectively to the treatment, and by utilisation of locating Mary Magdalene at the Cathedral, and correcting her story. By doing so, it has also corrected the misplaced myths surrounding the grail legends at Glastonbury, for as much as Glastonbury is thought to be a centre of great healing, it, too has needed healing.

It has an alleged Portal, a Gate ('agate' being a banded variegated chalcedony, Glastonbury's mythical 'chalice'), that Gateway which is now a term in computing allowing information to exchange from one computer network to another; dimensional contact. It too, has its musical clues waiting to be deduced from the carvings on the front of the Tower, brought about by the Collective Unconscious. The highest carving is that of our friend the Phoenix, the firebird of Arabia so called owing to its possession of a scarlet colour, the shade that is most prominent in its weird earth light displays. So why should this be above the Tor? Below it, to the left, we see St Michael and the devil, weighing souls. To their right is St Bridget milking a cow. Bridget was originally the Celtic, and possibly pre-Celtic, goddess Brigdhe. Her earliest representations associate her with fire. Why too should she be situated there, is it because both Bridget and Phoenix have this red, fire association? It is said that the Gateway to the Underworld opens only on the days of a fire festival, St Bridget having such a date on February 2nd. Using the Mother Tongue, when we look at the name 'Glastonbury', we can see 'Glass-stone-bury' or 'Glass-stone-ruby'. Is it that simple, a buried glass stone or buried glass ruby stone is somehow associated with the Tor?

Ruby is, of course, a pure transparent (as would be a glass stone) red corundum. The key word here may be 'transparent' from Latin 'parere' meaning 'to appear'. Back to Bridget-Brighde, and by consulting the phonetic, visual pun and anagrammatic of the Mother tongue, try pronouncing the name 'Bridget' without saying 'bridge shut'. Are we drawing attention to a shut bridge? 'Bridge' comes from the Old English 'Bryg' and a 'brig' is a two-masted, square-rigged vessel from the word 'brigantine'. Does this ship have a porthole? Or does this 'spaceship' have a 'portal'? Looking closer at the word 'bridge' we find that it is anything that connects across a gap or makes an electrical connection between, and its synonyms include 'arch, link, connection, connect'. Studying Mike Chenery's open portal photography under enlargement, the dazzling white shape caught on camera shows an outline not unlike a tomb headstone, and I wonder if we are seeing the actual archetype and origin for such a structure, something of an arch whereby the soul will pass through to liable voyage beyond. The dazzling bright light reminds me of the descriptions seen down a tunnel in near-death experiences. Is this, indeed, a space-time portal, a normally 'bridge shut' and a place of mystical rebirth of the Phoenix? Can such a portal exist on Glastonbury Tor and is this what Chenery has photographed physically open for a few moments of our known time? Is the Michael Tower with its two-sided arch you can walk through and out, a physical living unconscious memory of a replica, dimensional Portal?

Returning to the stonework images on the tower, we see Michael and the Pan-like figure of the devil weighing souls on a weighing scale, the devil having a foot on his scale attempting to weigh it down. The key words here are 'scales' and 'Way' (phonetic of 'weigh'). 'Way' means 'passage' and 'scales' in musical composition is a progression of single notes upwards or downwards in steps. The imagery of the devil tipping down his scale is to draw reference to the infamous Augmented 4th, or 'Devil's Chord' prohibited by the Church in the 12th Century. My friend, the Scottish author Brian Allen, has evidenced in his own work *Rosslyn, Between two Worlds*, a belief that there is a portal contained within Rosslyn Chapel and that this devil's chord is a key and sound frequency involved in opening the portal. I smile recalling how the devil was always represented holding a pitch fork, which I think we can now more correctly view as an acoustic resonating tuning fork which can be used to emit a pure musical tone. The Pan Pipes, or syrinx, of the god Pan also involve specific acoustic octave properties. As Allen suggests, does a specific frequency or harmonic note, along with this devil's chord, provide the science that opens a portal? It should therefore be no surprise that Glastonbury has this entwined musical connection with its annual festival. The word 'tone' refers both to one of the larger intervals between successive notes in the scale, as C and D (the original Solfeggio note 'C' used in DNA repair differing from our current diatonic 'C' owing to earlier tuning methods) and also to the harmony or general depth or brilliance of colour. And so there is a certain relationship with music and colour; upon the Tor the suspicion must be the red of the Phoenix and her earth lights.

We return next to the carved image of St Bridget seen milking a cow into a pitcher, the musical term for pitch means 'to set in a key'. With Bridget we are inviting in a 'bridge', which in classical music is also known as a 'transition', the word meaning 'a passage from one place'. Through the Portal, the mystical re-birth of the Phoenix allegory? With the wonder and revelation of synchronicity in mind, a bridge is formerly known as a bridge-passage in music. Michael Dan Archer placed 'The Portal', within Lincoln Cathedral, and outside of the Judgement Porch his gateway, was also entitled 'Between Two Worlds'. On 28th February 2005 legendary keyboard wizard Rick Wakeman, from the British progressive rock group Yes, performed - without an audience - solo piano pieces on the pipe organ within the Cathedral. 'Yes' is a word of affirmation or consent, and 'Wake man' sounds like a call to rouse from sleep. Was he unwittingly drawn to seeking crucial notes that could have momentarily opened a bridge?

Our amended biblical story concludes with the discovery of the final resting place of the enigmatic figure Mary Magdalene, not the Holy Grail, but the 'Holy Girl', led there by a genetic Code directive from the Collective Unconscious, the Mind of our pregnant living planet, the birth of a new consciousness awaiting. Religious history is now at last corrected, the battle between good and evil at Lincoln Cathedral is over, and the scar tissue associated with the Magdalene's demise can now heal. The birth she never had belongs now to the earth. At a time when all manners of significant world events are now occurring daily and are beginning to quicken, 'quickening' is the age-old name for feeling foetal movement when pregnant.

ADDENDUM

On April 16th 2011 an unofficial and unannounced Ground Penetrating Radar Scan was conducted at the Lincoln Cathedral Code marker tomb location by a well-known and prominent Rennes-le-Chateau investigator, and a German geophysicist from Hamburg, both wishing to remain anonymous.

The author of this book was contacted by both and kindly sent a copy of the scan, which reveals that at the exact location revealed by the Code, under an existing tomb, there is an anomaly measuring 2.50 metres x 0.70 metres and nearby, a metal object measuring 0.5 metres x 0.5 metres.

Speculation that here resides the sarcophagus and nameplate relating to Mary Magdalene continues.

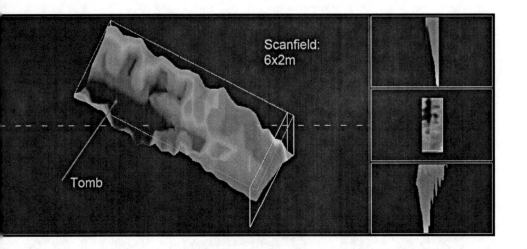

Sarcophagus shaped anomaly.

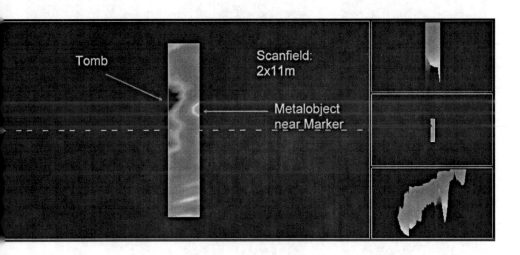

Oblong shaped anomaly.

11th Dimension Publishing

More books from 11th Dimension Publishing!

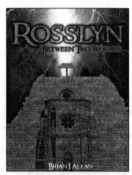

www.HealingsOfAtlantis.com

Lightning Source UK Ltd.
Milton Keynes UK
UKOW03f0917120813

215220UK00002B/186/P